A THOUSAND TONGUES

A THOUSAND TONGUES

The Wesley hymns as a guide to scriptural teaching

JOHN LAWSON

Paternoster:
thinking faith

LONDON ● ATLANTA ● HYDERABAD

First published 1987 by Paternoster Press
This edition first published 2007 by Paternoster
Paternoster is an imprint of Authentic Media
9 Holdom Avenue, Bletchley, Milton Keynes, Bucks, MK1 1QR, UK
285 Lynnwood Avenue, Tyrone, GA 30290, USA
OM Authentic Media, Medchal Road, Jeedimetla Village,
Secunderabad 500 055, A.P., India
www.authenticmedia.co.uk

Authentic Media is a division of Send the Light Ltd., a company limited by
guarantee (registered charity no. 270162)

British Library Cataloguing in Publication Data

A catalogue record for this book is available from the
British Library

ISBN 978-1-84227-550-4

Cover Design by fourninezero design.
Originally typeset by Photoprint, Torquay
Print Management by Adare Carwin
Printed and bound in Great Britain by J.H. Haynes & Co., Sparkford

Contents

Table of Sources

P.W. The Poetical Works of John and Charles Wesley. 13 volumes, collected by G. Osborn (London, 1868–72).

W.H. 'Wesley's Hymns', i.e. the historic 'Hymns for the Use of the People Called Methodists' (1780), compiled by John Wesley, who wrote a celebrated Preface to it. The writer has used his great-grandfather's hymn-book, that is, the 1876 edition 'With a new Supplement', which was the book customarily used by much of British Methodism until 1904. This volume contains more Wesley material than subsequent hymnals. It is worthy of note, furthermore, that the various nineteenth century hymn-books of the American Methodist Churches largely follow the contents of this book, and are interesting to students of this subject.

H.L.S. 'Hymns for the Lord's Supper'. The important sacramental manuals of the Wesleys consist of John Wesley's abbreviation of Dr. Daniel Brevint's 'On the Christian Sacrament and Sacrifice', and Charles Wesley's 166 'Hymns on the Lord's Supper', being a versification of extracts from Brevint. This was published first in 1745, and occurs in vol. 3 of Osborn's 'Collected Works'. It was also notably reprinted in 1948 in 'The Eucharistic Hymns of John and Charles Wesley', by J. Ernest Rattenbury. This invaluable book, though unfortunately out of print, is well worth seeking out.

M.H.B. 'The Methodist Hymn Book', 1933. The hymn-book of the British Methodist Church, now replaced.

M.H. 'The Methodist Hymnal', 1964. The official hymnal of the United Methodist Church of the United States.

H.P. 'Hymns and Psalms', 1983. The new hymnal of the British Methodist Church.

The attention of the careful student is also directed to 'Representative Verse of Charles Wesley', edited by Frank Baker, Abingdon Press and Epworth Press (1962), a work of very detailed and authoritative scholarship. There is also for research students the definitive scholarly edition of 'Hymns for the Use of the People Called Methodists', edited by Oliver Beckerlegge and Franz Hildebrandt, which is vol. 7 in the Oxford Edition of Wesley's Works.

Foreword

This republication of the late John Lawson's fine work on Charles Wesley is both very timely and very welcome. This year, 2007, is the tercentenary year of Charles' birth and Lawson's book is one of the very best ever published on his hymns. John Lawson was a biblical and theological scholar who worked and taught in Methodist colleges and universities both in Britain and America. He was also a life-long devotee of the hymns of Charles Wesley and this book is the product of those years of research, analysis and appraisal. The title, *A Thousand Tongues*, comes from the 18-verse hymn that Charles published in 1739, entitled 'For the Anniversary Day of one's Conversion.' The book's subtitle, 'The Wesley hymns as a guide to Scriptural teaching,' indicates its primary purpose and direction. Lawson was convinced that the hymns of both John and Charles Wesley faithfully represented the teaching of Scripture in memorable and moving poetry. While most of the examples of hymns used in this book are from the pen of Charles Wesley, some of John's translations of (mainly) German hymns are also included.

On Sunday 21 May 1738, Charles Wesley experienced his evangelical conversion and the next day he began his amazing output of evangelical hymns. Beginning with his 'conversion hymn,' 'Where shall my wondering soul begin?' he wrote in excess of 8000 pieces of religious verse in the next 50 years. That makes him the most prolific English poet of all time, producing more lines of poetry than Shakespeare, Milton, Pope or Wordsworth. In this anthology Lawson has retained some of Charles' most popular hymns, including, 'And can it be?', 'Christ the Lord is risen today', 'Hark, the herald angels sing', 'Jesus, Lover of my soul', 'Rejoice, the Lord is King', 'Thou Shepherd of Israel, and mine', and 'Wrestling Jacob'. In addition he has rightly included some truly great hymns by Charles Wesley that deserve to be much better known. These include, 'All ye that pass by', 'Come, O Traveller unknown', 'Entered the holy place above', 'Jesu, thou Sovereign Lord of all', 'O love divine, how sweet thou art', and 'Thy ceaseless, unexhausted love'.

While a number of books dealing with Charles Wesley's hymns have appeared over the years, this book has three particular strengths that make it both illuminating and delightful reading. First, Lawson outlines 53 Biblical doctrines, ranging from 'God the Sovereign Creator' to 'The Second Advent'. Along the way he deals with 'Revelation in Scripture,' 'The Incarnation,' 'The Atonement,' 'The Holy Trinity,' 'Original Sin,' 'Justification by Faith,' 'Communion with Christ,' 'The Lord's Supper' and much, much else. This makes the book a compendium of Biblical doctrines. Each of the 53 chapters is briefly and clearly introduced and the theme explained. In this way it could be used weekly for a whole year as a text book for group meetings dealing with Biblical doctrines.

Secondly, each of the 53 biblical themes is illustrated with a Charles Wesley hymn or, in a few places, a hymn translated by John Wesley. Thus, the chapter dealing with 'The Divine Son' is illustrated by the hymns, 'We know by faith, we surely know' and 'The Son of God is come'; the chapter 'Christ's Advent' by 'Come, Thou long-expected Jesus'; and 'The Preaching of the Gospel' by the hymn 'Come, sinners to the gospel feast'. So, in many of the chapters, more than one hymn is used—a reminder that in his huge output of hymns, Charles Wesley was pre-eminently a Scripture poet.

Thirdly, John Lawson shows how almost every poetic line that Charles Wesley wrote reflected one or more Biblical text. The hymns selected are helpfully printed with the Scripture verses following each appropriate line in each verse. Other great hymn writers like Isaac Watts, John Newton, William Cowper and James Montgomery were Scripture poets in that their hymns are based on the teaching of the Bible. Charles Wesley, however, was a Scripture poet in an additional way; his hymns incorporate the actual words, phrases and idioms of Scripture. When we sing a Charles Wesley hymn we are not only singing verses that teach Biblical doctrines but we are singing the very words of Scripture. Today this important fact is less understood because few congregations are now so familiar with the text of the Authorised Version of the Bible that Wesley used. Lawson has done an invaluable service here by painstakingly noting every Biblical reference in every Wesley hymn he has selected. One example will illustrate how well Charles Wesley knew and used the text of Scripture in his hymns. The four verses of the ever popular hymn, 'Love divine, all loves excelling', make use, directly or indirectly, of 46 Scripture texts from both Old and New Testaments.Writing this Foreword is, in St. Paul's words, 'a labour of love.' John Lawson (1909–2003) was an esteemed colleague and friend. This reprint of his *A Thousand Tongues* makes available, in the Charles Wesley tercentenary year, this very informative, very devotional and very delightful study of some of the best of the Wesley hymns. Whether used in personal reading and devotions or shared with others in groups, this book will demonstrate how well these hymns illustrate and explain the doctrines of the Christian faith.

Herbert B. McGonigle
Senior Lecturer in Historical Theology and Wesley Studies
Nazarene Theological College
Manchester
England

Introduction

It is the honoured tradition of the Church that Christian praise and worship is framed in the language of Holy Scripture. It is the business of Christian congregations to sing the Bible. Believers in the apostolic Church used the psalms of their Jewish background. The Canticles which enrich the opening of St. Luke's Gospel echo the language of the Old Testament, and doubtless represent a sample of the worship of the Church of New Testament times. The Church of the passing centuries continued to chant the Psalms. In the English Church at the Reformation, when the Latin services were translated into the stately and imperishable English of Coverdale and Cranmer, the mainspring of worship in our tongue continued to be the chanting of Psalms and Canticles.

However, the Anglican chant, though 'a thing of beauty and a joy for ever' when rendered by a competent choir, is not always easy for a congregation of limited musical gifts. Therefore in course of time the Psalms and Canticles were commonly paraphrased into metrical verse, as simpler for congregational singing. The best of the old Metrical Psalms have indeed provided our language with some of its greatest hymns, such as 'All people that on earth do dwell,' (Psalm 100), and 'Through all the changing scenes of life,' (Psalm 34). However, the Metrical Psalms were sometimes clumsy and wooden in style, through the attempt to paraphrase Scripture as closely as possible, verse by verse. All too often this filled the Church with pious doggerel, until the genius of Watts came to the rescue.

Isaac Watts (1674–1748), the older contemporary of the Wesleys, produced scriptural hymns which were both more poetical and more 'singable' by venturing upon a freer rendering of the sense of the Psalms, and also by skilfully weaving together texts from various parts of the Bible into metrical verse. He also showed the Christian application of Old Testament Scripture, and, as he put it, 'made David sing like a Christian'. Here then was established a tradition of evangelical hymns framed in the language of Scripture.

11

John and Charles Wesley then enriched this heritage in a most significant way. Watts the Nonconformist was of the Puritan tradition, and so did not celebrate the Christian Year, which in Puritan eyes savoured too much of Roman ritual. Hence 'When I survey the wondrous cross', which to us appears as a hymn for Holy Week or Good Friday, was written as a sacramental hymn, for Watts did not observe days like Good Friday, on the plea that the atoning death of Christ ought to be celebrated at all seasons. The Wesleys, however, were High Churchmen turned evangelist, and in them the two sides of Christian tradition, the churchly and the evangelical, flowed together into a new enriching synthesis. Charles Wesley, therefore, writes hymns for the great days of the Christian Year, proclaiming the Gospel truths associated with them.

Thus the Wesleys' pioneer hymn-book which was born of the 'first fine careless rapture' of the Evangelical Revival, 'Hymns and Sacred Poems' (1739), and which comprises so much of their finest work, contains, for example, such a seasonal hymn as the original form of 'Hark the herald-angels sing'. Here is a momentous advance in Christian worship. Charles Wesley's Christman hymn is no mere pleasant carol celebrating some old-world picturesque legend. It is a theologically serious Christmas hymn, setting forth in the language of Scripture, and in good poetical form, an adequate expression of the doctrine of the Incarnation.

Watts and Wesley are generally accepted as together the greatest hymnwriters in the English language. As befits one who came out of the Calvinist tradition, a main strength of Watts lies in reverent adoration of the power, the wisdom, and the goodness of the majestic God of creation. He sings:

> And will this sovereign King
>   Of Glory condescend?
> And will he write his name
>   My Father and my Friend?

This is the indispensable foundation of the Christian system, for the full marvel of the redeeming love of God is apprehended only if it be seen not as the partial and indulgent love of some small and private god, but as the love of the one great sovereign King of Glory. The Wesleys build upon this foundation. As befits those who by surprising divine grace had come to a deeper personal grasp of 'the experience of the heart strangely warmed', their chief strength is in celebrating the historic redeeming work of that great God, in the wonderful birth, death, resurrection, and ascension of the divine Son made man, and the continuing work of his Spirit in the hearts of believers. So:

He left his Father's throne above,
  So free, so infinite his grace!
Emptied himself of all but love,
  And bled for Adam's helpless race.

There are indeed other legitimate forms of Christian song, as well as the scriptural hymn. There is the hymn of Christian sentiment, of which the nineteenth century produced so many. These have their rightful place, for Christian redemption concerns the whole human personality and experience, its joys and griefs, its longings and aspirations, its doubts and fears. Thus a well-loved hymn of Christian sentiment, such as 'Abide with me; fast falls the eventide', may be accepted as one of the Church's great hymns, for it speaks to the condition of many believers. However, hymns of Christian sentiment remain open to this weakness. Too easily they can become introspective and subjective, and turn the thoughts of worshippers away from the great God and his saving work to little *me*, and my self-centred concern with my fleeting feelings.

There is likewise a place for the so-called 'contemporary' hymn directed towards the practical resolves and duties in the world of human affairs, and possibly framed in language derived from the social studies. Certainly the Christian experience of salvation and worship ought to result in lives of service in the community. So it is right on occasion to sing a hymn which invites us folk in our comfortable pews to repent of

  our wanton, selfish gladness,
Rich in things and poor in soul.

Certainly and sadly this is a diagnosis true of most industrial societies. Nevertheless, a weakness dogs the steps of hymns of social resolve. They likewise tend to be directed to the congregation, and not to God. The purpose of singing is indirectly to teach the singers, rather than the praise of God. This alternative branch of human self-centredness is as likely to move to despair over the social, economic, and international problems which afflict this fallen world, as it is to lift up the hearts of believers to renewed faith and courage.

By contrast, the scriptural hymn, so eminently associated with the Evangelical Revival, has this enduring virtue and strength. Because it is biblical it is centred upon God Almighty, his greatness, his goodness, his salvation. This is the salutary view of life, because God *is* the centre! There is indeed a great variety of writing in the Bible, from the pens of writers of many ages, many temperaments, many experiences, and directed to all sorts of situations. Yet in general it may be claimed that through all that variety the most important character in the story is always God. The Bible is eminently the God-aware and God-centred book, which is the mark of its divine inspiration. This is why it is so salutary a book, and brings so uncomfortable a rebuke to the typical secular-minded modern man, whose imagination is bemused by the all-encompassing things which can be weighed and measured, manufactured and possessed, bought and sold. Hymns celebrating the themes of Scripture, and written in the language of Scripture, convey the sense of God. This is why they excel all others.

It has to be admitted, nevertheless, that scriptural hymns also face a disability. This is that today even many of those who call themselves Bible-reading evangelical believers do not take the Bible as seriously as did those great masters. For example, when Charles Wesley launches off—

> None is like Jeshurun's God,
>   So great, so strong, so high—

most folk get no further than the first line! They exclaim: 'But who on earth is Jeshurun? What can he matter to us? Isn't all this very obscure, very antiquated?' The circumstance that this hymn contains some beautiful devotional lines, and is an aspiring prayer for the divine gift of holiness, totally escapes notice! The underlying reason for this common reaction is that those many folk whose study of the Bible is largely confined to a series of short 'daily readings', have never explored Deuteronomy 33, or even if they have read it have never supposed that it has anything to say to the Christian. Thus one of the great texts of the Bible, 'and underneath are the everlasting arms', is not known and loved in the manner of Wesley.

The scriptural hymns of the Wesleys, therefore, need an introduction. The present attempt to provide one seeks to operate in two ways. First, by providing an analysis of the biblical quotations and allusions in a selection of some of the more important works, the spiritual and theological depth of what is being said is made plain. Second, and perhaps even more importantly, the hymns, thus explained, give a guide as to how the Wesleys understood the Bible. It must be stated that a great heritage of Christian understanding is in danger of being lost, particularly with regard to the Old Testament. Modern academic study of the Bible has generally concentrated upon 'the historical-critical approach'. It has been assumed that the only meaning of Scripture which can concern the enlightened reader is what may have been in the mind of the original writer, in so far as this can be determined by reference to the background of the writer, personal, intellectual, social, or political. Discussion of what the Bible has come to mean in the experience and thought of later times has been dismissed as obscurantist and misleading.

the use of Scripture in the second line. The allusion here to Psalm 119:111 is made plain in the Book of Common Prayer (BCP) version of the Psalms, which it will be remembered the Wesleys would use daily for Morning and Evening Prayer. The reading here is: 'Thy testimonies have I claimed as mine heritage for ever: and why? they are the very joy of my heart'. This is much clearer than the Authorized Version, (KJV), where we read: 'They are the rejoicing of my heart'. However, the line may also contain reminiscence of Ecclesiastes 5:20, where 'the

The effect of this has been to relegate much of the Bible, particularly in the case of the Old Testament, to the status of a collection of data for the study of ancient religion (with the assumption in the mind of many critics that the data is not very reliable!) To do this is to cut off modern Christianity from its roots. There is of course a due place in academic study for the historical approach to the Bible. However, to ignore the splendid continuity of God's redeeming work in history, down through the centuries from patriarchal times, through Christ, to our own day, is a sad impoverishment of our heritage of Christian faith and devotion. The Wesleys interpret the Old Testament in the Christian manner, as the story of the preparation of the world for the coming of Christ, and the New Testament as the definitive witness to the accomplishment in Christ of what was prepared. The Old Testament therefore corresponds to the New Testament by way of promise, and the Wesleys do not hesitate to look for Christian truth in every part of the Bible. They find spiritually valuable 'leading texts' in parts which are often passed over with neglect. We may learn much of this way of looking at the Bible by tracing out their references. This will reward the careful reader with many spiritual insights. These can be both new apprehensions of familiar passages, and the discovery of Scripture treasures hitherto unfamiliar.

A glance at the pages which follow will indicate that Scripture references in the Wesley hymns are very numerous. More careful reading will show that they are of a variety of usage. In the first place, most obvious and striking, are direct and explicit quotations. For example:

> Sun of righteousness, arise,
> Triumph o'er the shades of night

is a clear citation of Malachi 4:2, 'shall the Sun of righteousness arise with healing in his wings'. This is the only place in the Bible where this precise phrase occurs. Here is one of Charles Wesley's favourite texts, which is quoted many times.

There are, however, very many clear allusions which fall short of explicit certainty, and these are often woven together with skill and poetic artistry, so that it is common to get more than one per line. For example:

> Thou Shepherd of Israel, and mine,
>   The joy and desire of my heart

may fairly be claimed to be a union of Psalm 80:1, 'Give ear, O Shepherd of Israel', with Psalm 23:1, 'The Lord is my shepherd'. Both these references to a shepherd are characteristically applied to Christ, following the example of our Lord's own reading of the Hebrew Scriptures. Less familiar to many modern readers, however, will be joy of his heart' also occurs. Furthermore, we have the word 'desire' as well as 'joy', and this is doubtless derived from such passages as Psalm 37:4 (BCP) 'and he shall give thee thy heart's desire', and perhaps Haggai 2:7, 'and the desire of all nations shall come'. The latter is a text traditionally applied to Christ, and certainly by Wesley, as seen in the familiar Christmas hymn:

> Come, Desire of nations, come,
>   Fix in us thy humble home.

Where, as frequently, there is citation of many possible texts, one has been content to give one or two of the most apposite. It is impossible, and not very useful, to seek to make exhaustive the Scripture analysis of these hymns.

The succeeding lines of this same hymn:

> For closer communion I pine,
>   I long to reside where thou art:
> The pasture I languish to find
>   Where all, who their Shepherd obey

contains allusions to the Song of Solomon (listed in our notation by the alternative title of Canticles), 5:8, 3:4, and 1:7. It may indeed appear strange to many modern readers to understand the outspoken imagery of the Song of Solomon as an allegory referring to Christ, the Bridegroom of the Church. However, it will be less strange if it be remembered that our Lord spoke of himself as the Bridegroom, and the imagery of the Church as the bride of Christ occurs in several places in the New Testament. There has been a well-established tradition in the Church down the ages that Canticles may be expounded with reference to Christ. The matter is clinched for this hymn because in the original the Wesleys printed the reference Canticles 1:7 at the head. Also there are many striking lines in other hymns which use this part of Scripture. One does not deny that historical criticism will seek to determine original meanings of texts, and will affirm that traditional Christian meanings have, in the case of much of the Old Testament, been read into them, and so are not 'historical'. The explorer of Wesley must be mentally prepared to follow him into many 'spiritual' and allegorical renderings of a variety of texts, which are of devotional rather than academic value.

The skill and intricacy of interwoven Scripture citation illustrated from the verse above is no isolated example. It is a characteristic usage. Sometimes a whole passage is paraphrased into verse in a masterly fashion, frequently with added allusions to other texts. For example, a less known but very moving verse of the prayer for growth in love and holiness entitled 'Desiring to love', which starts 'O Love divine, how sweet thou art', is a rendering of St. Peter's response to the challenge of the Risen Lord in John 21:15–17.

> O that with humbled Peter I
> Could weep, believe, and thrice reply
>   My faithfulness to prove,
> 'Thou know'st (for all to thee is known),
> Thou know'st, O Lord, and thou alone,
>   Thou know'st that thee I love!'

The type of references we have been considering concern largely the phraseology and literary derivation of the hymns. In addition, we have given a set of Scripture citations of another sort, which we hope will prove valuable. These are the 'Scripture proofs' of points of doctrine. Thus when Wesley refers, as he so often does, to 'full assurance of salvation', and 'the witness of the Spirit', we record in our references the one or two leading texts which we know would have been cited to establish these parts of the Gospel message, such as Romans 8:16, and 1 John 2:5, 5:10, etc. It is not possible to make this analysis exhaustive, for on many points of teaching the texts are very numerous. In such cases one or two of the more apposite references have been provided. For example, where Wesley mentions our Lord's Second Advent in a general manner one or two leading texts are cited, out of the very many. However, a number of striking lines depend upon reference to the Last Trumpet, which is mentioned in the Bible in a few distinctive places, which can be noted. If there are parallel savings on some subject in the Gospels it has not been found necessary to give more than one.

In some cases the choice of what is the apposite Scripture reference depends on what is known of the usage of the Wesleys in other parts of their writing. For example, a text which may be cited to uphold the proposition that salvation is by divine grace, and not by human merit, is the BCP version of Psalm 74:13: 'For God is my King of old: the help that is done upon earth he doeth it himself'. (KJV reads 'working salvation in the midst of the earth'.) We remember that John Wesley explicitly cites this text to this effect in *Sermon* XII. ii. 3.

The composition of the Wesley hymns is not simply the versification of a deliberate collection of biblical texts. It is the idiom of writers whose whole model of natural expression was moulded by familiarity with the Scriptures, and love of them. Thus when Charles Wesley wishes to say that at the Incarnation the divine Son took upon himself the form of a human baby he writes: 'Infant of days he here became'. The telling phrase, 'infant of days', is clearly derived from Isaiah 65:20, though there it can hardly be applied to Christ. It is just the prophet's poetical term for a baby. We see that Wesley is not looking round for Scripture references to ornament his verse. His poetic genius moves at a higher level than any such artificial device. He is just expressing himself spontaneously, and the phrase which comes naturally to him is the language of the English Bible.

In a few cases, indeed, this characteristic style can land the writer in a doubtful expression. A striking biblical allusion can be taken up and used in a sense inconsistent with the original. For example, in the verses opening with 'Jesus the Conqueror reigns', on the subject of the victory of the Cross, we come to the lines:

> He felt the mortal dart,
> The horror-breathing king
> Shot all our sin into his heart
> And death hath lost his sting.

Here Wesley would seem to have in mind Lamentations 1:13, 'From above hath he sent fire into my bones,' a text traditionally applied to Christ crucified. This has been read as a prophecy of the Father visiting the Son with expiatory suffering. However, in this hymn the 'dart' is shot by Satan! Here is an expression of the ancient patristic theology of *Christus Victor*, the Conqueror of Satan through the sufferings of the Cross, and triumphant Resurrection. This of course is sound New Testament doctrine, though we may question Wesley's use of this particular text.

It will be apparent that the reader who wishes to explore this Scripture analysis must use the Authorized Version (KJV) of the Bible. Many of the references become much less clear, and some disappear altogether, in modern versions of the Bible, particularly in those where there is an element of paraphrase. The reader must also be prepared on occasion to refer to the Coverdale version of the Psalms in the BCP, to which the Wesleys were even more attached than to the KJV on account of their regular use of them in daily Morning and Evening Prayer.

Nevertheless, it is important also to remember that although the Wesleys possessed a wonderful knowledge of the English Bible, and a great love of it, they were scholars who were familiar with the original Hebrew and Greek. Thus there are numbers of Scripture allusions in these hymns which are not fully plain from the traditional English text, but which require to be demonstrated from the original. A salient example of this occurs in the familiar lines from 'And can it be that I should gain?':

> Emptied himself of all but love,
> And bled for Adam's helpless race.

This is a reference to Philippians 2:7, but this is not plain from the KJV reading 'but made himself of no reputation'. The phrase 'emptied himself' is a more exact translation of the Greek. The method which has been adopted in the notation of this book to convey this information to readers who are not acquainted with the original languages lies in the circumstance that modern revisions, or at least their marginal readings, usually make the point required. It is not possible to record all the multitude of new versions, but it suffices to give a note of the Revised Version, sometimes with margin, as representative.

There are also in the Wesley hymns many allusions to other literary works, which include classical Latin verse, the ancient Fathers of the Church, mediaeval liturgies, and English poetry. To trace out all these would be an immense task, particularly as it would suppose acquaintance with English poetry now little read. As the present work is not a literary commentary upon Wesley no attempt has been made to compile an exhaustive index to such references. One has been content to record those more usually noticed, or more interesting.

The method of arrangement of the material selected is as follows. The system of Christian theology is surveyed in 53 numbered sections, each headed with a statement of the doctrine under consideration. In those many cases where there is nothing distinctive in the position of the Wesleys, and where they faithfully follow the accepted, orthodox, and scriptural teaching of the Church, particularly the Church of England of their upbringing, all that is required is a short note to summarize the position. When one comes to those matters which Methodists have traditionally described as 'our doctrines', wherein the Wesleys made it their distinctive calling to emphasize some particular position, a fuller and more careful introduction is naturally called for. Such points of teaching are universal grace, personally experienced faith as the gift of God, the necessity of evangelical conversion, full assurance of salvation by the witness of the Spirit, holiness or perfect love, and their sacramental doctrine. All sections are then illustrated by the most appropriate Wesley verse available.

In this selection we have not limited ourselves to that body of Wesley hymnody which has been more widely circulated in hymnbooks prepared for use in Church services. Many of the hymns here annotated are indeed loved and sung in the Churches, and certainly it is valuable to have additional information about these. However, it is also interesting to read some of these familiar items in a fuller form than appears in customary hymnals, or with original wording restored. We have not, indeed, tried to restore every precise detail of Wesley's original text. So the prolific use of capital letters, and of italics, has been reduced to modern style, and the frequent use of apostrophes, as 'reconcil'd' for 'reconciled', in like manner. Nor have we found it necessary to substitute the occasional polite 'mercies' for the scriptural 'bowels'. We have also included valuable hymns which have been commonly crowded out of Church hymnals, probably because they have appealed to the taste only of the few and discriminating. Finally there are examples of religious verse, often of real beauty, and expressive of important truths, which are more suitable for private reading and meditation than for congregational use.

It is not in every case possible to be certain what work is by John Wesley, and what by Charles, because their earlier publications, which contain the greater part of their most valuable work, were issued jointly without statement of the respective contributions. In general, however, the masterly translations from the German are the work of John Wesley, though he did compose a few early hymns in English, whereas the vast bulk of the work composed in English is from the prolific pen of Charles Wesley.

At the head of each poem selected there is a list of sources, and of hymnals where the verses in question may be found. It is not possible to list all the latter, because at least a few of the Wesley hymns have found their way into almost all hymn-books. The books referred to are shown on p. 7.

1. God the Sovereign Creator

The essential foundation of the whole system of scriptural Christianity is a conviction that the origin of the universe is no bare and remote principle of existence, but a sovereign Creator, a personal King of Glory, the Living God of the Bible. To say this does not involve that Christians believe that God is some sort of 'big man above the sky', for God is a spiritual Being, not having a body or physical desires, and not confined to time and space. To speak of God in terms of 'him', of 'fatherhood', 'love', etc. or as 'up in heaven' is symbolical language, not to be taken literally. It is highly significant and divinely revealed symbolical language, used to set forth God's spiritual and moral character. It should be made abundantly plain in this connection that 'he' is not the counterpart to 'she', but the opposite to 'it'. To speak of God as 'he' does not mean that he is male, but that he is personal, and not an impersonal Absolute, or principle of existence. To attempt to introduce into Christian theology and devotion unscriptural terms such as 'she', and 'mother', in rebuttal of supposed 'sexism' is a radical misunderstanding, and a counter-productive misunderstanding, because it brings into the discussion of the nature of God the issue of human sexuality which has no place here.

The religious consequences of this view of God are profound. (i) He can act through the processes of the world for the blessing of mankind. (ii) He is the supreme moral Governor of the race. (iii) Human beings can have personal fellowship with Him. The Wesleys, not being philosophers of religion, are not characteristically concerned to argue the reasonableness of this belief. They are men of practical religion, possessed of prophetic zeal to call their hearers to adoration, trust, moral obedience, and personal fellowship. It is perhaps significant that their chief celebration of God as the original principle and governor of creation comes in John Wesley's profound translation of the German of Johann Scheffler.

P.W. i. 141; W.H. 38; M.H.B. 67

O God, of good the unfathomed sea!	Ps. 77:19, 36, 6. Eph. 3:18
Who would not give his heart to thee?	Ps. 27:8, 86:12
Who would not love thee with his might?	Deut. 6:5
O Jesu, lover of mankind,	Wisd. 11:26
Who would not his whole soul and mind,	Mk. 12:30
With all his strength, to thee unite?	Jer. 50:5

Thou shin'st with everlasting rays;	Isa. 60:19, 20
Before the insufferable blaze	Ex. 3:6
Angels with both wings veil their eyes	Isa. 6:2
Yet free as air thy bounty streams	Acts 14:17
On all thy works; thy mercy's beams	Ps. 145:9
Diffusive as thy sun's arise.	Matt. 5:45

Astonished at thy frowning brow,	Rev. 20:11
Earth, hell and heaven's strong pillars bow;	Job. 9:6, Heb. 12:26
Terrible majesty is thine!	Job 37:22
Who then can that vast love express	1 Cor. 2:9, Eph. 3:19
Which bows thee down to me, who less	Phil. 2:8
Than nothing am, till thou art mine?	Gen. 18:27, 2 Cor. 6:10

High throned on heaven's eternal hill,	Ps. 103:19, Dan. 7:9
In number, weight, and measure still	Job 28:25
Thou sweetly orderest all that is:	Wisd. 11:20
And yet thou deign'st come to me,	Ps. 113:6
And guide my steps, that I, with thee	Ps. 37:23, Lk. 1:79
Enthroned, may reign in endless bliss.	Rev. 22:5

Fountain of good! all blessing flows	Joel 3:18
From thee; no want thy fulness knows;	Ps. 50:12
What but thyself canst thou desire?	
Yes; self-sufficient as thou art,	Gen. 22:16, Heb. 6:13
Thou dost desire my worthless heart;	Deut. 7:7
This, only this, dost thou require.	Deut. 10:12, Mic. 6:8

Hell's armies tremble at thy nod,	Isa. 24:21, James 2:19
And trembling own the Almighty God,	Gen. 17:1, Rev. 19:6
Sovereign of earth, hell, air, and sky:	Isa. 40:22–26
But who is this that comes from far,	Isa. 63:1–3
Whose garments rolled in blood appear?	
'Tis God made man, for man to die!	2 Cor. 5:14, Gal. 2:20

O God, of good the unfathomed sea!
Who would not give his heart to thee?
  Who would not love thee with his might?
O Jesu, lover of mankind,
Who would not his whole soul and mind,
  With all his strength to thee unite?

2. God the Holy One

The basic idea of 'the holy' is 'that which is separated unto God'—separated from the commonplace, from the passing and imperfect, from the merely human, and from that which is defiled. The awe with which one should approach God the King is set forth in John Wesley's fine translation from the German of Gerhardt Tersteegen.

P.W. i. 167; W.H. 494; M.H.B. 683; H.P. 531

Lo! God is here! let us adore,	Gen. 28:16–17
And own how dreadful is this place!	
Let all within us feel his power,	Ps. 111:6
And silent bow before his face;	Eccl. 5:2, Hab. 2:20
Who know his power, his grace who prove,	Rom. 9:22–3
Serve him with awe, with reverence love.	Ps. 33:8
Lo! God is here! him day and night	Gen. 28:16, Rev. 4:8
The united choirs of angels sing;	Rev. 5:11–14
To him, enthroned above all height,	Ps. 103:19, Heb. 8:1
Heaven's host their noblest praises bring;	Neh. 9:6
Disdain not, Lord, our meaner song,	Ps. 113:5, 6
Who praise thee with a stammering tongue.	Isa. 32:4
In thee we move: all things of thee	Acts 17:28
Are full, thou source and life of all;	Acts 17:25, Eph. 1:23
Thou vast unfathomable sea!	Ps. 77:19
Fall prostrate, lost in wonder fall,	Ps. 95:6
Ye sons of men, for God is man!	Jn. 1:14, Phil. 2:8
All may we lose, so thee we gain.	Phil. 3:8
As flowers their opening leaves display,	Cant. 2:10–12
And glad drink in the solar fire,	
So may we catch thy every ray,	Ps. 19:4–8
So may thy influence us inspire;	
Thou beam of the eternal beam,*	Ps. 36:9
Thou purging fire, thou quickening flame.	Mal. 3:2, 3

---

* Hail, holy Light, offspring of Heaven first-born!
Or of the Eternal coeternal beam.   (Milton, *Paradise Lost*, iii. 1–2)
Light from Light. *(Nicene Creed)*

3. The Unseen World

God's creation is by no means limited to those physical existences which can be 'seen' or 'felt', directly or indirectly. The unseen world of rational spiritual beings, or angels, joins in the worship of God. cf. *Gloria in excelsis.*

P.W. v. 279; W.H. 221; M.H.B. 17; H.P. 501

Meet and right it is to sing,*
   In every time and place, — Ps. 34:1, Mal. 1:11
Glory to our heavenly King, — Ps. 47: 6–8
   The God of truth and grace; — Jn. 1:17
Join we then with sweet accord, — Acts 1:14
   All in one thanksgiving join, — Ps. 95:2, 1 Cor. 14:16
Holy, holy, holy Lord, — Isa. 6:3, Rev. 4:8
   Eternal praise be thine! — 1 Tim. 1:17

Thee the first-born sons of light, — Job 38:7
   In choral symphonies,**
Praise by day, day without night, — Rev. 4:8, 21:25, 22:5
   And never, never cease;
Angels and archangels all — Ps. 148:2, Heb. 1:6
   Praise the mystic Three in One, — 1 Jn. 5:7
Sing, and stop, and gaze, and fall — Rev. 7:11, 8:1
   O'erwhelmed before thy throne.

Vying with that happy choir, — Heb. 12:22
   Who chant thy praise above,
We on eagles' wings aspire, — Ex. 19:4, Isa. 40:31
   The wings of faith and love; — Gal. 5:6, 22
Thee they sing with glory crowned, — Heb. 2:9
   We extol the slaughtered Lamb; — Rev. 5:6,12, 13:8
Lower if our voices sound, — Eccl. 5:2
   Our subject is the same.

Father, God, thy love we praise, — Jn. 3:16
   Which gave thy Son to die; — Rom. 8:32
Jesus, full of truth and grace, — Jn. 1:14, 17

Alike we glorify;	2 Thess. 1:12
Spirit, Comforter divine,	Jn. 14:16, 26, 15:26, 16:7
Praise by all to thee be given;	
Till we in full chorus join,	Phil 2:10–11
And earth is turned to heaven.	Rev. 21: 2–3, 10

---

* It is very meet, right, and our bounden duty. (*Book of Common Prayer*, Communion Service).

** for ye behold him, and with songs
   And choral symphonies, day without night,
   Circle his throne rejoicing. (Milton, *Paradise Lost*, v. 161–3)

4. Communion with God

In the passionate and eloquent poetry of an allegorical (*see 11*) treatment of Exodus 33:18–23 Charles Wesley celebrates the experience of personal communion with God. The 'Name' of God is a biblical phrase to convey the idea of the nature of God. Thus to 'know the Name' is to receive a divine revelation.

P.W. v. 92; W.H. 283

O God, my hope, my heavenly rest,	Ex. 33:14, Matt. 11:28, Heb. 4:9
My all of happiness below,	Ps. 144:15, 146:5
Grant my importunate request,	Gen. 18:23f., Isa. 62:7, Lk. 18:1f
To me, to me, thy goodness show;	Ex. 34:6, Ps. 27:15
Thy beatific face display,	Ex. 33:11
The brightness of eternal day.	Ex. 33:18
Before my faith's enlightened eyes	Eph. 1:18
Make all thy gracious goodness pass;	Ex. 33:19, 34:6
Thy goodness is the sight I prize,	Ex. 33:13
O might I see thy smiling face!	Ex. 33:11, 2 Cor. 4:6
Thy nature in my soul proclaim,	Ex. 3:13–14, 33:19
Reveal thy love, thy glorious name!	Ex. 33:12, Jn. 17:26
There, in the place beside thy throne,	Acts 1:9, Heb. 4:16, Rev. 3:21
Where all that find acceptance stand,	Acts 10:35
Receive me up into thy Son;	Eph. 1:6
Cover me with thy mighty hand;	Ex. 33:22, Isa. 51:16
Set me upon the rock, and hide	Ex. 33:21, Ps. 40:2, Isa. 26:4 (R.V
My soul in Jesu's wounded side.	Isa. 32:2, Jn. 19:34
O put me in the cleft; empower	Ex. 33:22
My soul the glorious sight to bear!	Tit. 2:13
Descend in this accepted hour,	Isa:49:8, 2 Cor. 6:2
Pass by me, and thy name declare;	Ex. 33:22, 34:6
Thy wrath withdraw, thy hand remove,	Ex. 33:23, Isa. 54:8, Hab. 3:2
And show thyself the God of love.	Ex. 34:6–7, 1 Jn. 4:8

To thee, great God of love! I bow,	Mich. 6:6, 1 Jn. 4:8
And prostrate in thy sight adore;	Ex. 34:8
By faith I see thee passing now;	Ex. 33:19, 22, 34:6
I have, but still I ask for more,	Jas. 1:5, 6, 4:6
A glimpse of love cannot suffice,	1 Cor. 13:12
My soul for all thy presence cries.	Ps. 84:2, Job 23:3
I cannot see thy face, and live,	Ex. 33:20
Then let me see thy face, and die!*	
Now, Lord, my gasping spirit receive,	Ps. 31:5, 42:1
Give me on eagles' wings to fly,	Ex. 19:4, Isa. 40:31
With eagles' eyes on thee to gaze,	Prov. 30:19
And plunge into the glorious blaze.	
The fulness of my vast reward	Gen. 15:1
A blest eternity shall be;	Matt. 5:12
But hast thou not on earth prepared	Rom. 9:28
Some better thing than this for me?	Heb: 6:9
What, but one drop! one transient sight!	1 Cor. 13:12
I want a sun, a sea of light.	Isa. 60:19, 1 Jn. 1:5
Moses thy backward parts might view,	Ex. 33:23
But not a perfect sight obtain;	Heb. 7:19, 11:40
The Gospel doth thy fulness show	Rom. 15:29, Eph. 3:19
To us, by the commandment slain;	Rom. 7:9, 11
The dead to sin shall find the grace,	Ex. 33:13, Rom. 6:2
The pure in heart shall see thy face.	Matt. 5:8
More favoured than the saints of old,	Heb. 11:40
Who now by faith approach to thee	Heb. 10:22
Shall all with open face behold	Gen. 32:30, Ex. 33:1
In Christ the glorious Deity;	2 Cor. 4:6
Shall see, and put the Godhead on,	Rom. 13:14, Gal. 3:27
The nature of thy sinless Son.	Jn. 8:46, Heb. 4:15

---

* Ah, Lord, let me die, that I may see Thee;   (Augustine, *Soliloquies, c. i.*)
  let me see Thee, that I may die.

5. Divine Providence

Though we would perhaps hesitate to say that God 'breaks' the laws of nature, which he has himself established, it is the scriptural Christian faith that the living and active God is in control of the processes of nature, and can effectually work through them to accomplish His blessing for the race and for individuals. Believers are therefore to trust God to guide and protect them.

P.W. vi. 461; W.H. 245; M.H.B. 59; H.P. 37

Good thou art, and good thou dost,	Matt. 19:17, Acts 14:17
Thy mercies reach to all,	Ps. 145:9
Chiefly those who on thee trust,	1 Tim. 4:10
And for thy mercy call;	Ps. 51:1
New they every morning are;	Lam. 3:23
As fathers when their children cry,	Matt. 7:11
Us thou dost in pity spare,	Ps. 103:13, Mal. 3:17
And all our wants supply.	Matt. 6:33, Phil. 4:19
Mercy o'er thy works presides;	Ps. 145:9
Thy providence displayed	Gen. 22:14 (R.V.), Ps. 65:9
Still preserves, and still provides	Gen. 45:5, Matt. 6:25f., Acts 14:
For all thy hands have made;	Isa. 64:8
Keeps with most distinguished care	1 Pet. 5:7
The man who on thy love depends;	1 Tim. 4:10
Watches every numbered hair,	Matt. 10:30
And all his steps attends.	Ps. 37:31
Who can sound the depths unknown	Rom. 11:33
Of thy redeeming grace?	Rom. 3:24, Eph. 2:5, 8,
Grace that gave thine only Son	Jn. 3:16
To save a ruined race!	1 Cor. 15:22
Millions of transgressors poor	Isa. 53:12, Lk. 22:37
Thou hast for Jesu's sake forgiven,	Eph. 4:32
Made them of thy favour sure,	Heb. 10:22
And snatched from hell to heaven.	Amos 4:11, Zech. 3:2,
	Jude 23

Millions more thou ready art	Ex. 20:6, 34:7, Jer. 32:18
To save, and to forgive;	Ps. 103:3, Dan. 9:9
Every soul and every heart	1 Tim. 2:4, 2 Pet: 3:9
Of man thou wouldst receive:	
Father, now accept of mine	1 Pet. 2:5
Which now, through Christ, I offer thee;	
Tell me now, in love divine,	1 Jn. 4:16
That thou hast pardoned me!	Isa. 55:7, Jer. 31:34,
	Rom. 8:16

The following is one of the poems written for his future wife by Charles Wesley when he was courting. We may presume, therefore, that the 'blessing', 'by heaven designed for me' was originally Sally Gwynne. And who will say that a happy choice in marriage is not a signal example of divine providence?

P.W. v. 448; W.H. 832; M.H.B. 510

Away my needless fears,	Ps. 27:1
And doubts no longer mine;	Matt. 14:31
A ray of heavenly light appears,	Acts 9:3
A messenger divine.	Acts 27:23
Thrice comfortable hope,	Phil. 2:1
That calms my stormy breast;	Mk. 4: 39–40
My Father's hand prepares the cup,	Matt. 20:22–23, Jn. 18:11
And what he wills is best.	Lk. 22:42
If what I wish is good,*	
And suits the will divine;	Rom. 12:2
By earth and hell in vain withstood,	Rom. 8:38–9
I know it shall be mine.	Mk. 11:24
Still let them counsel take	Ps.2:2, 7, Acts 4:25
To frustrate his decree,	Acts 5:38f., Rom. 9:19
They cannot keep a blessing back	Num. 22:12
By heaven designed for me.	Matt. 7:11
Here then I doubt no more,	Lk. 12:29
But in his pleasure rest,	Lk. 12:32
Whose wisdom, love, and truth, and power	
Engage to make me blest.	Eph. 1:3
To accomplish his design	Isa. 55:11
The creatures all agree;	1 Tim. 4:4
And all the attributes divine	Rom. 8:28
Are now at work for me.	

---

* Grant unto thy people, that they may love the thing which thou commandest, and desire that which thou dost promise. (B.C.P. Collect: Easter IV).

6. Revelation

As God is the Infinite One, an unseen spiritual Being throned in bright glory, we humans could know nothing of him were it not that of his grace he has made something of his nature known. This is the fact of divine revelation.

P.W. ii. 299; W.H. 144; M.H.B. 369

Come, Lord, and help me to rejoice	Ps. 51:15
In hope that I shall hear thy voice,	Cant. 2:14
Shall one day see my God;	Isa. 33:17
Shall cease from all my sin and strife,	Prov. 20:3, 1 Pet. 4:1
Handle and taste the word of life,	Heb. 6:5, 1 Jn. 1:1
And feel the sprinkled blood.	1 Pet. 1:2, Heb. 9:19, 10:22
Prisoner of hope, to thee I turn,	Zech. 9:12
And calmly confident, I mourn,	Isa. 30:15
And pray, and weep for thee:	Isa. 61:2, Matt. 5:4
Tell me thy love, thy secret tell,	Ps. 25:14, 1 Jn. 4:9
Thy mystic name in me reveal,	Gen. 32:29, Ex. 3:13–14, 33:19, 3
Reveal thyself in me.	Gal. 1:16
Descend, pass by me, and proclaim,	Ex. 34:5–6
O Lord of hosts, thy glorious name,	Ps. 24:10
The Lord, the gracious Lord,	
Long-suffering, merciful, and kind;	
The God who always bears in mind	Ps. 111:5, 115:12, Isa. 49:15
His everlasting word.	Rev. 14:6
Plenteous he is in truth and grace	Ex. 34:6–7, Jn. 1:17
He wills that all the fallen race	1 Tim: 2:4, 2 Pet; 3:9
Should turn, repent, and live;	Lk. 24:47, Acts 17:30
His pardoning grace for all is free;	Ex. 34:7, Eph. 2:8
Transgression, sin, iniquity,	
He freely doth forgive.	Lk. 7:42
Mercy he doth for thousands keep;	Ex. 34:7
He goes and seeks the one lost sheep,	Matt. 18:12–13

And brings his wanderer home;	Jer. 29:14, 31:8, 32:37
And every soul that sheep might be:	Ezek. 18:4
Come then, my Lord, and gather me,	Ps. 106:47, Mal. 3:17
My Jesus, quickly come!	*Joshua 10:6, Rev. 3:11,
	22:7, 12, 20

---

* Joshua in Hebrew and Jesus in Greek are the same name, see Heb. 4:8, A.V. and R.V.

7. Natural Religion

The vastness of the creation, and its admirable order, speak of the illimitable power and wisdom of God. There are thus some basic truths of religion which can be known to all men and women by reasonable observation of nature, and the facts of human life, apart from the revelation in the Bible.

This is the *General Revelation*, and provides the basis for *Natural Religion.*

Herein is a measure of common ground between the Christian faith and many other forms of religion. Natural religion is not specifically Christian, but is a part of the foundation of Christian faith.

P.W. vi. 388; W.H. 233

Happy man whom God doth aid!	Ps. 146:5
God our souls and bodies made;	Gen. 1:27, 2:7
God on us, in gracious showers,	
Blessings every moment pours;	Ezek. 34:26
Compasses with angel-bands,	Matt. 18:10, Lk. 16:22
Bids them bear us in their hands;	Ps. 91:11, Matt. 4:6
Parents, friends, 'twas God bestowed,	Ps. 68:6
Life, and all, descend from God.	Acts 17:28
He this flowery carpet spread,	Gen. 1:11, 2:8, Cant. 2:12
Made the earth on which we tread;	Gen. 1:9–10, Ps. 95:4–5
God refreshes in the air,	Acts. 17:25
Covers with the clothes we wear,	Gen. 3:21, Matt. 6:30
Feeds us with the food we eat,	Gen. 1:29, 8:22, 9:3, Matt. 6:3
Cheers us by his light and heat,	Gen. 1:16–18, Ps. 19:4–6
Makes his sun on us to shine;	Matt. 5:45
All our blessings are divine!	Acts 14:17
Give him, then, for ever give,	Ps. 30:13 (B.C.P.)
Thanks for all that we receive!	
Man we for his kindness love,	Matt. 5:46f.
How much more our God above?	Matt. 5:48
Worthy thou, our heavenly Lord,	Ps. 18:3, Rev. 4:11
To be honoured and adored;	
God of all-creating grace,	Gen. 1:1, Isa. 43:7, Rev. 4:11
Take the everlasting praise!	1 Tim. 6:16

8. Revelation in Scripture

The truths of Natural Religion are affirmed in the Bible, and this is a part of God's authoritative scriptural revelation. However, the determinative element in the Bible, which makes it into Christian Scripture, is the account of God's saving action in calling and disciplining his ancient People the Hebrews, in preparation for the coming of Christ, and of witness to Christ when he came. Here is a *Special Revelation* which could not have been discerned by the exercise of human faculties. This forms the basis for the *Revealed Religion* of salvation. The Holy Spirit, who is the Spirit of Christ, and who inspired the recording of Scripture, both guides the Church in the interpretation of the book of God, and brings the meaning home to the heart of the believer with personal conviction.

P.W. iv. 136; W.H. 90

Come, O thou Prophet of the Lord,	Deut. 18:15, Acts 3:22
Thou great Interpreter divine,	Lk. 24:27
Explain thine own transmitted word,	Jn. 16:13–15
To teach and to inspire is thine;	Lk. 24:32, Jn. 14:26
Thou only canst thyself reveal,	2 Pet: 1:20
Open the book, and loose the seal.	Rev. 5:5
What'er the ancient prophets spoke	2 Pet. 1:21
Concerning thee, O Christ, make known;	
Chief subject of the sacred book,	Jn. 5:39, 46
Thou fillest all, and thou alone;	Eph. 1:23, 4:10
Yet there our Lord we cannot see,	1 Cor. 12:3
Unless thy Spirit lend the key.	Lk. 11:52, Jn. 16:14
Now, Jesus, now the veil remove,	2 Cor. 3:13–14
The folly of our darkened heart;	Rom. 1:21
Unfold the wonders of thy love,	Ps. 119:18
The knowledge of thyself impart;	Eph. 4:13
Our ear, our inmost soul, we bow,	Prov. 22:17, Mich. 6:6
Speak, Lord, thy servants hearken now.	1 Sam. 3:10

P.W. i. 238; W.H. 87; M.H.B. 305; M.H. 131; H.P. 469

Come, Holy Ghost, our hearts inspire,	Acts 1:8
Let us thine influence prove,	
Source of the old prophetic fire,	Isa. 6:6–7, Jer. 20:9, Ezek. 1:4
Fountain of light and love.	Gal. 5:22
Come, Holy Ghost (for moved by thee	
The prophets wrote and spoke)	Isa. 61:1, 2 Pet. 1:21
Unlock the truth, thyself the key,	Jn. 14:6, Rev. 3:7
Unseal the sacred book.	Rev. 5:2, 5
Expand thy wings, celestial Dove,	Lk. 3:22
Brood o'er our nature's night;	1 Cor. 2:14
On our disordered spirits move,	Gen. 1:2, 8:9
And let there now be light.	Gen. 1:3
God, through himself, we then shall know,	1 Cor. 2:11–12
If thou within us shine,	Isa. 60:1–2, 2 Cor. 4:6
And sound, with all thy saints below,	Eph. 3:18
The depths of love divine.*	

P.W. xiii. 219; W.H. 885; M.H.B. 306; H.P. 468

Come, divine Interpreter,	Jn. 16:13–14
Bring me eyes thy book to read,	Acts 8:30–1
Ears the mystic words to hear,	
Words which did from thee proceed,	2 Tim. 3:16, 2 Pet. 1:21
Words that endless bliss impart,	Ps. 119:111, Isa. 51:11
Kept in an obedient heart.	Rom. 6:17
All who read, or hear, are blessed,	Rev. 1:3
If thy plain commands we do;	James 1:25
Of thy kingdom here possessed,	Lk. 12:32
Thee we shall in glory view;	1 Jn. 3:2, Rev. 22:4
When thou com'st on earth to abide	Mk. 13:26, Rev. 1:7, Acts 1:11
Reign triumphant at thy side.	Matt. 19: 28, Rev. 20:4

---

* 'All that has being in full concert join   (Young, *The Last Day*, ii; 47–8)
  And celebrate the depths of love divine!'

9. The Old Testament

The God-given ritual of Hebrew religion, and the inspired teaching of the prophets, embody authentic but partial glimpses of those truths which are fully seen in Christ.

P.W. iii. 307; H.L.S 123; W.H. 702

O thou, whose offering on the tree — Heb. 9:13–14, 1 Pet. 2:21
  The legal offerings all foreshowed, — Gal. 3:24, Lev. 16:15–16
Borrowed their whole effect from thee,
  And drew their virtue from thy blood. — Heb. 9:11–12

The blood of goats and bullocks slain — Heb. 10:4
  Could never for one sin atone:
To purge the guilty offerer's stain, — Heb. 5:3, 9:9, 10:11
  Thine was the work, and thine alone. — Ps. 74:13 (B.C.P.), Eph. 2:8

Vain in themselves their duties were, — Matt: 15:9
  Their services could never please, — Heb. 11:6
Till joined with thine, and made to share — Rom. 6:5–7
  The merits of thy righteousness. — Rom. 4:5

Forward they cast a faithful look — Rom. 3:21f., Heb. 9:10, 10:1
  On thy approaching sacrifice; — Acts 8:32–5
And thence their pleasing savour took, — 2 Cor. 2:15, Eph. 5:2
And rose accepted in the skies. — Ezek. 20:40–1

Those feeble types, and shadows old, — Heb. 9:24, 10:1
  Are all in thee, the Truth, fulfilled: — Jn. 14:6, Heb. 9:14, 22–3
We in thy sacrifice behold
  The substance of those rites revealed. — Heb.11:1

Thy meritorious sufferings past, — Mk. 10:45, Rom. 3:25, 1 Jn. 2:2
  We see by faith to us brought back; — 2 Cor. 5:14–15
And on thy grand oblation cast — Heb. 10:9–10
  Its saving benefits partake. — Ps. 103:2, Heb. 10:19–22

P.W. xii. 288; W.H. 883

Jesus I humbly seek,	Jn. 6:24, 12:21
And of himself inquire,	Lk. 7:19
Did not the prophet speak	Acts 8:34
Of thee, the world's Desire:	Hag. 2:7
Thou poor, despised, afflicted Man,	Isa. 53:3–4
His meaning to my heart explain.	Acts 8:35
Art thou the Lamb of God	Jn. 1:29, 36, Rev. 5:6
Who didst from heaven come,	Gen. 22:8, Jn. 6:38, 42
Led by the multitude,	Lk. 22:47, 23:1
Before thy shearers dumb,	Isa. 53:7, Matt. 27:14
The patient, speechless Man of woe,	Lam. 1:12
By sinners crucified below?	Lk. 24:7, Acts 2:23
Swept from the face of earth	Isa. 53:8, Jn. 19:15
Didst thou our sorrows bear,	Isa. 53:4
Whose everlasting birth	Jn. 1:1–2, 8:58, Rev. 1:8
God only can declare,	Isa. 53:8, Acts 8:33
Whose countless seed shall soon arise,	Gen. 22:17, Heb. 11:12
And shine as stars beyond the skies?	Dan. 12:3
Adopt me by thy grace	Gal. 4:5, Eph. 1:5
Into thy family,	Jer. 31:1, Eph. 3:15
My heart shall then confess	Rom. 10:9
The prophet spake of thee,	Acts 13:27
Then, to mine inmost soul made known,	
I feel he spake of thee alone.	Jn. 5:39

10. Revelation in Christ

The climax of divine revelation is the wonderful birth, life, acts, teaching, and supremely the sufferings, death, resurrection, and ascension of Christ. This revelation is determinative for Christian faith, though Christian faith is much more than the declaration of a body of moral and spiritual truths (12.) As this hymn is a classic example of how many Scripture references can sometimes be found in Charles Wesley we leave the complete set of references.

P.W. vii. 194; W.H. 128; M.H.B. 172; H.P. 184

1 With glorious clouds encompassed round,	Ex. 24:16, 17, 1 Kgs. 8: 10–11, Ps. 97:2, Ezek. 10:4
Whom angels dimly see,*	Isa. 6:2, 1 Pet. 1:12
Will the unsearchable be found,	Job 11:7, 23:3, 8, 9, 1 Tim. 6:16
Or God appear to me?	Jer. 31:3, Acts 7:2, Tit. 2:13, Heb. 9:26
2 Will he forsake his throne above,	Ps. 103:19, 113:5, 6, Isa. 6:1, Rev. 4:10–11, 7:10
Himself to worms impart?	Job 25:6, Ps. 22:6, Isa. 41:14
Answer, thou Man of grief and love,	Isa. 53:3, 4, 10, Jn. 11: 35–6, 13:1, 19:5, Gal. 2:20, Rev. 1:5
And speak it to my heart!	Rom. 10:9
3 In manifested love explain	Jn. 1:18, 14:21, 17:26, 2 Tim. 1:10, 1 Jn. 4:9
Thy wonderful design;	Isa. 28:21, Eph. 3:3, Col. 1:26, 1 Tim. 3:16
What meant the suffering Son of man,	Isa. 50:6, 53:4–8, 63:9, Lk. 24:26, Acts 8:34f., Heb. 2:10, 1 Pet. 1:11, 3:18
The streaming blood divine?	Mk. 15:39, Acts 20:28, Heb. 13:12, 1 Jn. 5:5–6, Rev. 1:5

4 Didst thou not in our flesh appear   Jn. 1:14, 1 Tim. 3:16, Tit. 2:13

    And live and die below,   Phil. 2:8, Heb. 2:16
  That I may now perceive thee near   Eph. 2:13
  And my Redeemer know?   2 Cor. 8:9, Eph. 3:18, 19, 2 Tim. 1:12

5 Come then, and to my soul reveal   Rom. 1:17, Gal. 1:16
  The heights and depths of grace,   Eph. 3:18
  The wounds which all my sorrows heal,   Isa. 53:4, 5, 1 Pet. 2:24
  That dear disfigured face.   Isa. 52:14, 53:2

6 Before my eyes of faith confessed,   Matt. 10:32, Rom. 10:9, 10, Phil. 2:11, 1 Jn. 4:2, 3

    Stand forth a slaughtered Lamb,   Isa. 53:7, Acts 8:32, Rev. 5:6
  And wrap me in thy crimson vest **   Isa. 63:1–3, Matt. 27:28, Jn. 19:2, 5

    And tell me all thy name.   Ex. 3:13, 33:19, Eph. 1:21, Phil 2:9, 10, Rev. 19:12, 16

7 Jehovah in thy person show,   Ex. 3:14, Ps. 83:18
  Jehovah crucified!   Mk. 15:39, Heb. 1:3, 2:14
  And then the pardoning God I know,   Mich. 7:18, 2 Cor. 5:19, Eph. 4:32, Ex. 34:6–7

    And feel the blood applied.   1 Pet. 1:2, Heb. 12:24, Rev. 7:14

8 I view the Lamb in his own light,   Jn. 8:12, 9:5, Rev. 21:23
  Whom angels dimly see,   Isa. 6:2, 1 Pet. 1:12
  And gaze, transported at the sight,   1 Cor. 2:9, 2 Cor. 12:2, 1 Tim. 3:16, Rev. 4:1

    Through all eternity.   Jn. 17:3

---

* To us invisible, or dimly seen.   (Milton, *Paradise Lost*, v. 157;
  In light unsearchable enthroned   S. Wesley, Jun. 'An Hymn to
    Which angels dimly see.   God the Father', *Poems* (1736) p. 2. ll. 5–6)

** So, in his purple wrapp'd, receive me, Lord.   (John Donne, 'Hymn to God
  His dying crimson, like a robe,   my God, in my Sickness'.)
    Spreads o'er his body on the tree.   (Isaac Watts, 'When I survey', v

11. Scripture Allegory

A prominent traditional method of expressing the spiritual continuity of the Old and New Testaments is to treat Old Testament prophecies and narratives as allegories referring to Christ, and to the Christian gospel. Christian 'hidden meanings' are discerned in the Old Testament text. Modern critical and historical scholarship has generally assumed that the only legitimate concern of the expositor is to recover so far as possible the sense which was originally in the mind of the writer. This attitude is surely to be upheld, so far as the interests of historical study are concerned. This has commonly led to the neglect, or even the repudiation, of scripture allegory, because the 'hidden meanings' have been later discerned by the mind of the Christian reader, and are therefore to be rejected as 'unhistorical'. However, it is not as easy as this to sweep aside this traditional method of scripture exposition, deeply rooted as it is in the spiritual devotion and theological methods of the Church, if only because the New Testament, and our Lord himself, to some extent make use of this method upon the Old Testament (e.g. Matt. 12:39–41, Mark 12: 1–12, Galatians 4:22–31, and widely in Hebrews). Certainly we cannot understand the Wesleys' attitude to scriptural doctrine without taking full account of the method of allegory. It provides some of the most effective of Charles Wesley's poetry and devotional writing. A number of leading examples are:

(i) Moses' encounter with God upon Sinai, mountain of the Mosaic Law, is viewed as a parable of the fuller communion with God and Christ, and the giving of the higher law of the Spirit. See (4).

(ii) The wrestling of Jacob, the ancestor of the traditional Twelve Tribes of Israel, with a theophany, or divine appearance, is interpreted as a type of the Christian encounter with God in Christ, involving penitence, faith, and a revelation of divine love (Genesis 32:24–32).

P.W. ii. 173; W.H. 140, 141; M.H.B. 339; M.H. 529; H.P. 434

Come, O thou Traveller unknown,	Isa. 63:1
Whom still I hold, but cannot see!	Ex. 33:20, Jn. 1:18

My company before is gone,   Gen. 32: 13–23
   And I am left alone with thee;   Gen. 32:24
With thee all night I mean to stay,   Lk. 6:12
And wrestle till the break of day.   Gen. 32:24, 26

I need not tell thee who I am,   Gen. 32:27
   My misery and sin declare;   Ps. 38:18, Isa. 3:9, Rev. 3:17
Thyself hast called me by my name,   Gen. 32:28, Isa. 43:1, 45:4
   Look on thy hands and read it there;   Isa. 49:16
But who, I ask thee, who art thou?   Gen. 32:29
Tell me thy name, and tell me now.   Ex. 3:13–14

In vain thou strugglest to get free,   Gen. 32:26
   I never will unloose my hold!
Art thou the Man that died for me?   Jn. 19:5, Gal. 2:20
   The secret of thy love unfold;   Ps. 25:14, Rom. 5:8, Eph. 3:4
Wrestling, I will not let thee go,   Gen. 32:26
Till I thy name, thy nature know.   Ex. 3:13–14

Wilt thou not yet to me reveal   1 Cor. 2:9, 2 Cor. 12:4
   Thy new, unutterable name?   Ex. 3:14, Rev. 19:12
Tell me, I still beseech thee, tell;   Gen. 32:29
   To know it now resolved I am: 1 Cor. 2:2
Wrestling, I will not let thee go,   Gen. 32:26
Till I thy name, thy nature know.   Ex. 3:13–14

'Tis all in vain to hold thy tongue,   Hab. 1:13
   Or touch the hollow of my thigh;   Gen. 32:25
Though every sinew be unstrung,   Gen. 32:32
   Out of my arms thou shalt not fly;   Cant. 3:4
Wrestling I will not let thee go,   Gen. 32:26
Till I thy name, thy nature know.   Ex. 3:13–14

What though my shrinking flesh complain,   Gen. 32:25
   And murmur to contend so long: Job 9:3
I rise superior to my pain,   2 Cor. 4:17
   When I am weak, then I am strong;   2 Cor. 12:10
And when my all of strength shall fail,   Ps. 73:26, Lam. 3:18, 22
I shall with the God-man prevail.   Gen. 32:28, 1 Sam. 2:9

My strength is gone, my nature dies,   Ps. 90:10, 1 Cor. 15:42ff.
   I sink beneath thy weighty hand,   Ps. 39:11 (B.C.P.), Ezek 3:14
Faint to revive, and fall to rise;   Isa. 40:29, Lk. 2:34
   I fall, and yet by faith I stand,   Rom. 11:20, 1 Cor. 2:5
I stand, and will not let thee go,   Ex. 14:13
Till I thy name, thy nature know.   Ex. 3:13–14

Yield to me now, for I am weak,   Ps. 6:2, Matt 26:41
   But confident in self-despair;   2 Cor. 4:8–10, 12:10, 13:4
Speak to my heart, in blessings speak,   Gen. 32:26, Eph. 1:3
   Be conquered by my instant prayer;   Ex. 32:9f., Lk. 18:1, Rom. 12:

Speak or thou never hence shalt move,	
And tell me if thy name is Love.	1 Jn. 4:8, 16
'Tis Love! 'tis Love! thou diedst for me!	Rom. 5:8, Gal. 2:20, 1 Jn. 4:16
I hear thy whisper in my heart;	1 Kgs. 19:12
The morning breaks, the shadows flee,	Gen. 32:31, Cant. 4:6
Pure, universal love thou art;	Jn. 3:16
To me, to all, thy mercies move;	Ezek. 33:11, Ps. 145:9,
	1 Tim. 2:4, 2 Pet. 3:9
Thy nature and thy name is Love.	1 Jn. 4:8, 16
My prayer hath power with God; the grace	Gen. 32:28, Jas. 5:16–18
Unspeakable I now receive;	2 Cor. 9:15
Through faith I see thee face to face,	1 Cor. 13:12, 2 Cor. 3:18
I see thee face to face, and live!	Gen. 32:30, Ex. 33:11, 20
In vain I have not wept and strove;	Isa. 30:19, Phil. 2:16
Thy nature and thy name is Love.	1 Jn. 4:8, 16
I know thee, Saviour, who thou art,	Mk. 1:24
Jesus, the feeble sinner's friend;	Matt. 11:19, Jn. 15:14–15
Nor wilt thou with the night depart,	Jer. 14:8
But stay and love me to the end,	Jn. 13:1
Thy mercies never shall remove;	Jer. 31:3, Ps. 138:8
Thy nature and thy name is Love.	1 Jn. 4:8, 16
The Sun of righteousness on me	Gen. 32:31
Hath risen with healing in his wings,	Mal. 4:2
Withered my nature's strength; from thee	Gen. 32:32, 2 Cor. 4:16
My soul its life and succour brings;	Ps. 66:9, Heb 2:18
My help is all laid up above;	Ps. 74:13 (B.C.P.), Ps. 121:1
Thy nature and thy name is love.	1 Jn. 4:8, 16
Contented now upon my thigh	Gen. 32:31
I halt, till life's short journey end;	Wisd. 5:13, Ps. 90:9–10
All helplessness, all weakness, I	
On thee alone for strength depend,	2 Cor. 12:9
Nor have I power from thee to move;	Jn. 6:68
Thy nature and thy name is Love.	1 Jn. 4:8, 16
Lame as I am, I take the prey,	Gen. 32:31, Num. 23:23f.
Hell, earth, and sin, with ease o'ercome;	Rom. 8:37–9
I leap with joy, pursue my way,	Ps. 30:11, 119:32, Lk. 6:23
And as a bounding hart fly home,	Ps. 42:1, Isa. 35:6
Through all eternity to prove	Wisd. 2:23
Thy nature and thy name is Love.	1 Jn. 4:8,16

(iii) When Aaron, the High Priest, and representative to God of the whole People of God, went into the Holy Place, he wore a breast-plate bearing twelve precious stones engraved with the names of the twelve tribes of Israel. (Exodus 28:15–21, 29–30) This is a type of Jesus Christ, our great High Priest, who is the Head of the body which is his Church. He is the true Representative in glory of the whole body of believers. In the following selection of verses the first two are from no. 129 of Charles Wesley's 166 'Hymns from the Lord's Supper', and the remainder from no. 110. They are based upon extracts from the Caroline divine Brevint (see intro. to section 49.) 'Let us ever turn our eyes and our hearts toward Jesus our eternal High Priest, who is gone up into the true sanctuary, and doth there continually present both his own Body and Blood before God, and, as Aaron did, all the true Israel of God in a memorial.—He delivers into our hands, by way of instrument and conveyance, the blessed Sacrament of his Body and Blood, in the same manner as kings used to bestow dignities by the bestowing of a staff.'

P.W. iii. 313, 297; H.L.S. 129, 110; H.S. 62; H.P. 622

1 See where our great High-Priest	Heb. 9:7, 11–12, 24f.
Before the Lord appears,	
And on his loving breast	Isa. 40:11, Jn. 13:23, 25
The tribes of Israel bears,	Ex. 28:15–21, 29–30
Never without his people seen,	Isa. 63:8–9, Hos. 1:10,
	Rom. 9:24f.
The Head of all believing men!	Eph. 1:22, 4:15–16, 5:23,
	Col. 1:18
2 With him the Corner-stone,	Ps.118:22, Isa. 28:16, Matt.
	21:42, Eph. 2:20, 1 Pet. 2:6
The living stones conjoin;	1 Cor. 3:12, 16, Eph. 2:21f.,
	1 Pet. 2:4–5
Christ and his Church are one,*	Cant. 6:9
One body and one vine;	Jn. 10:16, 11:52, 15:1–6,
	17:11, 23, Rom. 12:5, 1 Cor.
	10:17, 12:13, Eph. 2:14, 4:5
For us he uses all his powers,	Matt. 28:18, Acts 4:7, 10,
	Eph. 1:19, Heb. 6:5
And all he has, or is, is ours.	Lk. 15:31, Gal. 2:20,
	Phil. 4:19
3 Jesu, on thee we feed	1 Cor. 10:3–4
Along the desert way,	Ex. 13:18
Thou art the living Bread	Jn. 6:51
Which doth our spirits stay,	Cant. 2:5, Jn. 6:35, 48–51
And all who in this banquet join	Cant. 2:4, Isa. 25:6,
	Lk. 22:30
Lean on the staff of life divine.	Isa. 3:1, Heb. 11:21
4 O may we still abide	Jn. 15:4, 7, 10, 1 Jn. 2:27f.
In thee our pardoning God,	Ex. 34, 6–7, Neh. 9:17,
	Mic. 7:18
Thy Spirit be our guide,	Isa. 30:21, Jn. 16:13

Thy body be our food,	Jn. 6:51–8
Till thou who hast the token given	Ps. 86:17, Jn. 6:14, Acts 2:22
Shalt bear us on thyself to heaven.	Ex. 19:4, Isa. 40:11, 46:4, 1 Thess. 4:17

---

* (Cyprian: *De catholicae ecclesiae unitate*, 4.) 'To this one Church the Holy Spirit points in the Song of Songs, in the person of our Lord, saying, "My dove . . ." '

(iv) The institution of the Year of Jubilee reflects Hebrew feeling that one's holding of land was a sacred patrimony, which ought not to be alienated in perpetuity, (Ruth. 4:1–11, 1 Kings 21:2–3, Ezek. 46:16–18). Therefore it was only to be pledged on terms which allowed of its return to the original owner at the fiftieth year (Leviticus 25:8–17.) This passage, which contains the text which runs round the Liberty Bell, is made the basis of a stirring treatment of the gospel of free forgiveness.

P.W. vi. 12; W.H. 738; M.H. 100

Blow ye the trumpet, blow,	Lev. 25:9
The gladly solemn sound,	Num. 10:10
Let all the nations know,	Isa. 2:2–4, Matt. 28:19
To earth's remotest bound;	Ps. 98:3, Jer. 16:19
The year of Jubilee is come!	Lev. 25:8–9
Return, ye ransomed sinners, home.	Lev. 25:13, Isa. 35:10, Mk. 10:45, 1 Tim. 2:6
Jesus, our great High-Priest,	Heb. 9:11, 12, 14
Hath full atonement made:	Ex. 30:10, Rom. 3:25f., 5:11
Ye weary spirits, rest,	Matt. 11:28–9
Ye mournful souls, be glad!	Isa. 61:2, 3, Matt. 5:4
The year of Jubilee is come!	Lev. 25:8–10
Return, ye ransomed sinners, home.	Lev. 25:13, Isa. 35:10, Mk. 10:45, 1 Tim. 2:6
Extol the Lamb of God,	Ps. 145:1, Rev. 5:12–13
The all-atoning Lamb,	Jn. 1:29, 36
Redemption in his blood	Eph. 1:7, Col. 1:4
Throughout the world proclaim;	Mal. 1:11, Rev. 5:9
The year of Jubilee is come!	Lev. 25:8–9
Return, ye ransomed sinners, home.	Lev. 25:13, Isa. 35:10, Mk. 10:45, 1 Tim. 2:6
Ye slaves of sin and hell,	Lev. 25:47–54, Rom. 5:17, 6:17, 20, Heb. 2:15
Your liberty receive,	Isa. 61:1, Lk. 4:18
And safe in Jesus dwell,	Lev. 25:18
And blest in Jesus live;	Lev. 25:21, Eph. 1:3

The year of Jubilee is come!	Lev. 25:8–9
Return, ye ransomed sinners, home.	Lev. 25:13, Isa. 35:10, Mk. 10:45, 1 Tim. 2:6
Ye who have sold for nought,	Lev. 25–8
Your heritage above,	Matt. 6:20, Acts 20:32
Receive it back unbought,	Isa. 49:8, 55:1
The gift of Jesu's love:	Lk. 7:42, Rom. 6:23,
The year of Jubilee is come!	Lev. 25:8–9
Return, ye ransomed sinners, home.	Lev. 25:13, Isa. 35:10, Mk. 10:45, 1 Tim. 2:6
The gospel trumpet hear,	Lev. 25:9, 1 Cor. 14:8
The news of heavenly grace,	Acts 20:24
And saved from earth, appear	Gal. 1:4
Before your Saviour's face:	Rev. 22:4
The year of Jubilee is come!	Lev. 25:8–9
Return, ye ransomed sinners, home.	Lev. 25:13, Isa. 35:10, Mk. 10:45, 1 Tim. 2:6

(v) The slaughter of the Canaanites (taken to be the enemies of God), and the consequent possession of the Promised Land, is taken as an allegory of the victory of Christ over sin, and the growth of the believer in holiness. It is a pity that the apparent difficulty of the opening word 'Jeshurun', which is a poetic term for Israel, should perhaps have stood in the way of the wider appreciation of this hymn with its striking, though sometimes quaint, scriptural imagery. (Deuteronomy 33: 26–29)

P.W. ii. 305; W.H. 407; M.H.B. 68

None is like Jeshurun's God,	Deut. 33:26
So great, so strong, so high,	Deut. 10:17, Isa. 12:2, 26:4
Lo! he spreads his wings abroad,	Ps. 18:10
He rides upon the sky!	Deut. 33:26
Israel is his first-born son;	Ex. 4:22
God, the Almighty God, is thine;	Ps. 91:1
See him to thy help come down,	Deut. 33:7, Ps. 121:1
The excellence divine.	Deut. 33:26
Thee the great Jehovah deigns	Ex. 3:14, 6:3, Ps. 83:18
To succour and defend;	Ps. 121:5 (B.C.P.) 2 Cor. 6:2
Thee the eternal God sustains,	Deut. 33:27
Thy Maker and thy friend:	Isa. 17:7, Jas. 2:23
Israel, what hast thou to dread?	Isa. 44:2, Jer. 30:10
Safe from all impending harms,	1 Pet. 3:13
Round thee and beneath are spread	Deut. 33:27
The everlasting arms.	

God is thine; disdain to fear	Ps. 27:1, Isa. 43:1, 2
The enemy within:	Mk. 7:21, 23, 2 Cor. 7:5
God shall in thy flesh appear,	Jn. 1:14
And make an end of sin;	Dan. 9:24
God the man of sin shall slay,	2 Thess. 2:3, 8
Fill thee with exceeding joy;	Ps. 43:4, Jude 24
God shall thrust him out, and say,	Deut. 33:27
'Destroy them all, destroy!'	Deut. 7:2, 23, 24, 1 Jn. 3:8

All the struggle then is o'er,	Isa. 40:2
And wars and fightings cease,	Ps. 46:9
Israel then shall sin no more,	Jn. 5:14, 8:11, 1 Jn. 3:9
But dwell in perfect peace;	1 Chron. 22:9, Isa. 2:4
All his enemies are gone;	Deut. 12:10, Lk. 1:74
Sin shall have in him no part;	2 Cor. 6:15
Israel now shall dwell alone,	Deut. 33:28, Num. 23:9
With Jesus in his heart.	Jn. 15:4, 2 Cor. 6:16, Eph. 3:17

In a land of corn and wine	Gen. 27:28, Deut. 33:28
His lot shall be below;	Deut. 32:9
Comforts there, and blessings join,	Ps. 23:4, Isa. 57:18
And milk and honey flow;	Ex. 3:8, Josh. 5:6
Jacob's well is in his soul;	Deut. 33:28, Jn. 4:6
Gracious dew his heavens distil,	Deut. 32:2
Fill his soul, already full,	Jn. 4:11–14, Eph. 3:19
And shall for ever fill.	

Blest, O Israel, art thou!	Deut. 33:29
What people is like thee:	Deut. 4:7, 8, 32ff.
Saved from sin, by Jesus, now	Deut. 33:29, Matt. 1:21
Thou art, and still shalt be;	
Jesus is thy seven-fold shield,	Deut. 33:29, Eph. 6:16
Jesus is thy flaming sword;	Deut. 33:29, Eph. 6:17, Rev. 1:16, 19:15

Earth, and hell, and sin, shall yield	Rev. 19:11–13
To God's almighty Word.	

12.   The Divine Son

The Christian faith is that our Lord is much more than the greatest of the prophets, and the climax of divine revelation. In him God came not only to reveal something, but supremely to do something, to perform an historic divine saving act within our world, as a member of the human race, and on behalf of our race. By consequence our Lord is to be confessed as the eternal divine Son.

P.W. xiii. 210; W.H. 673; M.H.B. 88

We know, by faith we surely know, — Heb. 11:3, 6
    The Son of God is come; — 1 Jn. 5:20
Is manifested here below, — Jn. 2:11, 17:6, 1 Jn. 3:5, 8
    And makes our hearts his home: — Jn. 15:4, Eph. 3:7
To us he hath, in special love,
    An understanding given, — 1 Jn. 5:20
To recognise him from above — Jn. 8:23
    The Lord of earth and heaven. — Acts 10:36, Phil. 2:10–11

The true and faithful Witness, we — Jn. 5:36, Rev. 1:5, 3:14
    Jehovah's Son confess; — Ex. 6:3, Mk. 15:39, Jn. 8:58
And in the face of Jesus see — 2 Cor 4:6
    Jehovah's smiling face; — Num. 6:25
In him we live, and move, and are, — Acts 17:28
    United to our Head, — Eph. 4:15–16, Col. 2:19
And, branches of the Vine, declare — Jn. 15:5
    That Christ is God indeed. — Jn. 1:1, 20:28, Phil. 2:6, Heb.1:3

The self-existing God supreme, — Isa. 43:10–13, Jn. 5:26
    Our Saviour we adore, — Isa. 45:21, Acts 5:31, Jude 25
Fountain of life eternal, him — Jn. 3:16, 4:14
    We worship evermore; — 1 Thess. 5:16
Out of his plenitude receive — Jn. 1:16, Col. 1:19
    Ineffable delight, — 1 Cor. 2:9
And shall through endless ages live — Rev. 22:5
    Triumphant in his sight.

13. The Creative Word

The Son, who is the divine Reason and the creative Word, is the Agent of creation. As the Agent is in the proper sense of the word divine, creation by the Word is divine creation.

P.W. vi 458, vii 274, 277, 286; W.H. 234

Let all that breathe Jehovah praise,	Ps. 150:6
Almighty, all-creating Lord;	Gen. 1:1, Rev. 4:11
Let earth and heaven his power confess,	Ps. 69:34
Brought out of nothing by his Word!	Ps. 33:6, Jn. 1:3
He spake the word, and it was done,	Gen. 1:3
The Universe his word obeyed:	Heb. 1:3
The Word is his eternal Son,	Rev. 19:13
And Christ the whole creation made.	Jn. 1:3
Jehovah the almighty Lord,	Gen. 17:1, Rev. 4:8, 19:6
Father of Jesus Christ, and ours,	Jn. 20:17
The heavens created by his Word,	2 Pet. 3:5
And by his breath the heavenly powers:	Ps. 33:6
To Father, Son, and Holy Ghost	Matt. 28:19, 2 Cor. 13:14
Be equal adoration given,	Jn. 5:23, 1 Jn. 5:7
Maker of the celestial host,	Gen. 1:16, Job 26:13, Ps. 33:6
Maker of the new earth and heaven!	Rev. 21:1, 5
Baptized into one only name,	Acts 4:12
The Father, Son, and Holy Ghost,	Matt. 28:19
One nature we in three proclaim,	2 Cor. 13:14, 1 Jn. 5:7
One God for our salvation trust:	Isa. 43:10–11, Rom. 1:16
One God eternally abides,	Ps. 90:2, Rev. 4:9
One undivided Trinity,	Isa. 6:3, Rev. 4:8
And the whole Deity resides	Jn. 10:30, Rom 8:9
In each of the mysterious Three.	
Father, and Son, and Spirit join	1 Tim. 3:9, 16
To make the joyful secret known,	Eph. 1:9–10, 3:3–5, 19
The love unsearchable, divine,	Eph. 3:8, 19

Of One in Three, and Three in One:
This is the counsel of his grace,   Acts 2:23, 20:27, Eph. 1:11
   That him we here by faith should see,   Heb. 11:1, 27
Should see above his glorious face,   Rev. 22:4
   And gaze to all eternity.   Rev. 22:5

P.W. ix. 381

Rejoice in Jesu's birth!   Lk. 1:47, 2:13–14
   To us a Son is given,   Isa. 9:6
To us a Child is born on earth,
   Who made both earth and heaven!   Jn. 1:3, 14, Col. 1:16
His shoulder props the sky,   Isa. 9:6, Heb. 1:10
   This universe sustains!   Col. 1:17
The God supreme, the Lord most high,   Ps. 47:2
   The King Messiah reigns!   Lk. 1:33, 1 Cor. 15:25,
                                                     Rev. 11:15

His name, his nature, soars   Rev. 19:12
   Beyond the creatures' ken:
Yet whom the angelic host adores,   Rev. 5:11–12
   He pleads the cause of men!   Heb. 7:25
Our Counsellor we praise,   Isa. 9:6
   Our Advocate above,   Heb. 9:11–14, 24, 1 Jn. 2:1
Who daily in his Church displays
His miracles of love.   Acts 2:43, 46

The Almighty God is he,   Gen. 17:1, Rev. 19:6, 21:22
   Author of heavenly bliss,   Rev. 21:23, 22:3
The Father of eternity,   Isa. 9:6, Jer. 10:10
   The glorious Prince of Peace!   Isa. 9:6
Wider and wider still
   He doth his sway extend,   Isa. 9:7, Hab. 2:14
With peace divine his people fill,   1 Thess. 5:23
   And joys that never end.   Jn. 16:22

Now for thy promise sake,   Rom. 4:13, 2 Pet. 3:9
   O'er earth exalted be,   Isa. 2:11
The kingdom, power, and glory take,   Matt. 6:13
   Which all belong to thee;
In zeal for God and man   Isa. 9:7
   Thy full salvation bring,   Heb. 7:25
The universal Monarch reign,   Ps. 72:11
   The saints' eternal King.   Rev. 15:3

14. Christ's Advent

The Hebrew people believed that God had promised that the monarchy of the House of David, the symbol of nationhood, should continue for the future (2 Sam. 7:12–16). Long political misfortune gradually extinguished the hope that this could come about through any sort of human restoration. Strong religious faith inspired the prophets to declare that what could not happen through the political process would be brought about by divine intervention. God would send 'the Anointed One' (Hebrew, 'Messiah'; Greek, 'Christ'), that is, his King, his personal representative on earth, filled with power divine, to set up God's Kingdom, or sovereignty. Thus God would redeem his people, and vindicate his glory as the righteous ruler of the world. In this way the religion of the Old Testament led up to the expectation of the coming, or Advent, of the Messiah, the Christ.

P.W. iv. 116; W.H. 688; M.H.B. 242; M.H. 360; H.P. 81

Come, thou long-expected Jesus,	Isa, 2:2, 9:6–7,
	Dan. 7:13–14, Lk. 1:31–3,
.	Gal. 4:4, Heb. 1:2
Born to set thy people free,	Lk. 4:18, Jn. 8:36, Gal. 5:1
From our fears and sins release us,	Rom. 6:18, 22, 1 Jn. 4:18
Let us find our rest in thee.	Ex. 33:14, Matt. 11:29
Israel's strength and consolation,	I Sam. 15:29, Lk. 2:25
Hope of all the earth thou art;	Matt. 12:21, Rom. 15:12
Dear Desire of every nation,	Hag. 2:7
Joy of every longing heart.	Jer. 15:16, Ps. 107:9,
	119:111, Eccles. 5:20
Born thy people to deliver	Matt. 1:21
Born a child and yet a king,	Isa. 9:6, Lk. 1:31–3, 2:7
Born to reign in us for ever,	Lk. 1:33, Heb. 1:8, 11–12
Now thy gracious kingdom bring:	Rom. 5:21
By thine own eternal Spirit	Heb. 9:14
Rule in all our hearts alone;	Col. 3:15
By thine all-sufficient merit	Rom. 3:25–6, 4:5–7
Raise us to thy glorious throne.	2 Tim. 2:12, Rev. 22:3, 5,
	Matt. 25:31

15. The Incarnation

At the long-awaited and divinely appointed time the eternal divine Son united himself with our human nature, so as to live as a man, a genuine part of the human race. This is the Incarnation (='becoming flesh'). This mysterious union took place by a birth from a holy virgin mother, by the miraculous action of the Holy Spirit.

P.W. iv. 342; W.H. 772

O thou who hast redeemed of old,	Ps. 74:2, 12
And bidd'st me of thy strength lay hold,	Isa. 27:5
And be at peace with thee,	
Help me thy benefits to own,	Ps. 103:2
And hear me tell what thou hast done,	Mk. 5:19
O dying Lamb, for me!	Rev. 5:6, 9
Canst thou deny that love to me?	2 Tim. 2:13
Say, thou incarnate Deity,	Jn. 1:14
Thou Man of sorrows, say;	Isa. 53:3
Thy glory why didst thou enshrine	2 Cor. 4:6
In such a clod of earth as mine,	Gen. 2:7
And wrap thee in my clay?	Job 4:19
Ancient of days, why didst thou come,	Dan. 7:9, 13
And stoop to a poor virgin's womb,	Lk. 1:31, 34
Contracted to a span:*	Lam. 2:20
Flesh of our flesh why wast thou made,	Jn. 1:14, Heb. 2:14
And humbly in a manger laid,	Lk. 2:7
The new-born Son of man?	Matt. 8:20
Love, only love, thy heart inclined,	Gal. 2:20
And brought thee, Saviour of mankind,	1 Tim. 4:10, 2 Pet. 3:9
Down from thy throne above;	Phil. 2:7–8, Rev. 3:21, 22:3
Love made my God a man of grief,	Isa. 53:3, Jn. 3:16
Distressed thee sore for my relief:	Isa. 53:5
O mystery of love!	1 Tim. 3:16

---

* Let us (said he) pour on him all we can:	(G. Herbert, 'The Pulley',
Let the world's riches, which dispersed lie,	lines 4–5)
Contract into a span.	

P.W. iv. 109; W.H. 685; M.H.B. 142; H.P. 109

Let earth and heaven combine,	Ps. 148: 1–4, 11–13
Angels and men agree,	Lk. 1:13–14, 20
To praise in songs divine	Eph. 5:19, Col. 3:16
The incarnate Deity,	Jn. 1:14
Our God contracted to a span, *	Lam. 2:20
Incomprehensibly made man.	1 Tim. 3:16
He laid his glory by,	Jn. 10:18, 17:5
He wrapped him in our clay;	Gen. 2:7, Job 4:19
Unmarked by human eye,	Isa. 53:8, Jn. 6:42, Acts 8:33
The latent Godhead lay:	Phil 2:7–8
Infant of days he here became,	Isa. 65:20
And bore the mild Immanuel's name.	Isa. 7:14
See in that Infant's face	2 Cor. 4:6
The depth of Deity,	Jn. 14:9
And labour while ye gaze	
To sound the mystery:	1 Cor. 2:7
In vain; ye angels gaze no more,	1 Pet. 1:12
But fall, and silently adore.	Rev. 8:1
Unsearchable the love	Eph. 3:8
That hath the Saviour brought;	Gal. 2:20
The grace is far above	
Or man or angel's thought;	Eph. 3:19
Suffice for us that God, we know,	Jn. 14:8
Our God, is manifest below.	1 Jn. 3:8
He deigns in flesh to appear,	2 Cor. 8:9, Phil. 2:8
Widest extremes to join;	Ps. 113:5–6, Isa. 55:8–9
To bring our vileness near,	Ezek. 36:25–6, Heb. 10:22
And make us all divine:	1 Jn. 3:1–2
And we the life of God shall know,	1 Jn. 1:1–2
For God is manifest below.	Jn. 1:18
Made perfect first in love,	1 Jn. 4:17–18
And sanctified by grace,	1 Cor. 1:30, Eph. 2:8
We shall from earth remove,	Phil. 1:23, 1 Thess. 4:17
And see his glorious face:	1 Cor. 13:12
Then shall his love be fully showed,	1 Jn. 3:2
And man shall then be lost in God.	Rev. 21:3, 22:3–4

* See footnote, p. 50.

52   *The Theologian's Carol*

P.W. i. 183; W.H. 683; M.H.B. 117; M.H. 387, 388; H.P. 106

Hark how all the welkin rings,	Lk. 2:13–14
Glory to the King of kings,	Rev. 17:14, 19:16
Peace on earth, and mercy mild,	Lk. 2:14, 1 Tim. 1:2
God and sinners reconciled!	Rom. 5:11, 2 Cor. 5:18–20
Joyful all ye nations rise,	Ps. 67:4, Rom. 15:9–10
Join the triumph of the skies,	Lk. 2:15
Universal nature say	Rev. 5:13
'Christ the Lord is born today!'	Lk. 2:11
Christ by highest heaven adored,	Dan. 7:13, Heb. 1:6, Rev. 5:8
Christ, the everlasting Lord,	Isa. 63:16
Late in time behold him come,	Gal. 4:4, Heb. 1:2, 1 Pet. 1:20
Offspring of a virgin's womb.	Matt. 1:18, Lk. 1:34
Veiled in flesh, the Godhead see,	Heb. 10:20
Hail the incarnate Deity!	Jn. 1:14
Pleased as Man with men t'appear	1 Cor. 15:47, 2 Tim. 1:10
Jesus, our Immanuel here!	Isa. 7:14
Hail the heavenly Prince of Peace!	Isa. 9:6
Hail the Sun of Righteousness!	Isa. 32:1, Mal. 4:2, Jer. 23:6
Light and life to all he brings,	Jn. 1:4, 8:12
Risen with healing in his wings.	Mal. 4:2
Mild he lays his glory by,	Jn. 10:17–18, Jn. 17:5
Born that man no more may die,	Rom. 6:8, 1 Cor. 15:22, 2 Tim. 1
Born to raise the sons of earth,	1 Cor. 15:47, Heb. 2:10
Born to give them second birth.	Jn. 3:3
Come, Desire of nations, come,	Hag. 2:7
Fix in us thy humble home,	Isa. 57:15, Phil. 2:8
Rise, the woman's conquering Seed,	Gal. 3:16, Rev. 19:15–16
Bruise in us the serpent's head.	Gen. 3:15
Now display thy saving power,	Rom. 1:16
Ruined nature now restore,	Gen. 3:16, Rom. 8:21–2,
	1 Cor. 15:21–2
Now in mystic union join	
Thine to ours, and ours to thine.	Eph. 5:28–32
Adam's likeness, Lord, efface,	1 Cor. 15:47, 49
Stamp thine image in its place,	
Second Adam from above,	1 Cor. 15:45, 47
Reinstate us in thy love!	1 Cor. 15:22, 2 Cor. 5:18–20
Let us thee, though lost, regain,	1 Cor. 15:22, Phil. 3:7–8
Thee the Life, the inner Man;	Jn. 14:6, Eph. 3:16, 1 Pet. 3:4
O! to all thyself impart,	
Formed in each believing heart.	Gal. 4:19, Eph. 3:17

16. The Two Natures of Christ

Our Lord, being the eternal divine Son made man, is the personal presence of God, living and acting in our world. He has two natures, the divine nature eternally existing, and the human, derived from the Holy Mother at the time of his conception. The divine nature is divine in the fullest and most proper sense of the word. The human nature is genuinely like ours, though without sin. The union at the incarnation is an eternal one into a divine-human Person. Such is the intimacy of the union that what may be said of the one nature may spiritually and theologically be applied to the other. Thus the divine Son, as a spiritual Being, has no body, and cannot be born, suffer, or die. Christ was born, suffered, and died by virtue of his human nature. Yet on account of the union this can be described as the birth, the suffering, and the death of God. This profound truth of the incarnation can only be set forth in the language of daring paradox, to be interpreted symbolically. If God is defined in the terms of secular philosophy as a remote Absolute the incarnation is plainly a nonsensical contradiction in terms. The finite cannot be joined to the infinite. However, if God is defined in scriptural terms, as a personal Sovereign King, high and lifted up in glory, yet active in the creation which is His handiwork, the idea of incarnation becomes credible, though it remains a staggering wonder of divine condescension and love.

P.W. ii. 74; W.H. 28; M.H.B. 186; M.H. 420; H.P. 175

O love divine! what hast thou done!	Jn. 3:16, Rom. 5:8, Gal. 2:20
The immortal God hath died for me!	Mk. 15:39, 1 Tim. 6:16
The Father's co-eternal Son	Jn. 1:1–2
Bore all my sins upon the tree;	2 Cor. 5:21, 1 Pet. 2:24
The immortal God for me hath died!	
My Lord, my Love is crucified.*	1 Cor. 2:8, Rev. 11:8
Behold him, all ye that pass by,	Lam. 1:12
The bleeding Prince of life and peace!	Isa. 9:6, Acts 3:15

Come, see, ye worms, your Maker die,	Gen. 1:26, Job 25:6, Ps. 22:6
And say, was ever grief like his?	Isa. 53:3, Lam. 1:12
Come, feel with me his blood applied:	Rom. 3:25, Heb. 10:19
My Lord, my Love is crucified.	
Is crucified for me and you,	1 Thess. 5:10, 1 Pet. 3:18
To bring us rebels back to God:	Ezek. 2:3, 2 Cor. 5:18–20
Believe, believe the record true,	Jn. 20:31, Acts 16:31
Ye all are bought with Jesu's blood,	1 Cor. 6:20, 1 Pet. 1:19
Pardon for all flows from his side;	Jn. 19:34
My Lord, my Love is crucified.	
Then let us sit beneath his cross,	Jn. 19:25
And gladly catch the healing stream,	Zech. 13:1
All things for him account but loss,	Phil. 3:7–8
And give up all our hearts to him;	Acts 11:23, 1 Pet. 3:4
Of nothing think or speak beside,	1 Cor. 2:1–2
My Lord, my Love is crucified.	

---

* Some commentators have read 'my love is crucified' as a reference to St. Ignatius of Antioch's Epistle to the Romans vii. *2: ho emos erōs estaurōtai*. Lightfoot however translates this as 'my lust is crucified', which quite accords with the context.

P.W. iv. 108; W.H. 684; M.H.B. 134; H.P. 101

Glory be to God on high,	Lk. 2:14
And peace on earth descend!	
God comes down, he bows the sky,	Ps. 144:5
And shows himself our friend:	Ex. 33:11, Jn. 15:15, Jas. 2:23
God the invisible appears!	Jn. 1:18, Col. 1:15, 1 Tim. 6:16
God the blest, the great I AM,	Ex. 3:14, Rom 9:5, 1 Tim. 6:15
Sojourns in this vale of tears,	Ps. 84:6 B.C.P.
And Jesus is his name.	Lk. 1:31
Him the angels all adored,	Lk. 2:13
Their Maker and their King;	Ps. 104:4
Tidings of their humbled Lord	Ps. 113:6, Lk. 2:10, Phil 2:8
They now to mortals bring.	
Emptied of his majesty,	Phil. 2:7 (cf. R.V. etc.)
Of his dazzling glories shorn,	Jn. 17:5, 2 Cor. 8:9
Being's source begins to be,	Jn. 1:3, Rev. 4:11
And God himself is born.	Heb. 1:6, 8
See the eternal Son of God	Jn. 8:58, Heb. 1:8,10–12
A mortal Son of man;	Matt. 17:22–3
Dwelling in an earthly clod,	Gen. 2:7, Job 4:19
Whom heaven cannot contain!	1 Kgs. 8:27
Stand amazed, ye heavens, at this!	
See the Lord of earth and skies;	Ps. 104:3, 5, Zech. 6:5
Humbled to the dust he is,	Ps. 22:15, 113:6, Phil. 2:8
And in a manger lies.	Lk. 2:7,16

We, the sons of men, rejoice,	Ps. 8:4
The Prince of peace proclaim;	Isa. 9:16
With heaven's host lift up our voice,	Ps. 148:1–2, 11–12
And shout Immmanuel's name:	Isa. 7:14
Knees and hearts to him we bow;	Phil. 2:10
Of our flesh and of our bone,	Lk. 24:39, Heb. 2:14, 10:20
Jesus is our brother now,	Lk. 8:21, Heb. 2:11
And God is all our own.	Ps. 50:7, 118:28, Isa. 41:10, Ezek. 34:31

17. The Epiphany

In the coming of Christ 'the day-spring from on high hath visited us' (Luke 1:78). Christ, the Light of the world to the whole race, has manifested the glory of God.

P.W. xi. 114; W.H. 686; M.H.B. 135; H.P. 462

Stupendous height of heavenly love,	Isa. 55:8, 9, Eph. 3:18
Of pitying tenderness divine!	Ps. 103:13
It brought the Saviour from above,	Jn. 3:16, Gal. 2:20
It caused the springing day to shine;	Lk. 1:78
The Sun of righteousness to appear,	Mal. 4:2
And gild our gloomy hemisphere.	Isa. 60:1–3
God did in Christ himself reveal,	Jn. 1:18
To chase our darkness by his light,	Isa. 60:1–2, Jn. 1:4–5, 8:12
Our sin and ignorance dispel,	Acts 17:23, Rom. 10:3
Direct our wandering feet aright,	Ps. 56:8, 13, Isa. 30:21
And bring our souls, with pardon blest,	Isa. 55:6–7, Matt. 11:28, 29
To realms of everlasting rest.	2 Thess. 2:16, Heb. 4:9
Come then, O Lord, thy light impart,	Isa. 60:1, Jn. 8:12, Eph. 5:14
The faith that bids our terrors cease;	Isa. 41:10, Matt. 14:27, 30–1
Into thy love direct our heart,	2 Thess. 3:5
Into thy way of perfect peace;	Lk. 1:79
And cheer the souls of death afraid,	Isa. 43:2
And guide them through the dreadful shade.	Ps. 23:4
Answer thy mercy's whole design,	Act 20:27
My God incarnated for me;	Gal. 2:20
My spirit make thy radiant shrine,	1 Cor. 6:19
My light and full salvation be;	Ps. 27:1
And through the shades of death unknown	Ps. 23:4
Conduct me to thy dazzling throne.	Rev. 20:11–12

18.   Our Lord's Life and Teaching

Though the attention of the Wesleys is chiefly engaged upon the saving work of God in the suffering, death, resurrection, and ascension of Christ, the Gospel activity is also to be seen in the life, work, teaching, and miracles of our Lord. (See 'Ye neighbours and friends', p. 00.)

The second verse of the following striking hymn on the somewhat unusual subject (for Wesley at least), of our Lord's earthly occupation has been the subject of discussion. It describes Jesus as 'son of the carpenter', and this has been read by some as implying a veiled denial of the virgin birth. This is doubtless the reason why John Wesley omitted this verse in the 1780 hymnal, though significantly it was brought back in the 1933 Methodist Hymn Book. The phrase is derived from Matthew 13:55, and it is interesting to surmise why Matthew should have phrased it this way, seeing that his presumed source in Mark 6:3 reads 'is not this the carpenter, the son of Mary', no mention being made of a father. Clearly, Matthew does not intend to affirm that Joseph was literally the father of Jesus (Matt. 1:18). It is quite possible that he is inviting his reader to answer 'No!' when he comes to this question, the whole passge implying ignorance of our Lord's nature and mission among the people of his home town. This is surely the sense of the parallel John 6:41–2. The unbelieving Jews do not understand the heavenly descent of our Lord. Equally clearly, Charles Wesley does not intend in this bold verse to call in question the doctrine of the virgin birth, which he confidently affirms in so many passages.

P.W. i. 172; W.H. 322, 321; M.H.B. 575; H.P. 383

Servant of all, to toil for man	Mk. 10:44
Thou didst not, Lord, refuse;	Jn. 13:14–16
Thy majesty did not disdain	Mk. 10:45, Lk. 22:27
To be employed for us!	

Son of the carpenter, receive	Matt. 13:55
This humble work of mine;	Matt. 26:10, Lk. 21:1–3
Worth to my meanest labour give,	1 Cor. 2:6–7
By joining it to thine.*	
End of my every action thou,	Rom. 10:4
In all things thee I see:	Col. 3:11
Accept my hallowed labour now,	Rom. 12:1
I do it unto thee.	Matt. 25:40
What'er the Father views as thine,	Heb. 10:10
He views with gracious eyes;	
Jesus, this mean oblation join*	Rom. 12:1
To thy great sacrifice.	Heb. 10:12–14, 19–24
Thy bright example I pursue,	1 Pet. 2:21
To thee in all things rise;	Col:3:1–2
And all I think, or speak, or do,	1 Cor. 10:31
Is one great sacrifice.	Rom. 12:1

---

* 'Who made there (by his one oblation of himself once offered) a full, perfect, and sufficient sacrifice, oblation, and satisfaction for the sins of the whole world'—'And although we be unworthy, through our manifold sins, to offer unto thee any sacrifice, yet we beseech thee to accept this our bounden duty and service.'

(Communion Service), B.C.P.

19. The Cross

The crucifixion of Christ, in which the divine Son, as man, made himself one with fallen humanity to the point of a cursed death in agony and disgrace, is to be viewed as the supreme mark of the victory of God's power and love over the power of evil, and of his great and forgiving love towards the human race. Jn. Wesley here translates Paulus Gerhardt, 'O Welt, sieh hier dein Leben' (1648).

P.W. i. 232; W.H. 23; M.H.B. 388; H.P. 743

Extended on a cursed tree,	Deut. 21:22–3, Isa. 65:2, Rom. 10:21, 2 Cor. 5:21, Gal. 3:13
Besmeared with dust, and sweat, and blood,	Ps. 22:15, Lk. 22:44, Jn. 19:34
See there, the King of glory see!	Ps. 24:8, 10, Jas. 2:1
Sinks and expires the Son of God.	Mk. 15:39
I, I alone, have done the deed!	Acts 9:4, 5, 1 Tim. 1:13, 15
'Tis I thy sacred flesh have torn;	Zech. 13:6, 1 Pet. 3:18
My sins have caused thee, Lord, to bleed,	1 Cor. 15:3, 1 Pet. 2:24
Pointed the nail, and fixed the thorn.	Ps. 22:16, Matt. 27:29
The burden, for me to sustain	Ps. 38:4
Too great, on thee, my Lord, was laid;	Ps. 55:22, Isa. 53:6
To heal me, thou hast borne my pain;	Isa. 53:5
To bless me, thou a curse wast made.	Gal. 3:13
My Saviour, how shall I proclaim,	Isa. 61:2
How pay the mighty debt I owe?	Matt. 18:24, Rom. 8:12–13
Let all I have, and all I am,	Rom. 12:1, 1 Thess. 5:23
Ceaseless to all thy glory show.	1 Cor. 10:31, Eph. 1:6, 12
Too much to thee I cannot give,	1 Chron. 29:14
Too much I cannot do for thee;	Lk. 17:10
Let all thy love and all thy grief	Isa. 53:3, 4, Lam. 1:12, Jn. 11:36, Gal. 2:20
Graven on my heart for ever be!	Jer. 31:33, Heb. 10:16

20. The Atonement: Christ as a Victor

The word 'atonement' (= at-one-ment: a making at one, a means of reconciliation) indicates that in the death and resurrection of Christ God has done all that is necessary to release the guilt and conquer the power of sin in the human heart, and so restore believers to fellowship with himself. One way of expressing this truth prominent in the New Testament is that the divine Son, as man, placed himself within the sphere of influence of the spiritual enemies of mankind, such as the demonic powers, sin, the curse of the law, and death. On the cross he suffered their utmost assault. The glorious resurrection is the mark of his triumph. This theme naturally comes to joyous expression in the hymns for Easter and Ascension (22, 23). We print here a selection of verses from a number of associated compositions in the same style, which have been variously arranged as hymns.

P.W. v. 36–9, 271, ix. 466–489; W.H. 277, 314, 315; M.H.B. 243, 481; H.P. 262

Jesus the conqueror reigns,	Rev. 19: 11–16
In glorious strength arrayed,	
His kingdom over all maintains,	Ps. 103:19
And bids the earth be glad:	Ps. 67:4
Ye sons of men rejoice	Rom. 15:10
In Jesu's mighty love,	
Lift up your heart, lift up your voice	Isa. 40:9, Lam. 3:41
To him who rules above.	Ps. 103:19
See on the mountain-top	Isa. 18:3
The standard of your God!	Isa. 49:22
In Jesu's name I lift it up,	Isa. 13:2, 62:10
All stained with hallowed blood.	Isa. 63:2, Rev. 19:13
His standard-bearer, I	
To all the nations call,	Isa. 49:22, Acts 1:8
Let all to Jesu's cross draw nigh!	Eph. 2:13
The cross he bore for all.	2 Cor. 5:15
The world cannot withstand	Jn. 16:33
Its ancient conqueror;	1 Pet. 1:20, Rev. 13:8
The world must sink beneath that hand,	1 Jn. 5:4, 5
Which arms us for the war;	Eph. 6:11, 13

Our advocate with God,	1 Jn. 2:1
He undertakes our cause,	Isa. 38:14
And spreads through all the earth abroad	Rom. 10:18
The victory of his cross.	1 Cor. 1:18, 1 Jn. 5:4,
	Rev. 5:6, 9
That blood-stained banner see,	Isa. 63:2, Rev. 19:13
And in your Captain's sight,	Heb. 2:10, 12:2
Fight the good fight of faith with me,	1 Tim. 6:12, 2 Tim. 4:7
My fellow-soldiers fight.	Phil. 2:25, Philem. 2
In mighty phalanx joined,	Eph. 4:16
Undaunted all proceed,	
Armed with the unconquerable mind	1 Cor. 2:16, Eph. 6:10–11
That was in Christ your Head.	Eph. 1:22, 4:15, Col. 1:18
Jesu's tremendous name	Phil. 2:10, Rev. 19:16,
Puts all our foes to flight:	Ps. 60:12, Lk. 1:71
Jesus the meek, the angry Lamb,	Matt. 11:29, Rev. 6:16
A Lion is in fight.	Rev. 5:5
By all hell's host withstood,	Eph. 6:12
We all hell's host o'erthrow;	Rom. 8:37–9
And conquering them, through Jesu's blood	
We still to conquer go.	Rev. 12:11
Through much distress and pain,	Lk. 21:25
Through many a conflict here,	Phil. 1:30, Col. 2:1
Through blood ye must the entrance gain;	Acts 14:22, Heb. 12:4
Yet O! disdain to fear.	2 Cor. 7:5–6
Courage, your Captain cries,	Heb. 2:10
Who all your toil foreknew,	Heb. 12:2
Toil ye shall have; yet all despise,	2 Cor. 4:8–11
I have o'ercome for you.	Jn. 16:33
'Twas there our peace he bought;	Eph. 2:13–14
Though nailed to yonder tree,	Acts 5:30, 10:39, Col. 2:14
His hands have our salvation wrought,	1 Sam. 11:13, 19:5
And got the victory:	Ps. 98:1
He felt the mortal dart,	Eph. 6:16
The horror-breathing king	
Shot all our sin into his heart,*	
And death hath lost his sting.	1 Cor. 15:55, 56
Jesus shall soon appear,	Rev. 3:11, 22:7, 12
With royal glory crowned,	Matt. 25:31, Rev. 19:11–16
Our dust the trump of God shall hear,	Gen. 2:7, 3:19, Dan. 12:2
And kindle to the sound:	1 Cor. 15:52, 1 Thess. 4:16
Quickened by power divine,	Rom. 8:11
We all shall see, and know	
The Son of Man's triumphant Sign,	Matt. 24:30
The cross we bore below.	Mk. 8:34, 10:21, 15:21

---

* This reference is not very clear, for such references as Lam. 1:13 and 2 Cor. 5:21, which may be in mind, do not properly apply to the action of Satan.

21. The Atonement: Christ as a Sacrifice

Another way of expressing the doctrine of the cross is that it is a sacrifice for sin. To put this vitally important evangelical matter in its proper New Testament sense it is necessary to establish the general idea of sacrifice as it existed in the Old Testament. Two main ideas are united. A sacrifice was the offering to God of some object set apart by sacred custom, as an 'acted prayer' that the worshippers were offering to God in consecration all that they had, and themselves. A sacrifice was also a meal shared with God, a shared meal being the means of fellowship. When an animal was killed in sacrifice this was not to destroy or 'punish' it, but to make it available for the representative offering, and for the meal of fellowship. Thus a sacrifice is in general a God-appointed means whereby worshippers may approach God in consecration, and enjoy religious communion with him.

Clearly, therefore, the death and resurrection of Christ is the supreme means for doing this. It is the perfect sacrifice. The Old Testament sacrifices, though ordained by God, and to be reverenced, were ceremonial only, and resulted chiefly in ritual purity, and the release from 'tabu'. The sacrifice of Christ, by contrast, was a sacrifice of moral and spiritual obedience, offered as Man on behalf of mankind to the heavenly Father. This has the effect of real and inward moral and spiritual cleansing. This profound conception of the sacrifice of the cross comes to the fore in hymns celebrating the heavenly high priesthood of Christ (24), for example, the moving poem entitled 'Ecce Homo', printed below, and those on the Lord's Supper, being the Christian meal of fellowship (50). Again we choose to show a full analysis of the Scripture references in this hymn.

P.W. ii. 323; W.H. 202; M.H.B. 368; M.H. 122; H.P. 217

1 Arise, my soul, arise,	Isa. 60:1, Eph. 5:14
Shake off thy guilty fears;	Ps. 51:4, 14, Heb. 10:31,
	1 Jn. 4:18

The bleeding sacrifice	Lev. 16:14–16, 17:11, Rom. 3:25, Heb. 9:12–14, 10:19, 13:12, 1 Pet. 1:19
In my behalf appears;	Isa. 53:4–5, 1 Cor. 15:3, Gal. 2:20
Before the throne my Surety stands;	Heb. 4:14, 7:22, 25, Rev. 5:6
My name is written on his hands.	Isa. 49:16
2 He ever lives above, For me to intercede,	Heb. 7:25
His all-redeeming love,	Ps. 103:4, Jn. 3:16, Rom. 5:8
His precious blood, to plead;	Heb. 9:14, 1 Pet. 1:19
His blood atoned for all our race,	Mk. 10:45, Rom. 5:11, 17–19, 8:32, 2 Cor. 5:14, 1 Tim. 2:6
And sprinkles now the throne of grace.	Lev. 16:14–16, Heb. 9:7, 11–14, 12:24
3 Five bleeding wounds he bears,	Ps. 22:16, Zech. 13:6, Jn. 19:34, 20:27, Rev. 5:6
Received on Calvary;	Lk. 23:33
They pour effectual prayers,	Isa. 53:12, Jas. 5:16, Heb. 7:25
They strongly speak for me:	Heb. 5:7, 12:24
'Forgive him, O forgive,' they cry,	Lk. 23:34
'Nor let that ransomed sinner die'!	Ezek. 18:31–2, Mk. 10:45
4 The Father hears him pray, His dear Anointed One;	Jn. 11:42, Heb. 5:7 Hab. 3:13, Acts 4:27, 10:38, Heb. 1:9
He cannot turn away	Ps. 132:10–11
The presence of his Son:	Heb. 9:24
His Spirit answers to the blood,	1 Jn. 5:8
And tells me I am born of God.	Rom. 8:16
5 My God is reconciled* His pardoning voice I hear,	Rom. 3:25–6, 5:11 Num. 14:20, Mich. 7:18, Acts 5:31, Eph. 4:32
He owns me for his child,	Rom. 8:15, Gal. 4:5, Eph. 1:5
I can no longer fear,	Lk. 1:74, 1 Jn. 4:18
With confidence I now draw nigh,	Heb. 10:22
And Father, Abba, Father, cry!	Rom. 8:15, Gal. 4:6

---

* Romans 5:11 speaks of the saving work of Christ crucified as the atonement (A.V, K.J.V.), or as the reconciliation (R.S.V., N.E.B., etc.,) this being an alternative translation for the same word. By derivation the word atonement is 'at-one-ment', i.e., a means of making at one, of reconciliation. On account of the meritorious sacrifice of Christ's obedience God the Father can rightly declare forgiveness. In the Cross the rightful claims of God as the just Judge of all the earth, and of God as the loving Father, are

reconciled (Romans 3:25–6). Thus the sacrificial death of Christ is a propitiation. The basic meaning of this Bible word is 'that which wipes away what is offensive in the sight of God'. The Cross, provided indeed by the love of God (Jn. 3:16) is that which enables the just God fittingly to forgive the sinner. Thus it is a propitiation for sin. Evangelical theology has often expressed these profound propositions of Gospel truth by the statement that God is reconciled to mankind, as Wesley does here. In this connection we remember also that such notable passages as 2 Cor. 5:18, 20, and Col. 1:20–21, speak of men and women being reconciled to God.

Christian thought has known of a number of ways in which the rationale of the sacrifice of the cross has been expounded, in the attempt to bring home its force to Christian faith. It is inappropriate to fall into dispute about these, for it is the glorious fact of God's love and power made known in the cross which saves, not theological theories about the cross. The most usual way in which the Wesleys, in common with many evangelicals, have expounded the cross is in terms of the infinite merit of the sufferings of the divine Son.

God is the moral Governor of the human race, and cannot exercise free forgiveness in such a way as to allow men and women to suppose that sin is merely condoned. It is wholly for the good of mankind that the moral law should be fully upheld by due punishment for sin, and by due submission made to God. Therefore the wrath of God must be satisfied. (We carefully note that the true biblical sense of the phrase divine 'wrath' is *not* that of 'God in a bad temper', for God does not have human emotions. The notion of the divine wrath is that God's world is a moral order, wherein penalty for sin is inevitable.) Frail and sinful men and women are in no position to suffer the awful penalty for sin, and to make full and exacting submission to God. Their good conduct is totally insufficient to acquire merit in the sight of God. However, because the Representative Man who suffered with mankind and for mankind upon the cross was no human martyr, but the sinless divine Son, his penalty and his sufferings possess an infinite *merit*: i.e. they provide an all-sufficient vindication for the moral law. Thus on account of the cross the just and loving God can rightly forgive, and for Christ's sake has pledged that free forgiveness.

P.W. iv. 371; W.H. 707; M.H.B. 188

All ye that pass by,	Lam. 1:12
To Jesus draw nigh:	Jn. 19:25, Eph. 2:13
To you is it nothing that Jesus should die?	
Your ransom and peace,	Mk. 10:45, Eph. 2:14
Your surety he is:	Heb. 7:22
Come, see if there ever was sorrow like his.	Isa. 53:3, Lam. 1:12, 18

For what you have done	1 Tim. 1:13–15
His blood must atone;	Rom. 3:25, 5:10–11
The Father hath punished for you his	Isa. 53:6, 10, Mk. 15:34,
dear Son.	Col. 1:13
The Lord in the day	Isa. 13:13, Lam. 1:12
Of his anger did lay	Isa. 53:6
Your sins on the Lamb, and he bore	Lev. 16:21–22, Jn. 1:29,
them away.	1 Pet. 2:24
He answered for all:	Jn. 11:51, Rom. 5:19
O come at his call,	Matt. 11:28
And low at his cross with astonishment fall!	Isa. 52:14, 1 Cor. 1:23–4
But lift up your eyes	Zech 12:10, Jn. 13:37
At Jesus's cries:	Mk. 15:37, Heb. 5:7
Impassive, he suffers, immortal, he dies.	Phil. 2:8, 1 Tim. 1:17,
	1 Pet. 3:18, 4:1
He dies to atone	Rom. 3:25, 5:10–11
For sins not his own;	Dan. 9:26, 2 Cor. 5:21
Your debt he hath paid, and your work he	2 Cor. 8:9, Heb. 10:9–10
hath done	
Ye all may receive	
The peace he did leave,	Jn. 14:27
Who made intercession, My Father, forgive!	Lk. 23:34
For you and for me	
He prayed on the tree:	Isa. 53:12
The prayer is accepted, the sinner is free.	Rom. 6:6–7, Eph. 1:6
That sinner am I,	1 Tim. 1:13, 15
Who on Jesus rely,	2 Tim. 1:12
And come for the pardon God cannot deny.	Isa. 55:7, 1 Thess. 5:24,
	2 Tim. 2:13
His death is my plea;	2 Cor. 5;14–15
My advocate see,	1 Jn. 2:1
And hear the blood speak that hath answered	Heb. 12:24
for me.	
My ransom he was	Mk. 10:45, 1 Tim. 2:6
When he bled on the cross;	
And by losing his life he hath carried	Jn. 10:11, 15, Heb. 7:25
my cause.	

22. The Resurrection

Christ's resurrection, which was no mere survival of a disembodied spirit, or vision of Christ in glory, but the divine mystery of a triumphant 'more than reversal' of his death, is a mark that the cross is indeed a victory over the power of evil, and that the sacrifice is effectual.

P.W. i. 185; W.H. 716; M.H.B. 204; M.H. 439; H.P. 193

'Christ the Lord is risen today',   Mk. 16:6, Lk. 24:6
Sons of men and angels say!   Matt. 28:6, Lk. 24:34, Jn. 20:1
Raise your joys and triumphs high,   Col. 2:15
Sing ye heavens, and earth reply.   Isa. 49:13

Love's redeeming work is done,   Rom. 6:9–10
Fought the fight, the battle won: Lk. 11:22, Col. 2:15
Lo! our Sun's eclipse is o'er,   Mal. 4:2, Lk. 23:45
Lo! He sets in blood no more.   Isa. 60:20

Vain the stone, the watch, the seal;   Matt. 27:65–66
Christ has burst the gates of hell!   1 Pet. 3:18–20, Rev. 1:18
Death in vain forbids his rise: Acts 2:24
Christ has opened paradise!   Lk. 23:43

Lives again our glorious King,   Ps. 24:7–10, Rev. 1:18
Where, O death, is now thy sting?   1 Cor. 15:55
Dying once, he all doth save,   Rom. 6:10, 1 Cor. 15:22
Where thy victory, O grave?   1 Cor. 15:55

Soar we now where Christ has led?   Col. 3:1
Following our exalted Head,   Acts 2:33, Eph. 1:22, Col. 1:1
Made like him, like him we rise;   Rom. 6:5
Ours the cross, the grave, the skies!   Rom. 6:4, 6

King of glory, soul of bliss,   Ps. 27;4, 1 Pet. 1:3, 8
Everlasting life is this;   Jn. 3:16
Thee to know, thy power to prove,   Phil. 3:10
Thus to sing, and thus to love!   Isa. 26:19

The Lord's Day, the weekly celebration of Christ's resurrection, is to be devoted to Christian worship, to prayer, praise, the preaching of the gospel, and the Lord's Supper.

P.W. vi. 429; W.H. 953; M.H.B. 661; H.P. 575

Come, let us with our Lord arise,	Col. 3:1
Our Lord, who made both earth and skies;	Gen. 1:1
Who died to save the world he made,	Jn. 1:3, 11
And rose triumphant from the dead;	Acts 2:24
He rose, the Prince of life and peace,	Isa. 9:6, Acts 3:15
And stamped the day for ever his.	Ps. 118: 24, Jn. 20:1, Acts 20:7, 1 Cor. 16:2, Rev. 1:10
This is the day the Lord hath made,	Ps. 118:24
That all may see his love displayed,	1 Jn. 4:9
May feel his resurrection's power,	Phil. 3:10
And rise again to fall no more,	2 Pet. 1:10
In perfect righteousness renewed,	Eph. 4:23–4
And filled with all the life of God.	Jn. 10:10, 2 Pet. 1:4
Then let us render him his own,	1 Chron. 29:14, Mk. 12:17
With solemn prayer approach the throne,	Ps. 65:4, Heb. 4:16
With meekness hear the gospel-word,	Jas. 1:21
With thanks his dying love record;	1 Cor. 11:26, 14:16
Our joyful hearts and voices raise,	Eph. 5:19
And fill his courts with songs of praise.	Ps. 100:4
Honour and praise to Jesus pay	Eph. 1:6, Acts 20:7
Throughout his consecrated day;	1 Cor. 16:2, Rev. 1:7
Be all in Jesu's praise employed,	1 Pet. 2:9
Nor leave a single moment void;	
With utmost care this time improve,	Eph. 5:16, Col. 4:5
And only breathe his praise and love.	Ps. 150:6

23. The Ascension

The risen Christ in his visible 'glorious body' vanished for the last time by being received into the heavens. Since then he has been seen in visions only. This manner of disappearance was an impressive acted parable to teach that the incarnate Son's work on earth is now finished, so that he may reign in glory. The Shekinah, or cloud of glory, is the mark of the presence of the invisible God (Ex. 16:10, 40:34, 38, Lev. 16:2, 1 Kings 8:10, Ezek. 10:4, Mk. 9:7, 1 Cor. 10:1–2.) To have vanished 'into the clouds' no more indicates that our Lord is now in some kind of 'place' above the blue dome of heaven than the circumstance that he vanished from a room 'the doors being shut' (Jn 20:19–29) presupposes that he was then on the other side of the door. The language of 'up' is a natural symbol for advancement in glory and power. The risen Christ was, and is, present all the time, though not always seen.

P.W. i. 187; W.H. 718; M.H.B. 221; H.P. 197

Hail the day that sees him rise,	Lk. 24:51, Jn. 20:17
Ravished from our wishful eyes!	Acts 1:10–11
Christ, awhile to mortals given,	Jn. 3:16
Reascends his native heaven.	Acts 1:9, Eph. 4:9–10
There the pompous triumph waits:*	Col. 2:15
Lift your heads, eternal gates;	Ps. 24:7, 9
Wide unfold the radiant scene;	Rev. 4:1–2
Take the King of glory in!	Ps. 24:7, 9
Him though highest heaven receives,	Acts 3:21, Heb. 7:26
Still he loves the earth he leaves;	Jn. 14:18
Though returning to his throne,	Jn. 6:62, 14:28, Rev. 3:21
Still he calls mankind his own.	Jn. 1:11, 13:1
See, he lifts his hands above!	Deut. 32:40, Dan. 12:7
See, he shows the prints of love!	Zech. 13:6, Jn. 20:27
Hark, his gracious lips bestow	Lk. 4:22
Blessing on his church below!	Eph. 4:8, 11–12

Still for us his death he pleads;	1 Jn. 2:1
Prevalent he intercedes;	Heb. 7:25
Near himself prepares our place,	Jn. 14:2–3
Harbinger of human race.	Heb. 6:20
Grant, though parted from our sight,	2 Chron. 6:18, Lk. 24:51
High above yon azure height,	Heb. 4:14, 7:26, 9:24
Grant our hearts may thither rise,	Col. 3:1–2
Following thee beyond the skies.	

---

* A 'pomp' is an old word for a procession

P.W. iv. 154; W.H. 719; M.H.B. 219

God is gone up on high,	Ps. 47:5
With a triumphant noise;	Col. 2:15
The clarions of the sky	
Proclaim the angelic joys!	Lk. 15:10
Join all on earth, rejoice and sing;	Ps. 47:7, Zech 2:10–11
Glory ascribe to glory's King.	Ps. 24:8, 96:7, 8 (B.C.P.)
God in the flesh below,	Jn. 1:14, Heb. 2:14, 1 Jn. 4:2
For us he reigns above:	1 Cor. 15:25, Rev. 19:15–16
Let all the nations know	Ps. 98:1–2
Our Jesu's conquering love!	
Join all on earth, rejoice and sing;	Ps. 47:7, Zech. 2:10–11
Glory ascribe to glory's King.	Ps. 24:8, 96:7, 8 (B.C.P.)
All power to our great Lord	Matt. 28:18
Is by the Father given;	1 Cor. 15:27, Eph. 1:22
By angel-hosts adored,	Heb. 1:6, Rev. 5:11–13
He reigns supreme in heaven:	Eph. 1:20–22, Phil. 2:9–11
Join all on earth, rejoice and sing;	Ps. 47:7, Zech. 2:10–11
Glory ascribe to glory's King.	Ps. 24:8, 96:7, 8 (B.C.P.)
High on his holy seat	Ps. 2:6, Heb. 1:3, 10:12
He bears the righteous sway;	Ps. 96:13, Isa. 11:4–5
His foes beneath his feet	1 Cor. 15:25, Heb. 2:8
Shall sink and die away:	Jer. 51:64, Acts 2:35
Join all on earth, rejoice and sing;	Ps. 47:7, Zech. 2:10–11
Glory ascribe to glory's King.	Ps. 24:8, 96:7, 8 (B.C.P.)
His foes and ours are one,	Eph. 6:12, Col. 2:15
Satan, the world, and sin;	Mk. 1:13, Jn. 15:18, Heb. 2:14
But he shall tread them down,	Isa. 63:3, Rev. 19:15
And bring his kingdom in:	Mk. 1:14–15, Rev. 11:15
Join all on earth, rejoice and sing;	Ps. 47:7, Zech. 2:10–11
Glory ascribe to glory's King.	Ps. 24:8, 96:7, 8 (B.C.P.)

Till all the earth renewed	Rom. 8:21–22, Rev. 21:1, 5
In righteousness divine,	Isa. 11:4, 51:5–6, Eph. 4:24
With all the hosts of God	Ps. 148:2
In one great chorus join,	
Join all on earth, rejoice and sing;	Ps. 47:7, Zech. 2:10–11
Glory ascribe to glory's King.	Ps. 24:8, 96:7, 8 (B.C.P.)

24. Christ our High Priest

In the incarnation of the divine Son God showed himself to be united to the human race, and having shared human affliction, to be close to humanity in loving sympathy. However, Christ's ascension to glory has not broken off the union, or rendered God again remote. There is eternally within the nature of the God of glory One who knows what it is to be frail and tempted, and of whose sympathy we may be sure. Because he is there men and women may take confidence in coming to God. As an earthly priest represents the people to God in worship, so our true Representative with God in glory is our great High Priest. Thus Christ is both the sacrifice (21) and the priest.

P.W. xiii. 140; W.H. 726; M.H.B. 232*

Entered the holy place above,	Lev. 16:1–2, Heb. 9:12, 24
Covered with meritorious scars,	Matt. 27:26, Jn. 20:20, 27
The tokens of his dying love	Jn. 10:11, 15:13, Gal. 2:20
Our great High-priest in glory bears;	Heb. 4:14, 5;5
He pleads his passion on the tree,	Heb. 5:7, 9:14, 1 Pet. 2:24
He shows himself to God for me.	Heb. 9:24
Before the throne my Saviour stands,	Acts 5:31, Rev. 5:6–7
My Friend and Advocate appears;	Heb. 4:15–16, 7:25, 1 Jn. 2:1
My name is graven on his hands,	Isa. 49:16
And him the Father always hears;	Jn. 11:42
While low at Jesu's cross I bow,	Jn. 19:25–7
He hears the blood of sprinkling now.	Heb. 12:24, 1 Pet. 1:2
This instant now I may receive	2 Cor. 6:2, Heb. 3:13
The answer of his powerful prayer:	Lk. 23:34, Heb. 7:25
This instant now by him I live,	Jn. 6:57, 1 Jn. 4:9, Gal. 2:20
His prevalence with God declare;	Jn. 11:22, Gen. 32:28
And soon my spirit, in his hands,	Ps. 31:5
Shall stand where my Forerunner stands.	Jn. 14:3, 17:24, Heb. 6:20

---

* It is much to be regretted that this fine hymn is omitted in the new Methodist 'Hymns and Psalms'.

25. The Kingdom of God

The great Creator is the sovereign ruler of all things, but the condition of a fallen and rebellious world is a repudiation of that sovereignty. Faith affirms that God will show himself to be God by invading the world-order with his sovereign power, to overthrow the power of evil, and to rescue his distressed people. This message of divine hope is the gospel of the Kingdom. The bringer of the Kingdom is the Messiah, God's personal Representative on earth. God's saving act was declared in promise, and witnessed in its initial prevailing stages in the earthly career of Christ: his incarnation, life, teaching, miracles, death, and resurrection. That this divine victory is destined to prevail and grow is symbolized in the ascended Christ's reign in glory. The second Advent in glory is the promised climax of the coming of the Kingdom of God (54).

P.W. iv. 140; W.H. 729, M.H.B. 247; M.H. 483; H.P. 243

Rejoice, the Lord is King!	Ps. 24:10, 47:7, Isa. 32:1
Your Lord and King adore,	Ps. 95:6, Zech. 14:16
Mortals, give thanks and sing,	Ps. 145:21
And triumph evermore;	2 Cor. 2:14, 1 Thess. 5:16
Lift up your heart, lift up your voice,	Ps. 25:1, Isa. 24:14, 40:9
Rejoice, again I say, rejoice.	Phil. 4:4
Jesus the Saviour reigns,	Lk. 1:33, Acts 5:31, 1 Cor. 15
The God of truth and love;	Ps. 31:5, Jn. 1:14, 1 Jn. 4:8
When he had purged our stains,	Heb. 1:3
He took his seat above:	
Lift up your heart, lift up your voice,	Ps. 25:1, Isa. 24:14, 40:9
Rejoice, again I say, rejoice.	Phil. 4:4
His kingdom cannot fail,	Ps. 145:13, Isa. 42:4
He rules o'er earth and heaven;	Phil. 2:10–11
The keys of death and hell	Rev. 1:18
Are to our Jesus given:	
Lift up your heart, lift up your voice,	Ps. 25:1, Isa. 24:14, 40:9
Rejoice, again I say, rejoice.	Phil. 4:4

He sits at God's right hand,	Rom. 8:34, Eph. 1:20, Col. 3:1
Till all his foes submit,	1 Cor. 15:25
And bow to his command,	Phil. 2:10
And fall beneath his feet:	1 Cor. 15:27
Lift up your heart, lift up your voice,	Ps. 25:1, Isa. 24:14, 40:9
Rejoice, again I say, rejoice.	Phil. 4:4
He all his foes shall quell,	Ps. 89:23, Acts 2:35
Shall all our sins destroy,	Heb. 2:14, 1 Jn. 3:8
And every bosom swell	Ps. 13:5, Jn. 16:22
With pure seraphic joy;	Job 38:7
Lift up your heart, lift up your voice,	Ps. 25:1, Isa. 24:14, 40:9
Rejoice, again I say, rejoice.	Phil. 4:4
Rejoice in glorious hope,	Rom. 5:2, 12:12, Col. 1:27
Jesus the Judge shall come,	Jn. 5:22, 2 Cor. 5:10, Rev. 1:7
And take his servants up	1 Thess. 4:17
To their eternal home:	Matt. 25:46, Jn. 14:3
We soon shall hear the archangel's voice,	1 Thess. 4:16
The trump of God shall sound, Rejoice!	1 Cor. 15:52, Phil:4:4–5,
	1 Thess. 4:16

P.W. v. 120; W.H. 218; M.H.B. 263; M.H. 464; H.P. 781

See how great a flame aspires,	Jas. 3:5
Kindled by a spark of grace!	
Jesu's love the nations fires,	Isa. 55:5, Zech. 2:11
Sets the kingdoms on a blaze;	
To bring fire on earth he came,	Matt. 3;1, Lk. 12:49
Kindled in some hearts it is,	Rom. 5:5
O that all might catch the flame,	Acts 2:3
All partake the glorious bliss!	Col. 1:12, 2 Pet. 1:4
When he first the work begun,	Matt. 4:17, Phil. 1:6
Small and feeble was his day;	Zech. 4:10
Now the word doth swiftly run,	Ps. 147:15, 2 Thess. 3:1
Now it wins its widening way;	Ps. 119:96
More and more it spreads and grows,	Matt. 9:31
Ever mighty to prevail,	Acts 19:20
Sin's strong-holds it now o'erthrows,	2 Cor. 10:4
Shakes the trembling gates of hell.	Matt. 16:18, Jas. 2:19
Sons of God, your Saviour praise!	1 Jn. 3:1–2
He the door hath opened wide;	Acts 14:27, Rev. 3:8
He hath given the word of grace,	Ps. 68:11, Acts 20:32
Jesu's word is glorified;	Acts 13:48, 2 Thess. 3:1
Jesus, mighty to redeem,	Isa. 63:1
He alone the work hath wrought;	Num. 23:23, Ps. 74:13, (B.C.P.)

Worthy is the work of him,	Rev. 4:11
Him who spake a world from nought.*	Gen. 1:1, Heb. 11:3
Saw ye not the cloud arise,	1 Kgs. 18:44–5
Little as a human hand?	
Now it spreads along the skies,	
Hangs o'er all the thirsty land;	Isa. 44:3
Lo! the promise of a shower	Ezek. 34:26
Drops already from above;	
But the Lord will shortly pour	Joel 2:28, Acts 2:18, 33
All the Spirit of his love!	Gal. 5:22, 2 Tim. 1:7

---

* 'Twas great to speak the world from nought.'
  (S. Wesley, Jun. 'An Hymn for Sunday,' *Poems* (1736) p. 241, line 16).

26. The Holy Spirit

In the divine Son incarnate we see God's saving work actually performed 'once for all' as part of the history of our world, at a certain place and time, and within the circumstances of a certain race and social background. This represents 'the gospel of what God did'. The divine Presence who, on account of what God did then, carries on the work of salvation among all men and women, in all their variety, and in every time and place, is the Holy Spirit. He represents 'the gospel of what God does'. The Holy Spirit takes the effect of Christ's historic work and brings it home to the believing heart in personal experience and conviction. As the Evangelical Revival was the occasion of outstanding spiritual renewal, alike in Britain and America, it is not surprising that the Wesley hymns are especially rich in verse on the person, work, and gifts of the Spirit.

P.W. ii. 227; W.H. 759; M.H.B. 274; H.P. 307

Lord, we believe to us and ours	Lk. 24:49, Acts 1:4–5, 2:39
The apostolic promise given;	
We wait to taste the heavenly powers,	Lk. 24:49, Heb. 6:5
The Holy Ghost sent down from heaven.	Jn. 14:26, 1 Pet. 1:12
To every one whom God shall call	Acts. 2:39
The promise is securely made;	
To you far off; he calls you all;	Eph. 2:13
Believe the word which Christ hath said;	Jn. 16:4
The Holy Ghost, if I depart,	Jn. 16:7
The Comforter shall surely come,	Jn. 15:26
Shall make the contrite sinner's heart	Ps. 51:4, 11
His loved, his everlasting home.	Jn. 14:16
Assembled here with one accord,	Acts 2:1
Calmly we wait the promised grace,	Lk. 24:49, Acts 1:4
The purchase of our dying Lord;	Jn. 14:16, 16:7
Come, Holy Ghost, and fill the place.	Acts 2:1–2
If every one that asks may find,	Matt. 7:7–8, Lk. 11:13
If still thou dost on sinners fall,	Acts 10:44, 11:15

| Come as a mighty rushing wind; | Acts 2:2 |
| Great grace be now upon us all. | Acts 4:33 |

Behold, to thee our souls aspire,	2 Cor. 1:22
And languish thy descent to meet:	Rom. 8:23
Kindle in each the living fire,	Lk. 12:49
And fix in every heart thy seat.	Ps. 57:7

P.W. i. 188; W.H. 758; M.H.B. 277; H.P. 287

NOTE: *Some consider that this may well be the hymn sung by the Wesleys on the morning of Charles's evangelical experience, May 21, 1738.*

Granted is the Saviour's prayer,	Jn. 14:16
Sent the gracious Comforter;	Jn. 14:26
Promise of our parting Lord,	Jn. 15:26, 16:7, Acts 1:8–9
Jesus now to heaven restored.	Jn. 6:62, Eph. 4:8–10

Christ, who now gone up on high	Eph. 4:8
Captive leads captivity;	Ps. 68:18
While his foes from him receive	Rom. 5:10
Grace, that God with man may live.	Rom. 5:17, Eph. 2:8

God, the everlasting God,	Gen. 21:33, Isa. 40:28
Makes with mortals his abode;	Jn. 14:23
Whom the heavens cannot contain,	1 Kgs. 8:27
He vouchsafes to dwell in man.	2 Cor. 6:16, 1 Jn. 4:13

Never will he thence depart,	Jn. 14:16, Heb. 13:5,
Inmate of an humble heart;	Isa. 57:15
Carrying on his work within,	1 Cor. 12:6, Phil. 2;13
Striving till he casts out sin.	Gen. 6:3, 12:31, Jn. 16:8–9

There he helps our feeble moans,	Rom. 8:26
Deepens our imperfect groans,	
Intercedes in silence there,	
Sighs the unutterable prayer.	

Come, divine and peaceful Guest,	Lk. 19:7
Enter our devoted breast;	Cant. 1:13
Holy Ghost, our hearts inspire,*	
Kindle there the Gospel-fire.	Matt. 3:11, Lk. 12:19

Now descend, and shake the earth;	Hag. 2:6–7, Heb. 12:26
Wake us into second birth;	Jn. 3:3, Rom. 13:11, Eph. 5:1
Life divine in us renew,	Ps. 51:10
Thou the gift and giver too!**	Jn. 14:16, Acts 2:38, 1 Cor. 12:1, 14:1

---

* cf. *Veni Creator Spiritus*
** Phrases similar to this are found in the Latin hymns of Adam of St. Victor, and Augustine, *Enchiridion*, C. xxxvii

P.W. iv. 203; W.H. 760; M.H.B. 278; H.P. 296

Away with our fears,	2 Tim. 1:7
Our troubles and tears!	Acts 13:52
The Spirit is come,	Acts 2:33
The witness of Jesus returned to his home.	Jn. 16:7, 15, Heb. 10:12, 15
The pledge of our Lord	2 Cor. 1:22, 5:5
To his heaven restored	Jn. 6:62
Is sent from the sky,	Acts 1:8–9
And tells us our Head is exalted on high.	Phil. 2:9
Our Advocate there	1 Jn. 2:1
By his blood and his prayer	Jn. 14:16, Heb. 9:12, 14
The gift hath obtained,	
For us he hath prayed, and the Comforter gained.	Jn. 14:16
Our glorified Head	Jn. 12:23, Eph. 1:20–22
His Spirit hath shed,	Acts 2:33
With his people to stay,	Jn. 14:16
And never again will he take him away.	
Our heavenly guide	Isa. 30:21, Jn. 16:13
With us shall abide,	Jn. 14:16
His comforts impart,	Jn. 14:18, Acts 9:31
And set up his kingdom of love in the heart.	Dan. 2:44, Rom. 5:5
The heart that believes	
His kingdom receives,	Matt. 25:34
His power and his peace,	Jn. 14:27, Acts 1:8
His life, and his joy's everlasting increase.	Isa. 9:7, Rom. 8:2, Gal. 5:22
The presence divine	
Doth inwardly shine,	2 Cor. 4:6
The Shechinah rests	Ex. 40:34, 38, Num. 9:15–16
On all our assemblies, and glows in our breasts.	Acts 2–3, 1 Pet. 4:14
Then let us rejoice	1 Pet. 1:8
In heart and in voice,	Jn. 16:22
Our leader pursue,	Heb. 12:1–2
And shout as we travel the wilderness through.	Deut. 32:10, Isa. 35:6, 10, 42:11
With the Spirit remove,	Ezek. 8:3–4
To Zion above,	Gal. 4:26, Heb. 12:22, Rev. 21:2
Triumphant arise,	2 Cor. 2:14
And walk with our God, till we fly to the skies.	Gen. 5:24, 6:9, Mic. 6:8, 1 Thess. 4:17

27. The Divine Person of the Spirit

'The Spirit' is a biblical phrase to convey the idea of the more immediate and commanding sense of the presence of God, the more prevailing and significant mark of his operation. As God is personal (1) the Spirit is a personal divine presence. In particular, the Spirit brings to the believer the sense of the personal presence of the risen and glorified Christ, fulfilling the promise of Christ that he will continue for ever with his Church (Matthew 28:20, Jn. 14:16). Thus the Holy Spirit is both the Old Testament Spirit of Prophecy and the New Testament Spirit of Christ. We can distinguish in thought between God the Son, who operated once in history, and God the Spirit, who operates now, but in devotional experience we can hardly distinguish between the presence of the risen and glorified Christ and the presence of the Spirit. Thus the Spirit of God is also and equally the Spirit of Christ (Romans 8:9).

P.W. iv. 165; W.H. 377; M.H.B. 730; H.P. 300

Father of everlasting grace,	Ps. 103:17, Jer. 31:3
Thy goodness and thy truth we praise,	Ex. 34:6
Thy goodness and thy truth we prove;	Rom. 12:2
Thou hast, in honour of thy Son,	Jn. 8:54, 14:26
The gift unspeakable sent down,	2 Cor. 9:15, 1 Pet. 1:12
The Spirit of life, and power, and love.	Rom. 8:2, 2 Tim. 1:7
Send us the Spirit of thy Son,	Gal. 4:6
To make the depths of Godhead known;	1 Cor. 2:11
To make us share the life divine;	2 Pet. 1:4
Send him the sprinkled blood to apply,	Heb. 10:22, 12:24, 1 Pet. 1:2
Send him our souls to sanctify,	2 Thess. 2:13, 1 Pet. 1:2
And show and seal us ever thine.	2 Cor. 1:22, Eph. 1:13
	1 Pet. 1:2
So shall we pray, and never cease,	Acts 12:5, 1 Thess. 5:17
So shall we thankfully confess,	Rom. 10:9–10
Thy wisdom, truth, and power, and love;	Jn. 1:14, 1 Cor. 1:24

With joy unspeakable adore,	1 Pet. 1:8
And bless and praise thee evermore,	Ps. 86, 12, 115:18
And serve thee as thy hosts above;	Rev. 7:15, 22:3

Till, added to that heavenly choir,	Heb. 12:22–3
We raise our songs of triumph higher,	Ps. 47:1
And praise thee in a bolder strain,	
Out-soar the first-born seraph's flight,	Job 38:7, 1 Pet. 1:12
And sing, with all our friends in light,	Rev. 21:24
Thy everlasting love to man.	Jer. 31:3

P.W. v. 469; W.H. 486; M.H.B. 719; H.P. 763

See, Jesu, thy disciples see,	
The promised blessing give!	Matt. 28:20
Met in thy name, we look to thee,	Matt. 18:20
Expecting to receive.	

Thee we expect, our faithful Lord,	2 Thess. 3:3, Rev. 1:5, 19:11
Who in thy name are joined;	1 Cor. 1:10, Eph. 4:16
We wait, according to thy word,	Acts 1:4
Thee in the midst to find.	Matt. 18:20

With us thou art assembled here,	Jn. 20:19
But O thyself reveal!	Gal. 1:16
Son of the living God, appear!	Matt. 16:16, Mk. 15:39, Jn. 6:69
Let us thy presence feel.	1 Thess. 2:19, 2 Pet. 1:16

Breathe on us Lord, in this our day,	Jn. 20:22
And these dry bones shall live;	Ezek. 37:4–5
Speak peace into our hearts, and say,	Jn. 20:21
'The Holy Ghost receive!'	Jn. 20:22

Whom now we seek, O may we meet!	Matt. 28:9, Lk. 24:5, 15, 31
Jesus the crucified,	1 Cor. 1:23, 2:2
Show us thy bleeding hands and feet,	Lk. 24:39–40, Jn. 20:20, 27
Thou who for us hast died.	Rom. 5:6, 1 Thess. 5:10,
	1 Cor. 15:3

Cause us the record to receive,	Jn. 19:35, 20:30–1
Speak, and the tokens show;	Acts 1:30
'O be not faithless, but believe	Jn. 20:27
In me, who died for you!'	Gal. 2:20

P.W. ii. 271; W.H. 312; M.H.B. 478

Jesu, my Saviour, Brother, Friend,	Matt. 12:50, Lk. 2:11, Jn. 15:1
On whom I cast my every care,	1 Pet. 5:7
On whom for all things I depend,	Rom. 8:32
Inspire, and then accept, my prayer.*	Ps. 69:13, Lk. 11:1,
	Rom. 8:26
If I have tasted of thy grace,	1 Pet. 2:3
The grace that sure salvation brings,	Eph. 2:8
If with me now thy Spirit stays,	1 Pet. 4:14
And hovering hides me in his wings.	Ps. 17:8
Still let him with my weakness stay,	2 Cor. 12:9
Nor for a moment's space depart,	Isa. 59:21
Evil and danger turn away,	Matt. 6:13, Rev. 3:10
And keep till he renews my heart.	Ps. 51:10, Ezek. 26:36
When to the right or left I stray,	Isa. 30:21
His voice behind me may I hear,	
'Return, and walk in Christ thy way;	Jer. 7:23, Jn. 14:6, Heb. 10:20
Fly back to Christ, for sin is near.'	Ps. 143:9
His sacred unction from above	1 Jn. 2:20
Be still my comforter and guide;	Jn. 16:7, 13
Till all the hardness he remove,	Ezek. 11:19, 36:26, Mk. 3:5
And in my loving heart reside.	Rom. 8:9, 11
Jesus, I fain would walk in thee,	Col. 2:6
From nature's every path retreat;	1 Cor. 2:14, Eph. 2:3
Thou art my Way, my leader be,	Isa. 55:4, Jn. 14:6, Heb. 12:2
And set upon the rock my feet.	Ps. 40:2, 61:2, 1 Cor. 10:4
Uphold me, Saviour, or I fall,	Ps. 145:14
O reach me out thy gracious hand!	Matt. 14:31
Only on thee for help I call,	Ps. 124:8
Only by faith in thee I stand.	Rom. 11:20

---

* 'and, that we may obtain that which thou dost promise, make us to love that which
thou dost command.'   (BCP Collect, Trinity XIV)

28. The Holy Trinity

Christian faith confesses that the one God has made himself known to humankind through a three-fold experience. There is the great sovereign King, whom Jesus taught us to call the Father. There is the divine Son, who in a certain place and time was incarnate, lived, died, rose again, and ascended to glory. And there is the divine Spirit, the saving unseen Companion who indwells the Church, and the hearts of believers in every time and place. The question for Christian thought is: 'Is this three-fold experience so far a concession to human infirmity of thought as to be virtually an illusion, leaving the eternal God 'as he is in himself' in principle unknown and unknowable?' The Christian affirmation, drawing out the implication of the witness of scripture, is that, whereas we certainly do not claim to know all about God, that which God has revealed of himself in this three-fold experience is an entirely authentic and reliable revelation. It represents the utmost that the human mind can hope to apprehend regarding the nature of God.

Therefore, when in glory we shall with fuller knowledge adore God 'as he is in himself', we shall realize that there was no element of illusion in God's earthly revelation of himself to Christian faith. The nature of God as he eternally exists truly corresponds to the three-fold experience of Father, Son, and Holy Spirit. By consequence, the one God is to be confessed as the Holy Trinity. However, when the Father, Son, and Holy Spirit are set forth in the traditional and technical term 'Three Persons', this does not mean that the Three are to be thought of as entirely separate 'personalities', in the modern sense of that word. The three 'Persons' are more intimately united in love and moral will than any human personalities can ever be, and so are more fully 'personal'. It is no true objection that this Christian doctrine of God involves a mystery, for the nature of the Supreme God is bound to pass beyond the power of human thought. The human mind even of a genius cannot grasp all knowledge of the universe which God has created. Therefore the being of the Creator transcends human knowledge. Nevertheless, the knowledge of himself which he has revealed is secure knowledge. We are not left in ignorance. Thus hymns to the Trinity adore, rather than 'explain'.

P.W. vi. 433, vii. 305; W.H. 232

Young men and maidens, raise	Ps. 148:12–13
Your tuneful voices high;	
Old men and children, praise	
The Lord of earth and sky;	
Him Three in One, and One in Three,	Matt. 28:19, 2 Cor. 13:14
Extol to all eternity.	Ps. 145:1
His Son, on us bestowed,	Jn. 3:16
The Father hath revealed:	Matt. 11:27
The Son his Father showed,	Jn. 1:18
From mortal eye concealed;	1 Jn. 4:12
The indwelling Comforter attests	Jn. 14:16, Rom. 8:9
That One is Three, in faithful breasts.	1 Jn. 5:7*
Thrice holy God, in whom	Isa. 6:3, Rev. 4:8
We live, and move, and are,	Acts 17:28
To do thy will we come,	Ps. 40:7–8, Heb. 10:7, 9
Thy glory to declare,	Isa. 66:19
By all our converse here to show	1 Tim. 4:12, 1 Pet. 3:1–2
That God is manifest below.	1 Jn. 3:8
Baptized into thy Name,	Matt. 28:19
Mysterious One in Three,	
Our souls and bodies claim	1 Cor. 6:19–20
A sacrifice to thee:	Rom. 12:1
We only live our faith to prove,	Jas. 2:18
The faith which works by humble love.	Gal. 5:6, 1 Thess. 1:3

* We observe that this text does not occur in the best MSS of the New Testament, and so is omitted in most modern editions of the Bible. It would, however, be treated as a scripture proof by the Wesleys, though John is aware that the text has been controverted (see *Notes on the New Testament*.)

P.W. iv. 254; W.H. 253; M.H.B. 39; H.P. 4

Father, in whom we live,	Acts 17:28
In whom we are, and move,	
The glory, power, and praise receive	Rev. 4:11
Of thy creating love.	
Let all the angel-throng	Dan. 7:10, Rev. 19:16
Give thanks to God on high;	Ps. 148:1–2
While earth repeats the joyful song,	Ps. 148:7, 11–13
And echoes to the sky.	

Incarnate Deity,	Jn. 1:14, Heb. 2:14
Let all the ransomed race	Isa. 35:10, 51:10, Mk. 10:45
Render in thanks their lives to thee,	Rom. 12:1, 1 Cor. 6:20
For thy redeeming grace.	Rom. 3:23, Eph. 2:5, 8
The grace to sinners showed	Lk. 23:43, Rom. 5:8, 1 Jn. 1:9
Ye heavenly choirs proclaim,	Rev. 7:9–10
And cry, 'Salvation to our God	
Salvation to the Lamb!'	
Spirit of Holiness,	Rom. 1:4
Let all thy saints adore	
Thy sacred energy, and bless	Acts 1:8, Rom. 15:13, 19
Thy heart-renewing power.	Ezek. 36:26, Jn. 3:3, 5, 2 Tim. 1:7
Not angel-tongues can tell	1 Pet. 1:12
Thy love's ecstatic height,	2 Cor. 12:4
The glorious joy unspeakable,	1 Pet. 1:8, Rev. 8:1
The beatific sight.	Matt. 5:8, 1 Cor. 13:12,
	Heb. 12:14, 1 Jn. 3:2
Eternal, Triune Lord!	Isa. 6:3, Rev. 4:8
Let all the hosts above,	Rev. 5:11–12, 7:9–12, 19:1, 6
Let all the sons of men record	Ps. 145:8–9, 12
And dwell upon thy love.	
When heaven and earth are fled	Rev. 20:11
Before thy glorious face,	
Sing all the saints thy love hath made	Ps. 145:10, 149:1
Thine everlasting praise!	Ps. 41:13

29. Human Nature

The Bible takes a realistic view of our common human nature. We are neither merely part of the animal world, in the last resort conditioned by our physical environment, nor are we lofty and gifted creatures capable of immense self-improvement. Human beings were created 'in the image and likeness of God', that is to say, possessed of reason, moral responsibility, and the power of spiritual fellowship with God. Nevertheless, the human race has collectively fallen into sin, so that men and women are not capable of knowing and obeying God as they ought. All men and women are by nature in a condition of spiritual and moral bondage, and to some degree of intellectual infirmity, which they are not capable of resolving by human effort unaided by divine grace.

That the human race, created by a good God, should be in this evil condition is the last and darkest mystery of human thought. We observe that the Bible, not being a book of philosophical speculation, but of practical religious devotion, does not attempt to give a theoretical explanation of the presence of evil in the world. Thus the Bible does not seek to explain why there was a Serpent in the Garden, or why Adam and Eve should so irrationally have yielded to his blandishments. The early chapters of the Bible give us something much more valuable. They reveal God's authoritative diagnosis of the spiritual condition of the race. Men and women discovered within themselves wonderful powers, which in pride they used to seek to lift themselves up against God. The consequence was spiritual alienation from God, and an inevitable train of moral ruin in the individual, and in society.

P.W. iii. 84; W.H. 6–8; M.H.B. 327

Sinners, turn, why will ye die:	Ezek. 18:31, Rom. 6:23
God, your Maker, asks you why?	Gen. 1:26–7, 2:7, Isa. 17:7
God, who did your being give,	Acts 17:28
Made you with himself to live;	Wisd. 2:23

He the fatal cause demands,
Asks the work of his own hands,   Isa. 64:8
Why, ye thankless creatures, why   Lk. 6:35
Will ye cross his love, and die?   Hos. 11:1–3

Let the beasts their breath resign,   Ps. 104:29
Strangers to the life divine;   Ps. 49:12
Who their God can never know,   ps. 73:22
Let their spirit downward go.   Eccl. 3:21
You for higher ends were born,   Gen. 1:26
You may all to God return,   Isa. 55:7, Jer. 3:22, Hos. 6:1
Dwell with him above the sky;   Jn. 14:2–3, Rev. 7:13–17
Why will you resolve to die?   Ezek. 3:7, 18:31

You, on whom he favours showers,   Ezek. 34:26
You, possessed of nobler powers,   Gen. 1:26–7
You, of reason's powers possessed,   Rom. 1:20
You, with will and memory blest,
You, with finer sense endued,
Creatures capable of God;   Ps. 8:4–6, Heb. 2:6–8
Noblest of his creatures, why,
Why will you for ever die?   Matt. 25:46, 2 Thess. 1:9

You, whom he ordained to be   Gen. 1:26–7
Transcripts of the Deity;   Wisd. 2:23, Acts 17:28
You, whom he in life doth hold;   Ps. 66:9
You, for whom himself was sold;   Zech. 11:12, Matt. 26:15
You, on whom he still doth wait,   Isa. 30:18
Whom he would again create;   2 Cor. 5:17, Gal. 6:15
Made by him, and purchased, why   Gen. 1:27, Acts 20:28
Why will you for ever die?   Matt. 25:46, 2 Thess. 1:9

What could your Redeemer do   Isa. 5:4
More than he hath done for you?
To procure your peace with God,   Rom. 5:1
Could he more than shed his blood?   Mk. 12:6–8, 14:24, Jn. 15:13,
    Gal. 2:20, 1 Pet. 1:18–19

See! the suffering God appears!   Heb. 2:9
Jesus weeps! believe his tears!   Jn. 11:35, Heb. 5:7
Mingled with his blood, they cry,   Lk. 22:44
Why will you resolve to die?   Ezek. 18:31

30. Original Sin

It is a pity that this sombre phrase has been the occasion of so much misunderstanding, and of so much misrepresentation of the Christian faith. Original sin is not any actual and voluntary sin of thought or deed, for which men and women are individually responsible before God. Rather is it that inborn weakness of human nature, which is ours simply because we are human, and which is, as it were, the raw material for voluntary and actual sins. All men and women are responsible for it in the collective sense, in that we are all part of a defiled human race, which must needs appear with shame before the holy God, and of a morally and spiritually infirm human race, which cannot obey God in the manner we know is his due. It is an immediate and dreadful fact of human experience that there is a bias in human nature which all too commonly makes evil easier to do than good, and which secures that 'the line of least resistance' in human affairs is commonly down-hill. Even the best of men and women are tempted, and find temptation subtle in approach and hard to resist. Thus we observe that all men and women, even the respectable and the church-going, are sinners before God. All human societies, including the Church, are to some extent corrupt. The biblical phrase for ordinary human nature is 'the natural man', (1 Cor. 2:14). The natural man is alienated from God, in that he naturally, but quite unrealistically, tends to look upon himself, or his group, as the centre of things, rather than God. Though the natural man possesses a true measure of free will, and so is morally responsible before God for his conduct, yet his will is in bondage. He cannot by his own unaided powers make himself believe in God, or love God, or obey him in such a way as to merit a reward. This truth is set forth in this selection of verses translated by John Wesley from the work of Count Zinzendorf, the patron of the Moravians, and of his associates.

P.W. i. 265; W.H. 26; M.H.B. 449; H.P. 568

Ah, Lord! enlarge our scanty thought,	Isa. 55:8–9, Rom. 11:33–4
To know the wonders thou hast wrought;	Ps. 77:14, Isa. 28:21, 29:14
Unloose our stammering tongues, to tell	Isa. 32:4, Mk. 7:35
Thy love immense, unsearchable.	Rom. 5:8, Eph. 3:8, 19
What are our works but sin and death,	Gen. 6:5, Ps. 51:5, Rom. 6:23, Col. 1:21, Heb. 9:14
Till thou thy quickening Spirit breathe!	Jn. 6:63, 2 Cor. 3:6
Thou giv'st the power thy grace to move;	Zech. 12:10, Eph. 2:8
O wondrous grace! O boundless love!	Rom. 5:20, 11:32–3
How can it be, thou heavenly King,	Dan. 4:37, Rev. 15:3
That thou shouldst us to glory bring?	Heb. 2:10
Make slaves the partners of thy throne,	Matt. 19:28, Rom. 6:17–20
Decked with a never-fading crown?	1 Cor. 9:25, 1 Pet. 5:4
Hence our hearts melt, our eyes o'erflow,	Lam. 2:18, Ezek. 21:7, 36:26
Our words are lost; nor will we know,	Hab. 2:20, Rom. 3:19
Nor will we think of aught beside,	1 Cor. 2:2
My Lord, my Love is crucified.*	
First-born of many brethren thou!	Rom. 8:29
To thee, lo! all our souls we bow:	Ps. 44:25
To thee our hearts and hands we give:	Lam. 3:41
Thine may we die, thine may we live!	Rom. 14:8

* see footnote p. 54.

P.W. i. 249; W.H. 114; M.H.B. 357

Jesu, in whom the weary find	Matt. 11:28–9
Their late, but permanent repose,	Jer. 6:16, Heb. 4:9–11
Physician of the sin-sick mind,	Mk. 5:15, 2 Tim. 1:7
Relieve my wants, assuage my woes;	Ps. 34:9–10
And let my soul on thee be cast,	1 Pet. 5:7
Till life's fierce tyranny be past.	Ps. 57:1 (B.C.P.)
Loosed from my God, and far removed,	Isa. 29:13, Jer. 6:8, Gal. 1:6
Long have I wandered to and fro,	Gen. 8:7, Hos. 9:17
O'er earth in endless circles roved,	
Nor found whereon to rest below:	Gen. 8:9
Back to my God at last I fly,	
For O, the waters still are high!	Ps. 124:4–5, Isa. 43:2
Selfish pursuits, and nature's maze,	1 Cor. 2:14, 2 Tim. 3:2, 4
The things of earth, for thee I leave;	Mk. 10:28, Col. 3:2
Put forth thy hand, thy hand of grace,	Gen. 8:9, Rom. 10:21
Into the ark of love receive,	1 Pet. 3:20–1
Take this poor fluttering soul to rest,	Ps. 55:6–8
And lodge it, Saviour, in thy breast.	Isa. 32:2, Jn. 13:23

Fill with inviolable peace,	Jn. 14:27, 16:22
Stablish and keep my settled heart;	1 Pet. 5:10
In thee may all my wanderings cease,	Ezek. 34:6, 12
From thee no more may I depart;	Rev. 3:12
Thy utmost goodness called to prove,	Rom. 12:2
Loved with an everlasting love!	Jer. 31:3

P.W. i. 259; W.H. 143; M.H.B. 110; M.H. 125, 126; H.P. 528

Jesu, Lover of my soul,	Cant. 2:10, Wisd. 11:26
Let me to thy bosom fly,	Isa. 40:11, Jn. 13:23
While the nearer waters roll,	Ps. 69:1, Isa. 43:2
While the tempest still is high:	Isa. 32:2, Jonah 1:4
Hide me, O my Saviour, hide,	Ps. 27:5, 32:7, Lk. 2:11
Till the storm of life be past:	Matt. 14:32
Safe into the haven guide;	Ps. 107:30, Jn. 6:21
O receive my soul at last.	Acts. 7:59
Other refuge have I none,	Ps. 57:1, 90:1 B.C.P., Jn. 6:68
Hangs my helpless soul on thee:	Ps. 46:1, 60:11
Leave, ah! leave me not alone,	Ps. 27:9, 141:8
Still support and comfort me.	Ps. 23:4, Isa. 40:1–2
All my trust on thee is stayed;	Ps. 56:4, 141:8, 2 Tim. 1:12
All my help from thee I bring:	Ps. 121:1–2
Cover my defenceless head	Ps. 140:7
With the shadow of thy wing.	Ps. 17:8, 57:1
Wilt thou not regard my call?	Ps. 102:17
Wilt thou not accept my prayer?	Ps. 119:108
Lo! I sink, I faint, I fall,	Ps. 69:2, 84:2
Lo! on thee I cast my care:	1 Pet. 5;7
Reach me out thy gracious hand!	Matt. 14:31
While I of thy strength receive,	Phil 4:13
Hoping against hope I stand,	Acts 26:6, Rom. 4:18
Dying, and behold I live!	2 Cor. 6:9
Thou, O Christ, art all I want,	Ps. 23:1
More than all in thee I find:	Rom. 8:32
Raise the fallen, cheer the faint,	Mk. 6:50, 9:27
Heal the sick, and lead the blind,	Isa. 42:16, Matt. 4:24
Just and holy is thy name,	Acts 3:14
I am all unrighteousness,	Rom. 1:18
False and full of sin I am,	Jer. 17:9
Thou art full of truth and grace.	Jn. 1:14, 17
Plenteous grace with thee is found,	Ex. 34:6, Rom. 5:17, 20
Grace to cover all my sin:	Ps. 32:1, 85:2, Rom. 4:7
Let the healing streams abound,	2 Kgs. 5:14, Zech. 13:1

Make and keep me pure within: 1 Jn. 1:7, 3:3
Thou of life the fountain art: Ps. 36:9, Rev. 21:6
 Freely let me take of thee,   Jn. 4:10, Rev. 22:17
Spring thou up within my heart,   Jn. 4:14
 Rise to all eternity!

31. Grace

God's response to the spiritually alienated and morally infirm condition of fallen humanity is seen in his grace. The term 'grace' means, in the first place, that God loves, forgives, and receives into fellowship with himself sinful men and women not at all because they deserve, or can come to deserve, love and forgiveness. He loves and forgives simply because it is his mysterious nature so to do. And 'grace' means, in the second place, that God uses his power to liberate from bondage that fallen humanity which he loves. This two-fold aspect of divine grace is well expressed in a familiar line of Wesley: 'He *breaks* the power of *cancelled* sin'. Grace as free forgiveness first cancels the guilt of sin, and restores the believer to fellowship with God. Grace as the activity of the Holy Spirit then actually reforms the believer in inward character and outward conduct.

These two aspects cannot be separated, for if the power of sin is not on the way to being broken it is a sure sign that the believer is not properly reconciled. The doctrine of grace indicates that in the whole process of salvation, from beginning to end, God is always there first, exercising his initiative. The human soul can only say 'Yes' to God if God first chooses to call. The believer can only go to God's service as and when God opens the door, and provides the power. We are totally dependent upon God. Thus grace is the direct opposite to the idea of religious 'merit'. Acceptance with God is not to be earned as a reward for service rendered to God in our own strength.

P.W. v. 30; W.H. 808; M.H.B. 66*

1 Oh God of all grace,	2 Cor. 9:8
Thy goodness we praise;	Ps. 107:8, Rom. 2:4
Thy Son thou hast given to die in our place	Isa. 53:4–5, Jn. 3:16, 2 Cor. 5:14, 1 Pet. 3:18
2 He came from above	Jn. 8:23, 2 Cor. 8:9, Phil. 2:6–8

Our curse to remove,	Gen. 2:17, 3:19, 1 Cor. 15:22, 2 Cor. 5:21, Gal. 3:13
He hath loved, he hath loved us, because he would love.	Jn. 15:9, 16

3 Love moved him to die,   Jn. 15:13, Gal. 2:20
    And on this we rely,   Rom. 3:25
He hath loved, he hath loved us, we cannot   Rom. 9:15–16, 11:33–4,
    tell why.   Ex. 33:19, Deut. 7:7–8

4 But this we can tell,   Jn. 9:25
    He hath loved us so well,
As to lay down his life to redeem us from hell.   Jn. 10:15, 15:13, Eph. 1:7

5 He hath ransomed our race,   Mk. 10:45, 1 Tim. 2:6
    Oh how shall we praise
Or worthily sing thy unspeakable grace?   2 Cor. 9:15, 1 Pet. 1:8

6 Nothing else will we know   1 Cor. 2:2
    In our journey below,   Heb. 11:13,16
But singing thy grace to thy paradise go.   Lk. 23:43, Col. 3:16

7 We all shall commend   Acts 14:23, Rom. 5:8
    The love of our Friend,   Jn. 15:13, 15
For ever beginning what never shall end.   Ps. 146:2, Rev. 5:13, 14:3

---

* It is to be hoped that the omission of this theologically important hymn from *Hymns and Psalms* will not lead to its being forgotten.

P.W. v. 174; W.H. 294; M.H.B. 534

Jesu, thou sovereign Lord of all,	Acts 10:36
The same through one eternal day,	Ps. 102:25, Heb. 1:10–12, 13:8
Attend thy feeblest followers' call,	Heb. 12:12
And O instruct us how to pray!	Lk. 11:1
Pour out the supplicating grace,	Zech. 12:10
And stir us up to seek thy face.	Ps. 27:8

We cannot think a gracious thought,	Gen. 6:5, 1 Cor. 2:14
We cannot feel a good desire,*	
Till thou, who call'dst a world from nought,	Gen. 1:1, Heb. 11:3
The power into our hearts inspire;	Rom. 8:26
And then we in the Spirit groan,	Jn. 11:33
And then we give thee back thine own.	1 Chron. 29:14

To help our soul's infirmity,	Rom. 8:26
To heal thy sin-sick people's care,	Ps. 41:4, Isa. 1:5, Matt. 10:8
To urge our God-commanding plea,	Ex. 32:10–14, Jas. 5:16–18
And make our hearts a house of prayer,	Isa. 56:7

| The promised Intercessor give, | Jn. 14:16, 26, Rom. 8:26 |
| And let us now thyself receive. | Jn. 1:12 |

---

* O Almighty God, who alone canst order the unruly wills and affections of sinful men: Grant unto thy people, that they may . . . desire that which thou dost promise. (BCP, Collect, Easter IV)

32. Universal Grace

Why should it be, if God is indeed the loving Father of the whole human race, who has provided in Christ an all-sufficient remedy for sin, that all have not accepted the gospel, and become Christian believers? We submit that one is well-advised not to approach this question from the point of view of theoretical speculation regarding the destiny of all human souls under the government of God. To do this is to raise questions for which we have no certain answer, because the divine revelation in Scripture is directed to more practical and spiritually up-building issues. It is indeed the case that human beings are possessed of a measure of morally responsible free will, and so are able to say 'No' to God's invitation of grace. However, the interest of scriptural doctrine is not so much to establish the dignity of the human personality by affirming free will, as to vindicate the power, the wisdom, and the goodness, the love of God.

Some schools of Christian thought (commonly called 'Augustinian' or 'Calvinist', from the names of the teachers associated with them), have so strongly emphasized the determinative place of God's initiative of grace in the way of salvation as to affirm that the reason why some accept Christ is in the last resort wholly a matter of the sovereign and mysterious choice of God. This indeed provides a logical answer to the speculative question as to why some people are converted at the preaching of the gospel, and others not. However, it does so at the expense of the implication that God has apparently not chosen those who are not converted, but has allowed them to go to the fate which all sinners alike deserve. This appears to call in question the universal goodness and love of God.

It was for this latter reason that the Wesleys so strongly and so characteristically affirmed that God's grace is universal in operation. It is important to remember that the Wesleys are scriptural evangelists, concerned to set forth the glory of God, not humanists concerned to vindicate the dignity of free human personality. The saving work of Christ crucified and risen can apply to every human soul. There

are, of course, speculative difficulties here also, for it is not clear to us
in what way Christ is in fact offered to every man and woman. After
all, even in nominally 'Christian' countries like our own there are many
circles where no completely intelligible and effective presentation of
the Christian faith is ever made, and in many other countries our
faith, though perhaps vaguely heard of, is commonly misrepresented
as a subversive alien religion, or as a reactionary superstition. We do
happily know, however, that God can surprisingly convert people
even in these most unhelpful circumstances.

However, it is not the interest of a scriptural presentation of the
gospel to pursue speculations of this sort. The fact is, we cannot
know how much spiritual light other human beings have, and must
trust God to judge all with justice. It is a dangerous speculation, and
easily conducive to self-righteousness, to seek to classify other people
as 'saved' or 'unsaved'. The wise gospel preacher, who wishes to
follow the practical spiritual wisdom of the Bible, will declare as
plainly, earnestly, and lovingly as he or she can that the assured way
of salvation is by faith in Christ, and that this way is fully open to all
hearers of the gospel, however simple, overburdened, unprivileged,
excluded, or degraded—and also remind them of the sad spiritual
loss which faces those who deliberately and obstinately turn away
from Christ. Yet the evangelist will leave to God all judgment as to
who have in fact, on this side of eternity, accepted or rejected Christ

The joyful celebration of God's universal grace is a most important
element of the Wesley hymnody.

P.W. i. 205; W.H. 4

Ho! every one that thirsts, draw nigh!	Isa. 55:1, 7
'Tis God invites the fallen race:	Hosea 14:1, 1 Cor. 15:22
Mercy and free salvation buy;	Tit. 2:11
Buy wine, and milk, and gospel grace.	Isa. 55:1, Acts. 20:24,
	1 Pet. 2:1–2
For thus the mighty God hath said,	Isa. 55:8
My ways and thoughts ye cannot scan;	1 Cor. 2:16
Ye cannot, whom my hands have made,	Ps. 119:73
Your infinite Creator span.	Job 11:7
Me will ye mete with reason's line;	2 Cor. 10:5 (R.V. marg.)
Or teach my grace how far to move?	Ex. 33:19, Ps. 145:9, 1 Tim. 2
Fathom my mercy's deep design,	Rom. 11:33–4
My height, and breadth, and length of love?	Eph. 3:18
Far as the heavens that earth surpass,	Isa. 55:9
Far as my throne those nether skies	Ps. 103:19
My ways of love, and thoughts of grace,	Rom. 11:33, Eph. 3:19
Beyond your low conceptions rise.	Isa. 55:8

Son of my love, behold, to thee	Jn. 3:35
From all eternity I give	Jn. 6:39, 17:24, Rev. 13:8
Sinners who to thy wounds will flee;	Isa. 53:5
The soul that chooseth life shall live.	Deut. 30:19
Nations, whom once thou didst not own,	
Thou thine inheritance shalt call;	Isa. 54:3
Nations who knew not thee shall run,	Isa. 55:5, 60:3, 5
And hail the God that died for all.	Mal. 1:17, 2 Cor. 5:14, 1 Tim. 2:6
For I, the holy God and true,	Ps. 99:9, Jn. 17:3, 1 Jn. 5:20
To glorify thy name have sworn:	Isa. 55:5
And lo! my faithfulness I show,	Ps. 89:5, 24, Isa. 11:5
And lo! to thee the Gentiles turn.	Isa. 60:5, Acts 11:1, 15:3

The following verses are one of the great foundation-hymns of the Wesleys. It is as well to point out to the modern reader that they would have appeared controversial, or even paradoxical, to many who first read them. In the eighteenth century most Evangelicals were Calvinists, and to them God's 'sovereignty' meant the decree of Election whereby God had chosen, according to his inscrutable wisdom, some souls to be the objects of his saving grace. These were in the end bound to be saved, because no power can resist the sovereign God. In these terms, to speak of 'sovereign grace' as universal would imply the unscriptural doctrine of 'universalism', i.e. that every human soul is bound of necessity to be saved. Thus Wesley's great hymn could cause great offence! Clearly, by 'sovereign grace' Charles Wesley means something quite different. He means that the divine initiative of grace is essential at every step of the Christian experience. Man cannot of his own free will turn to God, and render God service. At every stage God has to call, and to enable. Man's morally responsible freedom consists in this—though he cannot make himself be called he can refuse the call. But in some way or other the God of universal love does call all. It remains to be said that the chief Scripture which would be quoted by the Calvinists in support of the doctrines of Particular Election and Predestination is Romans 9–11. The Wesleys would expound this as an account of God's providential dealing in history with different nations, rather than as a discussion of the destiny of individual souls for salvation or perdition (see Wesley, *Notes on the New Testament*, Romans 9).

P.W. iv. 445; W.H. 216; M.H.B. 77; M.H. 130; H.P. 46

What shall I do my God to love?	Cant. 7:10–12
My loving God to praise	Ps. 106:2

The length, and breadth, and height to prove,	Eph. 3:18
And depth of sovereign grace?	Ex. 33:19, Rom. 11:5–6,
	Eph. 2:5, 8

Thy sovereign grace to all extends,	Rom. 11:32, 2 Pet. 3:9
Immense and unconfined;	Ps. 145:9, 1 Tim. 2:4
From age to age it never ends;	Jer. 31:3
It reaches all mankind.	Jn. 3:16

Throughout the world its breadth is known,	Ps. 145:9
Wide as infinity;	
So wide, it never passed by one,*	Jn. 1:9
Or it had passed by me.	1 Tim. 1:12–15

My trespass was grown up to heaven;	Ezra. 9:6
But far above the skies,	Ps. 108:4
In Christ abundantly forgiven,	Isa. 55:7
I see thy mercies rise.	Ps. 57:10

The depth of all-redeeming love	Gal. 3:13, 1 Pet. 1:18, 19
What angel-tongue can tell?	1 Pet. 1:12
O may I to the utmost prove	Rom. 12:2
The gift unspeakable!	2 Cor. 9:15

Deeper than hell, it plucked me thence,	Ps. 139:8
Deeper than inbred sin,	Ps. 51:5, Rom. 5:12
Jesus's love my heart shall cleanse	Ps. 51:2, 13, 1 Jn. 1:7, 9
When Jesus enters in.	Rev. 3:20

Come quickly, gracious Lord, and take	Rev. 3:11, 22:7, 12, 20
Possession of thine own;	1 Cor. 6:20, 1 Pet. 2:9
My longing heart vouchsafe to make	Ps. 107:9, 119:20
Thine everlasting throne!	Ps. 93:2

* but cf. Rom. 9:18

P.W. iii. 3; W.H. 39; M.H.B. 75; H.P. 520

Father, whose everlasting love	Jer. 31:3
Thy only Son for sinners gave,	Jn. 3:16
Whose grace to all did freely move,	1 Tim. 2:4, 4:10, 2 Pet. 3.9
And sent him down the world to save;	Jn. 3:16, 4:42, 17:21, 2 Cor. 5

Help us thy mercy to extol,	Ps. 145:1, 9
Immense, unfathomed, unconfined;	
To praise the Lamb who died for all,	2 Cor. 5:14, 15, 1 Tim. 2:6
The general Saviour of mankind.	Jn. 1:29, 36, 1 Tim. 4:10,
	1 Jn. 4:14

Thy undistinguishing regard	1 Tim. 2:4, 2 Pet. 3:9
Was cast on Adam's fallen race;	Gen. 3:17–19, Rom. 5:14, 19
For all thou hast in Christ prepared	2 Cor. 5:19

Sufficient, sovereign, saving grace.	Ex. 33:19, Ps. 67:2, Rom. 9:18, 2 Cor. 12:9
The world he suffered to redeem;	Jn. 4:42, Rev. 5:9
For all he hath the atonement made:	2 Cor. 5:19, 1 Jn. 2:2, 4:14
For those that will not come to him	Jn. 5:40, Rom. 10:21
The ransom of his life was paid.	Mk. 10:45, 1 Tim. 2:6
Arise, O God, maintain thy cause!	Ps. 140:12
The fulness of the Gentiles call;	Isa. 49:6, 60:5, Rom. 11:25
Lift up the standard of thy cross,	Isa. 62:10, Jn. 3:14, 12:32
And all shall own thou diedst for all.	Isa. 45:21–2, Rom. 8:32, 2 Cor. 5:14, 19, 1 Tim. 2:6

P.W. ix. 55; W.H. 250; M.H.B. 49; H.P. 48

Thy ceaseless, unexhausted love,*	Jer. 31:3
Unmerited and free,	Deut. 7:7–8, Rom. 9:15–16
Delights our evil to remove,	Ps. 121: 7, Jn. 17:15
And help our misery.	Ps. 116:6 (B.C.P.)
Thou waitest to be gracious still;	Ex. 34:6, Isa. 30:18
Thou dost with sinners bear,	Hosea 11:8, Rom. 2:4, 2 Pet. 3:9
That saved, we may thy goodness feel,	Ps. 23:6, 27:13, Jer. 31:14
And all thy grace declare.	Ps. 40:10, 66:16
Thy goodness and thy truth to me,	Ex. 34:6
To every soul abound,	
A vast, unfathomable sea,	Ps. 36:6, 92:5
Where all our thoughts are drowned.	Rom. 11:33
Its streams the whole creation reach,	Ps. 145:9
So plenteous is the store,	Ps. 103:8, 130:7
Enough for all, enough for each,**	
Enough for evermore.	Ps. 89:29
Faithful, O Lord, thy mercies are,	Lam. 3:22–3
A rock that cannot move!	Ps. 62: 2, 6
A thousand promises declare	2 Cor. 1:20
Thy constancy of love.	Jer. 31:3
Throughout the universe it reigns,	Ps. 145:9 (B.C.P.)
Unalterably sure;	2 Tim. 2:19, Heb. 6:19
And while the truth of God remains,	Ps. 100:5
The goodness must endure.	Ps. 52:1

---

* By wond'rous unexhausted love' (S. Wesley Jun., 'An Hymn to God the Father'.
Poems (1736) p. 2 l. 15)
** 'The springs of mercy are always full, the streams of mercy always flowing. There is mercy enough in God, enough for all, enough for each, enough for ever.'
(Matthew Henry, Commentary on Ex. 34:5–9)

33. Conviction of Sin

It is the Christian faith that the Holy Spirit of grace is working to some extent, guiding and prompting, in the lives even of those who are apparently careless of the claims of religion, and who are seemingly unaware of any spiritual experience. This divine initiative of grace, exerted before there is any kind of conscious response in evangelical experience, is called *prevenient* grace, i.e. 'the grace that goes before'. The great gulf fixed between the Christian faith, and what often passes as moral advice in those circles dominated by purely secular thought, is observed when we consider the first stage of definite Christian salvation. Non-religious thought too often and too easily inclines to the view that what the sinner must do is to free himself or herself from feelings of guilt, by coming to a persuasion that one need not be unduly deeply ashamed, because one's fault is so largely the result of unfriendly environment, unfortunate circumstance, inborn weakness, or ignorance and inexperience. One must learn to 'accept' oneself, and one's companions must learn to 'accept' one, and to silence any element of moral condemnation.

The Christian faith, by contrast, lays down the proposition that the first decisive step towards salvation is that men and women should come to a renewed realization that sin is something for which they are deeply and inexcusably guilty, and for which they certainly ought to be ashamed before God. "'Twas *grace* that taught my heart to *fear*, And grace that fear relieved.' This first stage of the genuine evangelical experience is conviction of sin. The wise Christian advocate will not try to produce conviction of sin by denouncing the open and grievous faults of general human society. This only tends to produce self-righteousness in the respectable people in the Church. Nor is the effective way to threaten the hearers with damnation hereafter. The wise and constructive note of the Wesleys at this point (though they did believe in the eternal loss of the finally impenitent, and did on occasion speak plainly of social wrongs), was to speak of the greatness and majesty of the holy God, of his righteous claim that men and women should reverence, love, and serve him, of the dreadfulness of trifling with his claim, and of the blessed offer of grace and hope.

P.W. iv. 405; W.H. 106

Jesu, let thy pitying eye	Ps. 103:13, Matt. 9:36
Call back a wandering sheep!	Matt. 18:12, Jn. 10:3
False to thee, like Peter, I	Zech 13:6, Mk. 14:66–72
Would fain, like Peter, weep:	Lk. 22:61–2
Let me be by grace restored,	Ps. 51:12, Eph. 2:5, 8
On me be all long-suffering shown;	Ex. 34:6, 1 Tim. 1:16
Turn, and look upon me, Lord,	Lk. 22:61
And break my heart of stone.	Ps. 51:17, Ezek. 11:19, 36:26
Look, as when thine eye pursued	Gen. 3:15, Jer. 17:10
The first apostate man,	
Saw him weltering in his blood,	Ezek. 16:4–6
And bade him rise again:	Lk. 5:23
Speak my paradise restored,	Gen. 3:23, Lk. 23:43, Rev. 2:7
Redeem me by thy grace alone;	Rom. 4:16, Gal. 2:16, Eph. 2:8
Turn, and look upon me, Lord,	Lk. 22:61
And break my heart of stone.	Ps. 51:17, Ezek. 11:19, 36:26
Look, as when thy weeping eye	Lk. 19:41
The bloody city viewed,	Ezek. 22:2, 24:6
Those who stoned and doomed to die	Lk. 13:34
The prophets, and their God:	Matt. 21:35–9
I deserve their sad reward,	1 Tim. 1:13–14
But this my gracious day I own:	Ezra 9:8, Eph. 5:16, Heb. 3:13
Turn, and look upon me, Lord	Lk. 22:61
And break my heart of stone.	Ps. 51:17, Ezek. 11:19, 36:26
Look, as when thy grace beheld	Lk. 7:37–8
The harlot in distress,	
Dried her tears, her pardon sealed,	Lk. 7:44–8
And bade her go in peace:	Lk. 7:50
Vile, like her, and self-abhorred,	Job 42:6, Rom. 7:24
I at thy feet for mercy groan;	Lk. 8:41, 17:13
Turn, and look upon me, Lord,	Lk. 22:61
And break my heart of stone.	Ps. 51:17, Ezek. 11:19, 36:26
Saviour, Prince, enthroned above,	Acts 5:31
Repentance to impart,	Acts 11:18
Give me through thy dying love	Jn. 15:13, Gal. 2:20
The humble contrite heart:	Isa. 57:15
Give what I have long implored,	Phil. 3:10
A portion of thy grief unknown;	Mk. 15:34, Lk. 22:44
Turn, and look upon me, Lord,	Lk. 22:61
And break my heart of stone.	Ps. 51:17, Ezek. 11:19, 36:26

P.W. v. 63; W.H. 9; M.H.B. 325, 326

Sinners, obey the gospel-word!
Haste to the supper of my Lord!
Be wise to know your gracious day;
All things are ready, come away!

Jer. 26:13, 38:20, Zech. 6:15
Lk. 14:17
Eph. 5:16, Heb. 3:7, 13

Ready the Father is to own
And kiss his late-returning son;
Ready your loving Saviour stands,
And spreads for you his bleeding hands.

Lk. 15:20

Tit. 3:4
Isa. 65:2, Zech. 13:6,
Jn. 20:27, Rom. 10:21

The Father, Son, and Holy Ghost
Is ready, with their shining host:
All heaven is ready to resound,
'The dead's alive! the lost is found!'

Matt. 28:19, 2 Cor. 13:14
Job. 38:7, Rev. 5:11–12
Lk. 15:7, 10
Lk. 15:32

Come then, ye sinners, to your Lord,
In Christ to paradise restored;
His proffered benefits embrace,
The plenitude of gospel grace:

Lk. 14:21–3, 2 Cor. 5:20
Gen. 3:23, Lk. 23:43, Rev. 2:
Ps. 116:12
Jn. 1:16

A pardon written with his blood,

Matt. 26:28, Heb. 9:28,
1 Jn. 1:7, Rev. 5:9

The favour and the peace of God;
The seeing eye, the feeling sense,
The mystic joys of penitence;

Prov. 8:35, Phil. 4:7
Jn. 9:25, Acts 17:27
2 Cor. 7:9–10

The godly grief, the pleasing smart,
The meltings of a broken heart,
The tears that tell your sins forgiven,
The sighs that waft your souls to heaven;

2 Cor. 7:11, 1 Pet. 1:6
Ps. 51:17
Lk. 7:38, 47
Ps. 12:5

The guiltless shame, the sweet distress,
The unutterable tenderness,
The genuine, meek humility,
The wonder, 'Why such love to me?'

Rom. 8:1, 2 Cor. 12:10
2 Kgs. 22:19, Rom. 8:26
Isa. 57:15, Jas. 4:6, 1 Pet. 5:5
1 Jn. 3:1

The o'erwhelming power of saving grace,
The sight that veils the seraph's face;
The speechless awe that dares not move,
And all the silent heaven of love.

2 Cor. 12:9, Eph. 2:5, 8
Isa. 6:2, 1 Pet. 1:12
Ps. 33:8, Eccl. 5:2
Hab. 2:20, Rev. 8:1

34. Penitence

The work of grace in the heart of those who, convinced of sin, have come to see their great need of forgiveness, is penitence. Christian penitence is much more than sincere regret that one is not a better man or woman. There is no particular virtue in this regret, which can be felt by any realistic person. Penitence involves a real effort of the moral will to turn away from evil to good. This is why men and women cannot repent as and when they so desire. Our wills are in bondage, and we can only repent when God calls us, and offers the power of grace to do so.

P.W. iv. 195; W.H. 165; M.H.B. 294

Come holy celestial Dove,	Matt. 3:16
To visit a sorrowful breast,	Jn. 16:20, 22
My burden of guilt to remove,	Ps. 51:3–5, 10–11, Rom. 3:19
And bring me assurance and rest!	Rom. 8:16, Heb. 4:9, 10:22
Thou only hast power to relieve	Jn. 6:68, Acts 4:12
A sinner o'erwhelmed with his load,	Matt. 11:28–9
The sense of acceptance to give,	Eph. 1:6
And sprinkle his heart with the blood.	Heb. 10:22, 12:24, 1 Pet. 1:2
With me if of old thou hast strove,	Gen. 6:3
And strangely withheld from my sin,	Gen. 20:6
And tried, by the lure of thy love,	Hos. 2:14, 19
My worthless affections to win;	Prov. 10:20, Matt. 8:8
The work of thy mercy revive,	Hab. 3:2
Thy uttermost mercy exert,	Heb. 7:25
And kindly continue to strive,	Gen. 6:3, 32:24, 29
And hold, till I yield thee my heart.	Heb. 12:11, Rom. 6:13
Thy call if I ever have known,	Eph. 4:4, 2 Tim. 1:9
And sighed from myself to get free,	Ps. 119:32 (B.C.P)
And groaned the unspeakable groan,	Rom. 8:26
And longed to be happy in thee;	Ps. 144:15, Prov. 3:13, 18
Fulfil the imperfect desire,	Ps. 145:19, Phil. 3:12
Thy peace to my conscience reveal,	Jn. 14:27, Heb. 10:22

The sense of thy favour inspire,   Ps. 106:4, Isa. 60:10
    And give me my pardon to feel.   Isa. 40:2, 55:7, Dan. 9:9,
                                                             Acts 26:18

If when I had put thee to grief,   Eph. 4:30
    And madly to folly returned,   Ps. 85:8, Prov. 26:11
Thy pity hath been my relief,   Isa. 63:9
    And lifted me up as I mourned;   Jas. 4:9–10
Most pitiful Spirit of grace,   Zech. 12:10
    Relieve me again, and restore,   Ps. 51:12
My spirit in holiness raise,   Rom. 1:4, Col. 3:12
    To fall and to suffer no more.   Jude 24

35. Legal Religion

The awakened and sincere penitent will return with renewed effort to the life of dutiful obedience to God, in order by serious self-discipline in prayer and practical good deeds to win through to a sense of acceptance with God, to a clear conscience, and to a better character. This form of discipleship is described as 'legal' Christianity, because it expresses somewhat the same principle as the pre-gospel religion of the Law of Moses, namely, that one must first carry out God's law by one's own resolve, and so come to merit God's blessing. This legal step is good so far as it goes, and represents the religion of many conscientious and morally upright people. Indeed, the legal step is a step forward in the spiritual life, in the sense that if those who profess penitence do not use their best effort to carry out their moral duties, and do not wait upon God in prayer and worship, they are very unlikely to advance any further.

Nevertheless, legal Christianity falls very far short of genuine Christian faith, and of God's gracious purpose for us. It remains a burden of devotional discipline and moral duty which the Christian has to carry as best he may, whereas the offer of God in Christ is of a life of fellowship with himself, and of praise and prayer, which carries the believer, and which brings to the performace of moral duty and devotional discipline a deep inward satisfaction, and often great joy. The effect of legal religion is to bring home to the sincere and earnest disciple more clearly than before the sombre truth that by one's own moral resolve one cannot carry out the law of God. Thus the benefit of legal religion is to confirm conviction of sin.

P.W. iv 477; W.H. 911

O how shall a sinner perform	Deut. 23:23
The vows he hath vowed to the Lord?	Gen. 28:20, Jonah 2:9
A sinful and impotent worm,	Ps. 22:6
How can I be true to my word?	Jas. 1:22, 23, 1 Jn. 3:18
I tremble at what I have done:	Deut. 28:65

O send me thy help from above;	Ps. 144:7, Isa. 41:14
The power of thy Spirit make known,	Acts 1:8, Rom. 15:13, 19
The virtue of Jesus's love!	Mk. 5:30
My solemn engagements are vain,	Jer. 31:32, Hosea 11:7, Rom. 7:21–3
My promises empty as air;	
My vows I shall break them again,	Eccl. 5:2–4
And plunge in eternal despair;	Eccl. 2:20
Unless my omnipotent God	Gen. 17:1, Rev. 19:6
The sense of his goodness impart,	Rom. 2:4
And shed by his Spirit abroad	Rom. 5:5
The love of himself in my heart.	
O Lover of sinners, extend	Rom. 5:8
To me thy compassionate grace;	Ps. 86:15, Rom. 9:15
Appear my affliction to end,	Isa. 63:9, Acts 7:10
Afford me a glimpse of thy face!	Ex. 33:11, 13, 20, 23
That light shall enkindle in me	Lk. 12:49
A flame of reciprocal love;	1 Jn. 4:19
And then I shall cleave unto thee,	Deut. 10:20, Acts 11:23
And then I shall never remove.	Jer. 4:1
O come to a mourner in pain,	Isa. 61:3
Thy peace in my conscience reveal!	Jer. 33:6, Heb. 10:22
And then I shall love thee again,	Rev. 2:4–5
And sing of the goodness I feel:	Ps. 107:8, 15, 21, 31
Constrained by the grace of my Lord,	2 Cor. 5:14
My soul shall in all things obey,	2 Cor. 2:9
And wait to be fully restored,	Joel 2:25
And long to be summoned away.	Phil. 1:23

36.   The Gift of Faith

Christian faith in the full and proper sense of the word, that is to say, evangelical saving faith, is much more than a sincere conviction of the truth of scriptural Christian doctrine. It is also much more than an emotional experience. The necessary foundation of faith is indeed conviction of the truth, but there must be built upon that foundation a strong movement of the emotions, the affections, and the moral will, toward that truth. In short, faith takes up the whole of the human personality, both that which we may call 'the head', and also 'the heart'. It is 'the faith that worketh by love' (Gal. 5:6).

That this must be so is seen from the circumstance that whereas the settled and reasonable convictions of the mind are the rudder in life, giving direction, the emotions are the engine, bringing power actually to perform. A set of religious opinions in the mind which has failed to move the heart leaves the disciple still in that legal position of insecure inward conflict, of trying to compel the reluctant will to obey. Yet a wave of powerful emotion in the heart, unenlightened by a grasp of God's truth in the mind, is at best religious sentimentality, and at worst, superstition, or even fanaticism. So to true faith there are two contrasting elements, to be held together. As Wesley puts it in his celebrated definition: 'It is not barely . . . a cold, lifeless assent, a train of ideas in the head; but also a disposition of the heart', (*Sermons*, I.i.4). The due place of 'ideas in the head' is not denied. Religious faith must be illuminated by knowledge of God's revelation. Yet 'ideas' by themselves do not suffice, for if the emotions and affections are not powerfully engaged the moral will remains largely impotent.

This is why evangelical saving faith is the gift of God. An intelligent searcher may to a certain extent convince himself, or herself, of the reasonableness of the Christian position, and of the authority of the scriptural revelation. But he cannot make himself 'feel', deep down in the heart, that God is 'there', that he is important, that he loves him, and that worship is a joy. Unless he can 'feel' he is a poor, feeble Christian. And to move the 'heart' is the work of the Holy Spirit.

P.W. iv. 196; W.H. 85; M.H.B. 363; M.H. 137; H.P. 325

Spirit of faith, come down,	2 Cor. 4:13
Reveal the things of God;	1 Cor. 2:10–11
And make to us the Godhead known,	Rom. 1:20, Eph. 3:5
And witness with the blood:	1 Jn. 5:6, 8
'Tis thine the blood to apply,	Jn. 16:14–15, 1 Pet. 1:2
And give us eyes to see,	Jn. 9:25, Eph. 1:17–18
Who did for every sinner die,	2 Cor. 5:14–15, 1 Tim. 2:6
Hath surely died for me.	Gal. 2:20
No man can truly say	1 Cor. 12:3
That Jesus is the Lord,	
Until thou take the veil away,	2 Cor. 3:13–16
And breathe the living word;	Heb. 4:12 (R.V.)
Then, only then, we feel	
Our interest in his blood,	Eph. 1:14
And cry with joy unspeakable,	1 Pet. 1:8
'Thou art my Lord, my God!'	Jn. 20:28
O that the world might know	Eph. 3:9
The great atoning Lamb!	Jn. 1:29, Rom. 5:11
Spirit of faith, descend, and show	2 Cor. 4:13
The virtue of his name;	Acts 3:16
The grace which all may find,	Acts 2:21, 39, 1 Tim. 2:4
The saving power impart;	Rom. 1:16, 1 Cor. 1:18
And testify to all mankind,	1 Pet. 1:11
And speak in every heart.	1 Cor. 12:7
Inspire the living faith,	Jn. 11:26
Which whosoe'er receives,	Jn. 3:16
The witness in himself he hath,	Rom. 8:16, 1 Jn. 5:10
And consciously believes;	2 Cor. 1:12
The faith that conquers all,	Rom. 8:37
And doth the mountain move,	Zech. 4:6–7, Matt. 17:20
And saves who'er on Jesus call,	Rom. 10:13
And perfects them in love.	1 Jn. 2:5

P.W. i. 209; W.H. 95; M.H.B. 362; M.H. 139; H.P. 662

Author of faith, eternal Word,	Jn. 1:2, Heb. 12:2
Whose Spirit breathes the active flame;	Matt. 3:11, Acts 2:3
Faith, like its Finisher and Lord,	Acts 20:21, Heb. 12:2
Today as yesterday the same.	Heb. 13:8
To thee our humble hearts aspire,	Isa. 57:15, Jas. 4:6, 1 Pet. 5:6
And ask the gift unspeakable;	2 Cor. 9:15, Eph. 2:8
Increase in us the kindled fire,	Lk. 12:49
In us the work of faith fulfil.	2 Thess. 1:11

By faith we know thee strong to save;	Isa. 63:1, Heb. 11:39–40
Save us, a present Saviour thou!	Ps. 46:1
Whate'er we hope, by faith we have,	Heb. 11:1
Future and past subsisting now.	
To him that in thy name believes	Acts 3:16
Eternal life with thee is given;	Jn. 3:13
Into himself he all receives,	
Pardon, and holiness, and heaven.	Acts 26:18
The things unknown to feeble sense,	1 Cor. 2:9
Unseen by reason's glimmering ray,*	1 Cor. 1:21
With strong, commanding evidence,	Heb. 11:1
Their heavenly origin display.	
Faith lends its realizing light,	Heb. 11:1
The clouds disperse, the shadows fly;	Isa. 9:2, Matt. 4:6, Lk. 1:79
The Invisible appears in sight,	Jn. 1:18, Col. 1:15, Heb. 11:27
And God is seen by mortal eye.	Gen. 32:30, 1 Jn. 1:1–3

---

*'So reason's glimmering ray
Was lent, not to assure our doubtful way,
But guide us upward to a better day.'   (J. Dryden; *Religio Laici*, ll.5–7)
Cf. also 'reason's glimmering light' in Prior, *On Exodus*, iii.14, ll.100–1.
Cf. Milton, *Paradise Lost*, ii. 1034–7.

If 'the faith that works by love' is indeed the gift of God the conseqence follows that the seeking human soul cannot simply 'decide' to have faith, as and when it will. There is little spiritual profit for 'blaming' other folk for not having faith, when it is not in their power to do so, simply by 'trying harder'. We have to pray to God for the gift of faith, believing that it is his good purpose to give it. But how can one pray believingly for faith, if one does not have faith? Are we not trapped in a vicious circle? The answer to this common dilemma is the initiative of God's prevenient grace, that is to say, the measure of grace which God exercises upon those who have not yet come to any apparent degree of religious awakening or conscious spiritual experience. As St. John writes, there is a true Light 'which lighteth every man that cometh into the world,' (John 1:9). And of this Light Wesley writes: 'By what is vulgarly termed natural conscience, pointing out at least the general lines of good and evil. And this light, if man did not hinder, would shine more and more to the perfect day.' (*Notes on the New Testament*, John 1:9.) A vague sense of unease, that one is living a pointless kind of life, or a perhaps dim and unformed sense that it would be a happy thing to have Christian faith, if only that were possible, is the work of the Spirit in the heart. We may say that this is that 'faith as a grain of mustard seed' which enables the troubled soul to cry out, 'Lord I believe, help thou mine unbelief'. This first rudimentary prayer can be answered in the gift of more faith.

Furthermore, the searcher who is sincere will join in fellowship with the people of God to be prayed for, and by example, to learn better how to pray. In this way a more mature prayer can be offered which will open the door for God to grant the unspeakable gift of full, evangelical, saving faith. Thus we are obediently and expectantly to wait upon God in the use of the means of grace, in order to receive grace (46). It is not to be accounted reprehensible that a man or woman has honestly to confess that he or she does not possess the gift of faith, does not enjoy the sense that God is real, present, and loving. What is blameworthy as spiritual blindness is that he or she should be indifferent and careless as to this lack of faith, or that one who does profess to desire to grow up into faith should inconsistently neglect to join with the Christian fellowship in worship, in praise and in prayer.

P.W. iv. 227; W.H. 148, 130

Father of Jesus Christ the Just,	Acts 7:52, 1 Pet. 3:18
My Friend and Advocate with thee,	Jn. 15:14–15, 1 Jn. 2:1
Pity a soul that fain would trust	Mk. 9:24
In him who lived and died for me;	Rom. 6:10
But only thou canst make him known,	Matt. 11:27, Jn. 1:18
And in my heart reveal thy Son.	Gal. 1:15–16
A hidden God indeed thou art!	Job 23:8–9, Isa. 45:15
Thy absence I this moment feel;	Job 23:3
Yet must I own it from my heart,	Col. 2:2
Concealed, thou art a Saviour still;	Job 23:10, Isa. 28:21
And though thy face I cannot see,	Ex. 33:20
I know thine eye is fixed on me.	Gen. 16:13, Ps. 11:4
Thee without faith I cannot please,	Heb. 11:6
Faith without thee I cannot have;	1 Cor. 12:3, Eph. 2:8
But thou hast sent the Prince of peace	Isa. 9:6
To seek my wandering soul, and save;	Ps. 119:10, Matt. 18:12
O Father, glorify thy Son,	Jn. 12:23, 17:1
And save me for his sake alone!	Eph. 4:32
The gift unspeakable impart;	2 Cor. 9:15
Command the light of faith to shine,	2 Cor. 4:6
To shine in my dark, drooping heart,	Isa. 60:2
And fill me with the life divine:	Jn. 1:4, 10:10, 2 Pet. 1:4
Now bid the new creation be!	2 Cor. 5:17, Rev. 21:1, 5
O God, let there be faith in me!	Mk. 9:24, Lk. 17:5

37. Justification by Faith

The gracious message of our Lord is that the great God, who is the Judge and Father of mankind, does not wait for sinful human beings to embark upon the hopeless task of making amends for sin. There is no possibility of acquiring 'merit' in his sight, and he does not look for it. God freely forgives, and graciously accepts, the penitent sinner. It is, however, only the sincerely penitent sinner who can be assured of forgiveness, for the moral Governor of the race cannot forgive in such a way as to lead men and women to suppose that sin is condoned, on account of God's free grace.

This salvation works on the principle that we are one body with Christ. The divine Son made himself one with the human race so that as man, and on our behalf, he might offer to the Father in glory the atoning sacrifice of obedience, even to the Cross. Thus his sacrificial divine death is a matter of infinite merit. If in response we by faith make ourselves one with Christ, who is our meritorious sacrifice, his merit belongs to us, so that we come to have a secure standing of acceptance and forgiveness before God, such as we cannot have on our own. These merits of Christ which we come to possess are not to be thought of as a coat of heavenly 'whitewash', whereby God treats us as other than we really are. There is no idea of pretence or deception, or of a merely formal change of status. The faith by which we make ourselves one with Christ is much more than a sincere profession of certain beliefs about God and Christ. It is that personal 'faith which worketh by love', which takes up the whole human personality, the affections, the emotions, the moral will, and the actions. The union with Christ is a real one, of unreserved personal loving trust, and moral obedience. Believers are part of a supportive fellowship, and the dominating Person in that fellowship is the Spirit of Christ.

In the New Testament, and most characteristically in the writings of St. Paul, we find that this proposition 'free forgiveness of the penitent sinner', is translated into law-court language, to read:

'Justification by faith, and not by the works of the law'. The word translated 'to justify' means 'to bring in a verdict of not guilty', 'to acquit'. The Jewish religion of the old covenant characteristically thought of God largely as the Judge of mankind. Mankind is in the dock, and the momentous issue is always: 'What is the verdict?' The leading answer of the religion of the Law was that mankind must obey the Law, and so come to merit a right standing in the court of God, and receive his blessing. The first Christians were all Jews, and the first Church a sub-section of Judaism. The conversion of Gentiles raised the issue as to whether these Gentile believers, in order to be recognized as Christians of proper status, had to become Jewish proselytes, be circumcised, and keep the whole Law of Moses. The freedom party in the Church, of which the most prominent advocate was St. Paul, held that this was not necessary in order for Gentile believers to be 'justified', i.e. accepted before God. Faith in Christ was sufficient. In fact, Christianity is not a revised religion of law, but a religion of the Spirit. This position was crystallized in the formula 'Justification by faith, and not by the works of the Law'. Free forgiveness has here been translated into legal terms. At the Reformation the Protestant party emphasized this position by speaking of 'Justification by faith alone'.

P.W. i. 276; W.H. 127; M.H.B. 343

Wherewith, O God, shall I draw near,	Mic. 6:6
And bow myself before thy face?	
How in thy purer eyes appear?	Hab. 1:13
What shall I bring to gain thy grace?	Ex. 33:13, 19, Heb. 4:16
Will gifts delight the Lord most high?	Ps. 50:9–13, Isa. 40–16
Will multiplied oblations please?	Mic. 6:6
Thousands of rams his favour buy,	
Or slaughtered hecatombs appease?	
Can these avert the wrath of God:	Eph. 5:6, Col. 3:6
Can these wash out my guilty stain?	Heb. 10:1, 4, 11
Rivers of oil, and seas of blood,	Mic. 6:7
Alas! they all must flow in vain.	
Whoe'er to thee themselves approve,	2 Cor. 7:11
Must take the path thy word hath showed;	Mic. 6:8
Justice pursue, and mercy love,	
And humbly walk by faith with God.	Gen. 5:22, 2 Cor. 5:7, Heb. 11:5
But though my life henceforth be thine,	2 Cor. 5:15
Present for past can ne'er atone;	Matt. 18:24–5, Lk. 7:42
Though I to thee the whole resign,	1 Cor. 6:19–20
I only give thee back thine own.	1 Chron. 29:14

What have I then wherein to trust?	Isa. 36:5, Jer. 13:25, 17:5
I nothing have, I nothing am;	2 Cor. 6:10, 12:11
Excluded is my every boast,	Rom. 3:27
My glory swallowed up in shame.	Hos. 4:7
Guilty I stand before thy face,	Rom. 3:19
On me I feel thy wrath abide;	Jn. 3:36
'Tis just the sentence should take place;	Ps. 7:12 (B.C.P.), Rom. 3:5–6
'Tis just; — but O thy Son hath died!	Rom. 3:26, Jas. 2:13
Jesus, the Lamb of God hath bled,	Isa. 53:7, Rev. 5:6
He bore our sins upon the tree;	1 Pet. 1:19, 2:24, 3:18
Beneath our curse he bowed his head;	Deut. 21:23, Lam. 1:12–13,
	Mk. 15:34, Jn. 19:30,
	2 Cor. 5:21, Gal. 3:13
'Tis finished! he hath died for me!	Gal. 2:20
See where before the throne he stands,	Heb. 8:1, 9:11–12, Rev. 5:6
And pours the all-prevailing prayer;	Heb. 7:25
Points to his side, and lifts his hands,	Lk. 24:50, Jn. 20:27
And shows that I am graven there.	Isa. 49:16
He ever lives for me to pray;	Heb. 7:25
He prays that I am with him may reign:	Rom. 5:17
Amen to what my Lord doth say!	Ps. 106:48, Rev. 22:30
Jesus, thou canst not pray in vain.	Isa. 53:11

———————————

These verses, a notable expression of the characteristic Reformation doctrine of Justification, are John Wesley's translation of Count Zinzendorf's *Christi Blut und Gerechtigkeit*, of 1739.

P.W. i. 346; W.H. 190; M.H.B. 370; M.H. 127; H.P. 225

Jesu, thy blood and righteousness,	2 Cor. 5:21, Phil. 3:9
My beauty are, my glorious dress;	Isa. 52:1, 61:10, Ecclus. 27:8
Midst flaming worlds in these arrayed,	2 Pet. 3:10
With joy shall I lift up my head.	Lk. 21:28
Bold shall I stand in thy great day,	1 Jn. 4:17
For who aught to my charge shall lay?	Rom. 8:33
Fully absolved through these I am,	Matt. 26:28
From sin and fear, from guilt and shame.	
The holy, meek, unspotted Lamb,	Ex. 12:5, 1 Pet. 1:19–20,
Who from the Father's bosom came,	Jn. 1:18, 29, 36
Who died for me, even me, to atone,	Rom. 5:11, 2 Cor. 5:18, Gal. 2:20
Now for my Lord and God I own.	Jn. 20:28
Lord, I believe thy precious blood,	1 Pet. 1:19
Which at the mercy-seat of God	Lev. 16:14, Heb. 9:11–12, 14

For ever doth for sinners plead,	Heb. 7:25, 9:24
For me, even for my soul, was shed.	Mk. 14:24, Heb. 9:22–3, 26

Lord, I believe were sinners more	
Than sands upon the ocean shore,	Heb. 11:12
Thou hast for all a ransom paid,	Mk. 10:45, 1 Tim. 2:6
For all a full atonement made.	Rom. 5:11, 2 Cor. 5:18–20

Jesu, be endless praise to thee,	1 Pet. 4:11
Whose boundless mercy hath for me,	Ps. 145:9
For me and all thy hands have made,	Isa. 64:8, Ps. 119:73
And everlasting ransom paid.	Mk. 10:45, 1 Tim. 2:6,
	Rev. 13:8

Ah! give to all thy servants, Lord,	Acts 4:29, 20:32
With power to speak thy gracious word,	Lk. 4:22, 1 Thess. 1:5
That all who to thy wounds will flee,	Zech. 13:1, 6
May find eternal life in thee.	Jn. 3:16, 1 Jn. 5:11

Thou God of power, thou God of love,	1 Cor. 1:18, 1 Jn. 4:8
Let the whole world thy mercy prove!	Isa. 54:5, Rom. 11:32
Now let thy word o'er all prevail;	Acts 19:20
Now take the spoils of death and hell.	Mk. 3:27, Rev. 1:18

O let the dead now hear thy voice,	Jn. 5:25, Eph. 5:14
Now bid thy banished ones rejoice,	2 Sam. 14:13, Isa. 43:5–7
Their beauty this, their gracious dress,	Isa. 52:1, 61:10, Ecclus. 27:8
Jesu, thy blood and righteousness!	2 Cor. 5:21

38. Adoption

This is another New Testament name for that new standing before God which is granted to those who have saving faith in Christ. Those who are justified, forgiven, accepted by God, are also actually incorporated spiritually into the family of his children. They are adopted. Adoption could be of much significance in the ancient world. An emperor could actually adopt some hopeful young man of the royal family to be his heir, to be designated and trained to succeed in due course to the imperial office. This is used as a picture of the spiritual dignity which belongs to believers. They are united to the family of God, and are possessed of such a strong personal awareness that God is the loving Father that in exultant prayer they cry out 'Abba, Father!' (Rom. 8:15).

P.W. viii. 202; W.H. 614; M.H.B. 399; M.H. 196; H.P. 703

What shall I render to my God	Ps. 116:12, 1 Thess. 3:9
For all his mercy's store?	1 Pet. 1:3
I'll take the gifts he hath bestowed,	Ps. 116:13, 1 Chron. 29:15
And humbly ask for more.	Jas. 4:6
The sacred cup of saving grace	Ps. 116:13, 1 Cor. 11:25–6
I will with thanks receive,	Ps. 116:17, 1 Cor. 14:16
And all his promises embrace,	Heb. 11:13
And to his glory live.	1 Cor. 10:31, Eph. 1:12
My vows I will to his great name	Ps. 116:14, Ezek. 36:23
Before his people pay,	Ps. 22:25, 66:13
And all I have, and all I am,	
Upon his altar lay.	Gen. 22:9
Thy lawful servant, Lord, I owe	Ps. 116:16, 1 Tim. 1:8
To thee whate'er is mine,	Ex. 12:48–9, 1 Chron. 29:14
Born in thy family below,	Rom. 8:23, Eph. 3:15
And by redemption thine.	Lev. 25:47–9, Rom. 3:24,
	Gal. 4:5, Eph. 1:7

ATT-H

Thy hands created me, thy hands	Ps. 119:72
From sin have set me free,	Rom. 6:18, 22, Gal. 5:1
The mercy that hath loosed my bands	Ps. 116:16
Hath bound me fast to thee.	1 Cor. 7:22
The God of all-redeeming grace	Ps. 130:7
My God I will proclaim,	Ps. 40:9–10, Isa. 12:4
Offer the sacrifice of praise,	Ps. 116:17, Jer. 33:11
And call upon his name.	Gen. 4:26, Ps. 105:1, Rom. 10:13
Praise him, ye saints, the God of love,	Ps. 30:4, 116:19, 1 Jn. 4:8
Who hath my sins forgiven,	Acts 13:38, 1 Tim. 1:12–15
Till, gathered to the Church above,	Eph. 1:10, Heb. 12:22–3
We sing the songs of heaven.	Rev. 5:9, 14:3, 15:3

39. Assurance

The believing soul has always craved for spiritual assurance, for 'an anchor of the soul both sure and stedfast' (Heb. 6:19). In Wesley's time the great Bishop Joseph Butler could indeed aim to establish a reasonable degree of religious conviction upon the maxim that 'probability is the guide to life'. Yet it is impossible to face with abounding courage and settled peace of mind the troubles of this life, and the awesome mystery of the life to come, upon the basis of a judicious balance of probabilities. The soul craves for a faith which will enable one to cry out: 'I *know* whom I have believed'. (2 Tim. 1:12)

This question of the assurance of salvation was a subject of much controversy in the time of the Wesleys. Then, as now, the multitude who were not committed to vital religion were prepared to say that assurance is impossible. A chief strength of the Calvinist position was precisely because it claimed to have a doctrine of assurance. The technical name for this is 'the final perseverance of the saints', expressed popularly in the maxim 'once saved, always saved'. If a believer could suppose that he was in a state of saving Christian grace solely because God had mysteriously chosen him to be such, and that God's grace in carrying out this purpose was irresistible, then he could feel assured of his final salvation. It is important to remember that the Wesleys questioned this doctrine not primarily on theoretical grounds of human freedom, but for practical and moral reasons. The fear was that, at least in the case of superficial and careless minds, the idea of 'final perseverence' could lead to dangerous presumption. One who trusted that final salvation was assured simply by the action of God might fall into the error of supposing that one might be saved even if one lacked moral and spiritual discipline.

Wesley's wise and balanced grasp of the evangelical principle was always that salvation by grace through faith was to lead to fuller obedience to the law of God, not to a fancied release from the duty of obedience. Thus the gospel promise was that God would grant to the full believer the privilege of *a present* assurance of salvation, bringing a confident standing in the sight of God, release from fear, and peace of mind, but that this privilege would not continue in the future if the disciple failed to walk steadfastly in the devotional and moral discipline of the Christian life. Thus Wesley can say of those who have the gift of evangelical saving faith: 'They are also saved from the fear, though not from the possibility, of falling away from the grace of God.' (*Sermon* I.ii.4.)

Wesley's doctrine of the full assurance of salvation, which was a characteristic and important part of Methodist preaching, came to expression in the exposition of Romans 8:16 'The Spirit himself beareth witness with our spirit, that we are the children of God.' It will be remembered that the association of this text with the preaching of assurance was by no means new, though Wesley gave to it an enhanced emphasis. He observed that the text speaks of two 'witnesses'. There is first 'the witness of my own spirit', that is to say, a profound awareness of a great change of inward moral character and outward conduct worked by the Spirit in the believer. There is also 'the witness of the Spirit of God', which is an inherently mysterious 'inward impression on the soul, whereby the Spirit of God directly witnesses to my spirit, that I am a child of God.' (*Sermon* X.i.7.) When the two 'witnesses' chime together the believer is granted the full privilege of a present assurance of salvation.

It is to be observed that according to Wesley's more mature and careful teaching 'the witness of my own spirit' is essential to the experience of every true believer. To claim 'full assurance' on account of an 'inward impression on the soul' alone, apart from the profound moral change, is a mark of diabolical self-deception. Therefore Wesley's doctrine is certainly not the simplistic emotional argument '*I feel* saved, therefore I am saved.' 'The witness of the Spirit' is the *privilege* of the believer, to be expected and prayed for, as part of the spiritual equipment of a fully effective witness. But it is not essential to salvation, in the sense that the sincere believer who is aware that one lacks the gift of 'full assurance' need be in a state of anxious fear that one is not on the road to eternal salvation.

P.W. v. 363; W.H. 96; M.H.B. 377; M.H. 114; H.P. 728

How can a sinner know	2 Tim. 1:12, 1 Jn. 2:4
His sins on earth forgiven?	Matt. 9:6
How can my Saviour show	Lk. 2:11
My name inscribed in heaven?	Lk. 10:20
What we ourselves have felt, and seen,	Acts 4:20
With confidence we tell,	Acts 28:31
And publish to the sons of men	Acts 10:37, 13:49
The signs infallible.	Acts 1:3

We who in Christ believe   Jn. 3:15, Acts 15:11
   That he for us hath died,   Rom. 5:6, 1 Cor. 15:3
His unknown peace receive,   Phil. 4:7
   And feel his blood applied: Heb. 12:14, 1 Pet. 1:2
Exults for joy our rising soul,   Lk. 24:41
   Disburthened of her load,   Ps. 55:22
And swells, unutterably full   1 Pet. 1:8
   Of glory, and of God.

His love, surpassing far
   The love of all beneath,   Ps. 43:4, Col. 3:2, 1 Pet. 4:13
We find within, and dare   Rom. 5:5
   The pointless darts of death:*   Eph. 6:16
Stronger than death, or sin, or hell, Cant. 8:6, Rom. 8:38–9
   The mystic power we prove,   Phil. 3:10
And conquerors of the world we dwell Rom. 8:37
   In heaven, who dwell in love.   1 Jn. 4:16

The meek and lowly heart,   Matt. 11:29
   Which in our Saviour was,
He doth to us impart,   1 Cor. 2:16, Phil. 2:5
   And signs us with his cross:**   Gal. 6:17
Our nature's course is turned, our mind*** Jas. 3:6
   Transformed in all its powers,   Rom. 12:2
And both the witnesses joined,   Rom. 8:16
   The Spirit of God with ours.

We by his Spirit prove,   Rom. 12:2
   And know the things of God,   1 Cor. 2:9–10
The things which of his love
   He hath on us bestowed: 1 Jn. 3:1
His glory is our sole design,   1 Cor. 10:31
   We live our God to please,   1 Thess. 4:1, Heb. 11:6
And rise with filial fear divine   Ps. 111:10, Prov. 14:27
   To perfect holiness.   Acts 9:31, 2 Cor. 7:1

The Spirit of my God   Rom. 8:16, 1 Cor. 6:11
   Hath certified him mine,   2 Tim. 1:11, 1 Jn. 5:10
And all the tokens showed,   Ps. 86:17
   Infallible, divine: Acts 1:3
Hereby the pardoned sinner knows   1 Jn. 3:24, 4:13
   His sins on earth forgiven,   Matt. 9:6
And thus my gracious Saviour shows Acts 15:11, 1 Pet. 2:3
   My name inscribed in heaven.   Lk. 10:20, Rev. 20:12, 21:27

---

* Death's pointless darts, and hell's defeated storms

                                     (Young, *Night Thoughts*, vi. 752)

** Ministration of Baptism, B.C.P.

*** This phrase is possibly suggested by this text, though the sense is not the same.

P.W. i. 307; W.H. 376; M.H.B. 280; H.P. 291

I want the Spirit of power within,	2 Tim. 1:7
Of love, and of a healthful mind;	
Of power, to conquer inbred sin,	Mic. 3:8, Jn. 13:10, 16:8
Of love, to thee and all mankind,	Lk. 10:27–9, 36–7, Gal. 5:22
Of health, that pain and death defies,	Lk. 5:17
Most vigorous when the body dies.	2 Cor. 6:9
When shall I hear the inward voice	1 Kgs. 19:12, Rom. 7:22
Which only faithful souls can hear?	Jn. 14:17
Pardon, and peace, and heavenly joys	Jn. 14:27, 16:22
Attend the promised Comforter;	Jn. 15:26
O come, and righteousness divine,	2 Cor. 5:21, Gal. 5:5
And Christ, and all with Christ, are mine!	Rom. 8:32, Phil. 3:9
O that the Comforter would come!	Jn. 15:26
Nor visit as a transient guest,	Jer. 14:8
But fix in me his constant home,	Jn. 14:16
And take possession of my breast,	Cant. 1:13
And fix in me his loved abode,	Jn. 14:17, 21
The temple of indwelling God!	1 Cor. 3:16, 6:19
Come, Holy Ghost, my heart inspire!	Job 32:8, Jn. 15:26
Attest that I am born again;	Jn. 3:3, Rom. 8:16, 1 Jn. 5:10
Come, and baptize me now with fire,	Matt. 3:11, Acts 2:3
Nor let thy former gifts be vain;	2 Cor. 6:1
I cannot rest in sins forgiven,	Lam. 2:18
Where is the earnest of my heaven?	Eph. 1:14
Where the indubitable seal	Eph. 1:13, 2 Tim. 2:19
That ascertains the kingdom mine?	Lk. 12:32
The powerful stamp I long to feel,	1 Cor. 15:49
The signature of love divine;	Hag. 2:23
O shed it in my heart abroad,	Rom. 5:5
Fulness of love, of heaven, of God!	Eph. 3:19

40. The New Birth

The believer, who is granted free forgiveness, gracious acceptance by God, or justification, also receives the gift of the new birth, or regeneration. These two are not to be thought of as successive stages in a process, but as the first decisive closing with Christ by faith looked at from two points of view. The term justification has in mind one's standing before God, regeneration that renewed life of inward moral character and outward righteous conduct which is the work of the Spirit in those who are justified. That these two are linked is manifest, because if the essence of human moral weakness is alienation from God, the load of a guilty conscience, and self-despising despair of the prospect of goodness in one's life, then the experience of forgiveness and acceptance by God ought to occasion in the human heart a spring of new moral resolve. It is a cardinal point of all well-considered evangelical teaching that these two, forgiveness and the new birth, justification and regeneration, are linked in this way. God's gracious offer of free forgiveness on account of the saving work of Christ is never to be misrepresented as bringing release from the duty of obedience to the moral law of God. It is the means by which the believer may be able to obey as he ought to obey, not in bare outward action for fear of punishment or hope of reward, but from the heart, and gladly, moved by the power of love. Any claim to the possession of Christian salvation purely on the emotional basis of an experience of peace and joy, and in the absence of real moral renewal, is to be regarded as a mistaken and spurious claim. Union with Christ by faith takes up the whole of the human personality, affections, emotions, intellectual convictions, the moral will, and actions.

To emphasize this vital union of moral renewal with evangelical experience was a salient concern of the teaching of the Wesleys. The new birth is the first decisive step in a life of progressive growth in grace, in which the believer is by experience to learn clearer ideals and new duties, and by more consistent discipline come to carry them out. This process is called sanctification. It is important to remember,

119

however, that this sanctification is not a self-imposed moral discipline, by which we gradually improve ourselves as Christians by our own efforts. It is throughout the work of the Spirit in believers, though they must co-operate. We may sum this matter up in Wesley's definition. 'God in justifying us does something *for* us; in begetting us again, he does the work *in* us. The former changes our outward relation to God, so that of enemies we become children; by the latter our inmost souls are changed, so that of sinners we become saints. . . . The one is the taking away the guilt, the other the taking away the power, of sin.' (*Sermon* XV.2.)

We turn to Charles Wesley's splendid paraphrase of the Beatitudes.

P.W. i. 258; W.H. 134; M.H.B. 349; H.P. 529

Jesu, if still the same thou art,	Heb. 13:8
If all thy promises are sure,	Rom. 4:16
Set up thy kingdom in my heart,	Col. 3:15
And make me rich, for I am poor:	Lk. 6:20, 2 Cor. 8:9
To me be all thy treasures given,	Lk. 12:33, 18:22
The kingdom of an inward heaven.	Lk. 17:21
Thou hast pronounced the mourners blest;	Matt. 5:4
And lo! for thee I ever mourn:	Ps. 38:6
I cannot, no, I will not rest,	Lam. 2:18
Till thou, my only rest, return;	Matt. 11:28–9
Till thou, the Prince of peace, appear,	Isa. 9:6
And I receive the Comforter.	Jn. 14:16, 15:26, 20:22
Where is the blessedness bestowed	Matt. 5:6
On all that hunger after thee?	
I hunger now, I thirst for God;	Ps. 42:2, 63:1, 143:6
See the poor fainting sinner, see,	Matt. 9:36, Ps. 107:5
And satisfy with endless peace,	Jn. 14:27, 16:22
And fill me with thy righteousness.	Matt. 5:6
Ah, Lord! if thou art in that sigh,	Jer. 45:3
Then hear thyself within me pray;	
Hear in my heart thy Spirit's cry,	Rom. 8:23
Mark what my labouring soul would say;	Matt. 11:28, Col. 4:12,
Answer the deep unuttered groan,	Rom. 8:26
And show that thou and I are one.	1 Cor. 6:17
Shine on thy work, disperse the gloom,	Ps. 119:135, 2 Cor. 4:6
Light in thy light I then shall see,	Ps. 36:9
Say to my soul, 'Thy light is come,	Isa. 60:1–2
Glory divine is risen on thee,	
Thy warfare's past, thy mourning's o'er;	Isa. 40:2, 51:11, 60:20
Look up, for thou shalt weep no more.'	Isa. 30:19, 65:19, Lk. 21:28

Under Charles Wesley's title 'Desiring to love' we have this earnest prayer for growth in grace and spiritual experience, with its rather quaint third verse, and the too frequently neglected fifth and sixth verses. This is one of the three Wesley hymns distinguished in that Handel wrote a tune for it, 'Wentworth'. The modern Methodist book has, however, dropped it.

P.W. iv. 341; W.H. 147; M.H.B. 434; M.H. 285

O Love divine, how sweet thou art!	Cant. 5:16
When shall I find my willing heart	Ex. 35:5
All taken up by thee?	Ps. 27:10
I thirst, I faint, I die to prove	Ps. 27:13, 42:2, Rom. 12:2
The greatness of redeeming love,	Eph. 2:4, 3:18
The love of Christ to me!	Gal. 2:20
Stronger his love than death or hell;	Cant. 8:6, Rom. 8:38–9
Its riches are unsearchable;	Eph. 3:8
The first-born sons of light	Job. 38:7
Desire in vain its depths to see,	Eph. 3:18, 1 Pet. 1:12
They cannot reach the mystery,	1 Cor. 2:6–7, Eph. 3:3–4
The length, and breadth, and height.	Eph. 3:18
God only knows the love of God;	Eph. 3:19
O that it now were shed abroad	Rom. 5:5
In this poor stony heart!	Ezek. 36:26, Mk. 3:5, 16:14
For love I sigh, for love I pine:	Cant. 2:5, 5:8
This only portion, Lord, be mine,	Ps. 16:5
Be mine this better part.	Lk. 10:42
O that I could for ever sit	Lk. 10:39
With Mary at the Master's feet!	
Be this my happy choice:	Lk. 10:42
My only care, delight, and bliss,	Ps. 37:4, Cant. 2:3, Phil. 4:6
My joy, my heaven on earth, be this,	Ps. 43:4, Heb. 6:4–5
To hear the Bridegroom's voice!	Matt. 25:6, Jn. 3:29
O that with humbled Peter I	
Could weep, believe, and thrice reply	Lk. 22:62, Jn. 21:15–17
My faithfulness to prove,	Deut. 8:2
'Thou know'st (for all to thee is known),	Jn. 21:17
Thou know'st, O Lord, and thou alone,	
Thou know'st that thee I love!'	
O that I could with favoured John	Jn. 13:23
Recline my weary head upon	Matt. 11:28
The great Redeemer's breast!	Jer. 50:34
From care, and sin, and sorrow free,	Jn. 16:20, Rom. 6:18, Phil. 4:6
Give me, O Lord, to find in thee	
My everlasting rest.	Matt. 11:28–29, 2 Thess. 1:7, 2:16, Heb. 4:9

P.W. v. 10; W.H. 429; M.H.B. 572; H.P. 788

Behold the servant of the Lord!	Lk. 1:38
I wait thy guiding eye to feel,	Ps. 32:8
To hear and keep thy every word,	Deut. 17:19, Jn. 8:47
To prove and do thy perfect will,	Rom. 12:2, 1 Jn. 2:17
Joyful from my own works to cease,	Heb. 4:10
Glad to fulfil all righteousness.	Matt. 3:15
Me, if thy grace vouchsafe to use,	2 Tim. 2:21
Meanest of all thy creatures, me,	Eph. 3:8
The deed, the time, the manner choose,	Ps. 25:12
Let all my fruit be found of thee;	Hos. 14:8, Phil. 3:9
Let all my works in thee be wrought,	Isa. 26:12
By thee to full perfection brought.	Heb. 13:21, Jas. 1:4
My every weak, though good design,	Rom. 14:1
O'errule, or change, as seems thee meet;	2 Cor. 12:8–9
Jesus, let all my work be thine!	1 Cor. 12:6, Phil. 2:13
Thy work, O Lord, is all complete,	Jn. 17:4
And pleasing in thy Father's sight;	Heb. 13:21
Thou only hast done all things right.	Heb. 3:1–2
Here then to thee thy own I leave;	1 Chron. 29:14
Mould as thou wilt thy passive clay;	Jer. 18:6, Rom. 9:21
But let me all thy stamp receive,	1 Cor. 15:49, Gal. 6:17
But let me all thy words obey,	Ps. 119:57
Serve with a single heart and eye,	Matt. 6:22, Col. 3:22
And to thy glory live and die.	Rom. 14:8, Eph. 6:5

The following is John Wesley's well-loved translation of the Halle Pietist Joachim Lange's verses 'O Jesu, süsses Licht' (1670–1744).

P.W. i. 159; W.H. 431; M.H.B. 573; H.P. 801

O God, what offering shall I give	Mic. 6:6
To thee, the Lord of earth and skies?	Isa. 66:1
My spirit, soul, and flesh receive,	Rom. 12:1
A holy, living sacrifice;	
Small as it is, 'tis all my store;	1 Kgs. 17:9, Lk. 21:4, 1 Cor. 1(
More shouldst thou have, if I had more.	
Now then, my God, thou hast my soul,	Ezek. 18:4
No longer mine, but thine I am;	1 Cor. 6:19–20
Guard thou thine own, possess it whole,	2 Tim. 1:12
Cheer it with hope, with love inflame;	Isa. 4:6, Rom. 12:12
Thou hast my spirit, there display	Ps. 31:5
Thy glory to the perfect day.	Prov. 4:18

Thou hast my flesh, thy hallowed shrine,	1 Cor. 3:16–17, 6:19
Devoted solely to thy will;	Ps. 40:8, Heb. 10:7, 9
Here let thy light for ever shine,	Jn. 1:5, 9
This house still let thy presence fill;	2 Chron. 5:14
O Source of life, live, dwell, and move	Acts 17:25
In me, till all my life be love!	1 Jn. 2:5
Send down thy likeness from above,	Gen. 1:26, 1 Cor. 15:47, 49
And let this my adorning be;	1 Pet. 3:3–4
Clothe me with wisdom, patience, love,	Job 28:12
With lowliness and purity,	1 Tim. 2:9, 1 Pet. 5:5
Than gold and pearls more precious far,	Job. 28:17–18
And brighter than the morning star.	2 Pet. 1:19, Rev. 2:28
Lord, arm me with thy Spirit's might,	Eph. 3:16, 6:11, Col. 1:11
Since I am called by thy great name;	Jer. 14:9, 15:16
In thee let all my thoughts unite,	Ps. 94:19
Of all my works be thou the aim;	Heb. 12:2
Thy love attend me all my days,	Ps. 23:6
And my sole business be thy praise!	Ps. 34:1

41. Conversion

That whole progression of response to divine grace which lifts 'the natural man' from the self-centred life of neglect of the offered love of God, and of carelessness in obedience to his law, to a transforming personal experience of salvation, is summed up in the term 'conversion'. It is to be noted, however, that this word is used in two senses. 'Conversion' in the fullest sense of the word indicates a change from definite unbelief, or from attachment to some other religion, to Christian faith. There are, however, many people who are summoned by grace from the background of a decent moral life, and of a sincere though perhaps somewhat superficial attachment to the institutions of religion, to the deep personal experience of saving faith. This momentous change is also frequently spoken of as 'conversion', even though those converted were in some sense 'Christians' beforehand. Thus one can be 'converted' from formal or 'legal' Christianity. It would appear that the momentous 'conversions' of the Wesleys, and of the majority of the leaders of early Methodism, were of this type.

An issue is presented at this point upon which it is necessary to have a cautious and reticent judgment. On the one hand, it is an essential part of the evangelical witness that all God's people are called to the privilege of a personal experience of saving Christian faith. It is not enough that Christian disciples should settle down to a conventional level of Churchgoing and respectable behaviour. At the same time, it is precarious to dismiss apparently sincere disciples who have not come to a distinct conversion experience as 'not Christians'. This can easily land one in uncharitable and self-righteous judgment, which does not commend the Christian faith. The rule surely is that it is the business of the evangelist to proclaim the terms of salvation as plainly and lovingly as possible, but not to venture upon judgment that particular classes of hearers are, or are not, 'saved', or in a state of Christian grace. Only God can judge this.

It is natural to find that the Wesley hymnody contains a great volume of writing celebrating the glory of the conversion experience. Charles Wesley came to his evangelical experience while on a sick-bed, lodging at the house of, and receiving evangelical counsel from 'Mr. Bray, a poor ignorant mechanic, who knows nothing but Christ; but by knowing him, knows and discerns all things.' On Pentecost Sunday he was visited by John Wesley and friends on their way to Church, and during the morning came to a remarkable experience, an account of which is well worth reading in Charles' *Journal* for May 21st 1738. On Tuesday, May 23rd, he continues in his *Journal*: 'I waked under the protection of Christ, and gave myself up, soul and body, to him. At nine I began an hymn upon my conversion, but was persuaded to break off for fear of pride. (It is generally assumed that this point came after the second verse.) Mr. Bray coming, encouraged me to proceed in spite of Satan. I prayed Christ to stand by me, and finished the hymn.' Of Wednesday evening, May 24th, after John Wesley's momentous experience at Aldersgate Street, Charles Wesley writes; 'Towards ten, my brother was brought in triumph by a troop of our friends, and declared, "I believe". We sang the hymn with great joy, and parted with prayer.'

P.W. i. 91; W.H. 30; M.H.B. 361; M.H. 528; H.P. 706

Where shall my wondering soul begin?	Isa. 25:1
How shall I all to heaven aspire?	Ps. 57:5; Eccl. 5:2
A slave redeemed from death and sin,	Lev. 25:48, Eph. 1:7
A brand plucked from eternal fire,	Amos 4:11, Zech. 3:2
How shall I equal triumphs raise,	2 Cor. 2:14
Or sing my great Deliverer's praise?	Rom. 11:26
O how shall I the goodness tell,	Ps. 145:7
Father, which thou to me hast showed:	Ps. 31:21, 66:16
That I, a child of wrath and hell,	Matt. 23:15, Eph. 2:3
I should be called a child of God,	Rom. 9:26
Should know, should feel my sins forgiven,	Rom. 8:16, 1 Jn. 3:14, 5:13
Blest with this antepast of heaven!	Heb. 6:4–5
And shall I slight my Father's love?	Heb. 10:29
Or basely fear his gifts to own?	Jn. 19:38
Unmindful of his favours prove?	Deut. 32:18
Shall I, the hallowed cross to shun,	Rom. 1:16, 1 Cor. 1:18
Refuse his righteousness to impart,	Ps. 40:9–10
By hiding it within my heart?*	Jer. 20:9
No! though the ancient dragon rage,	Rev. 20:2
And call forth all his hosts to war,	Rev. 20:8
Though earth's self-righteous sons engage,	Jn. 8:33, 41–5, Gal. 3:1–2
Them and their god alike I dare;	2 Cor. 4:4
Jesus, the sinner's friend, proclaim;	Matt. 11:19
Jesus, to sinners still the same.	Heb. 13:8

Outcasts of men, to you I call,	Lk. 14:23
Harlots, and publicans, and thieves!	Lk. 15:1
He spreads his arms to embrace you all;	Isa. 65:2, Rom. 10:21
Sinners alone his grace receives;	Mk. 2:17
No need of him the righteous have;	Matt. 9:12
He came the lost to seek and save.	Lk. 19:10

Come all ye Magdalens in lust,	Lk. 7:37–38, 8:2
Ye ruffians fell in murders old;**	
Repent, and live: despair and trust!	Ezek. 18:21, 23, Rom. 7:24–5
Jesus for you to death was sold;	Matt. 27:3–6
Though hell protest, and earth repine,	Ps. 99:1 (B.C.P.), Zech. 3:1–2
He died for crimes like yours — and mine.	Rom. 5:6, 8, 1 Cor. 15:3,
	Gal. 2:20, 1 Tim. 1:12–15

Come, O my guilty brethren come,	Isa. 55:6–7
Groaning beneath your load of sin!	Rom. 7:24
His bleeding heart shall make you room,	Isa. 32:2
His open side shall take you in.	Jn. 19:34, 20:27
He calls you now, invites you home;	Lk. 14:17
Come, O my guilty brethren, come!	Isa. 53:6

---

* It is possible that the wording of this line is a reminiscence of Job 10:13, though this is
not the sense of the original.
** This line is from a poem by Samuel Wesley Jnr. (*Poems*, 1862, p. 433.)

Charles Wesley's 'For the Anniversary Day of one's Conversion'
extended to eighteen verses, of which selections have been used in
later hymnals.

P.W. i. 299; W.H. 1; M.H.B. 1; M.H. 1; H.P. 744

Glory to God, and praise, and love	Ps. 86:12
Be ever, ever given;	
By saints below, and saints above,	Heb. 12:22–3
The Church in earth and heaven.	Eph. 1:10

On this glad day the glorious Sun	Ps. 118:24
Of Righteousness arose,	Mal. 4:2
On my benighted soul he shone,	Jn. 1:5, 11:10, 2 Cor. 4:6
And filled it with repose.	Matt. 11:28–9

Sudden expired the legal strife,	Rom. 7:9–11, 15–25
'Twas then I ceased to grieve,	Lam. 3:32–3
My second, real, living life	Jn. 3:3, 10:10
I then began to live.	

Then with my *heart* I first believed,	Rom. 10:9–10
Believed with faith divine,	Rev. 14:12
Power with the Holy Ghost received	Acts 1:8
To call the Saviour mine.	1 Cor. 12:3

I felt my Lord's atoning blood	Rom. 5:11, 1 Pet. 1:2
Close to *my* soul applied;*	1 Cor. 12:3, Heb. 12:24
Me, me he loved, the Son of God,	Gal. 2:20
For me, for me, he died!	
O for a thousand tongues to sing**	Ps. 35:28, 69:30, 71:23
My dear Redeemer's praise!***	Cant. 2:16, Col. 1:13
The glories of my God and King,	Ps. 21:5, 44:4, 74:12
The triumphs of his grace.	Rom. 8:37, 2 Cor. 2:14
My gracious Master, and my God	Ps. 86:15, 1 Pet. 2:3
Assist me to proclaim,	Lk. 12:3, Acts 16:9
To spread through all the earth abroad	Matt. 9:31, Acts 1:8
The honours of thy name.	Matt. 13:57, Jas. 2:7,
	2 Pet. 1:17
Jesus, the name that charms our fears,	Isa. 61:1–3, Lk. 4:18–19
That bids our sorrows cease;	Jn. 16:22
'Tis music in the sinner's ears,	Lk. 15:25
'Tis life, and health, and peace!	Lk. 5:17, Rom. 8:6
He breaks the power of cancelled sin,	Rom. 6:1–2, 18
He sets the prisoner free;	Isa. 61:1
His blood can make the foulest clean;	Zech. 13:1
His blood availed for me.	Gal. 2:20, 1 Tim. 1:13–14
He speaks; and listening to his voice	Mk. 5:41–42, Jn. 11:43–44
New life the dead receive,	
The mournful, broken hearts rejoice,	Isa. 61:3, Matt. 5:4
The humble poor believe.	Matt. 11:5, Jas. 2:5, Lk. 6:20
Hear him ye deaf, his praise ye dumb	Matt. 11:5, Mk. 7:34
Your loosened tongues employ;	Mk. 7:35
Ye blind, behold your Saviour come,	Lk. 18:35, 37, 42–3
And leap, ye lame, for joy.	Acts 3:6, 8
Look unto him, ye nations, own	Isa. 45:22
Your God, ye fallen race!	Isa. 45:21, Rom. 5:12–14
Look, and be saved through faith alone;	Hab. 2:4, Rom. 1:17
Be justified, by grace!****	Rom. 4:16, Eph. 2:8
See all your sins on Jesus laid;	Isa. 53:6
The Lamb of God was slain,	Isa. 53:7, Rev. 5:6, 9, 12, 13:8
His soul was once an offering made	Isa. 53:10, Heb. 10:12, 14
For every soul of man.	Ezek. 18:4, Jn. 3:16,
	1 Tim. 2:4, 2 Pet. 3:9
With me, your chief, you than shall know,	1 Tim. 1:15–16
Shall feel your sins forgiven;	Acts 13:38
Anticipate your heaven below,	Eph. 2:6, Heb. 6:5
And own, that love is heaven.	1 Jn. 4:7

* 'I felt my heart strangely warmed—and an assurance was given me, that he had taken away *my* sins, even *mine*, and saved *me* from the law of sin and death.' (Wesley, *Journal*, May 24, 1738.)

** It is related that in May, 1738, Charles Wesley spoke to Peter Böhler about confessing Christ, and that Böhler said: 'Had I a thousand tongues, I would praise him with them all.' For the German original to this see H. Bett, 'The Hymns of Methodism', p. 95.

*** 'dear' was later changed by John Wesley in published hymnals to the familiar 'great', doubtless through the sentiment that it is inappropriate to address the language of human endearment to the Almighty. We observe that John Wesley also toned down the language of some of the German Pietist hymns which he translated, making it more restrained, and likewise passed over 'Jesu, Lover of my soul' for his 1780 hymnal.

**** In relation to these well-known lines it is as well to observe the careful usage adopted by the Wesleys of those two formulae which rose to prominence in much Reformation theology, 'faith alone', and 'grace alone'. The penitent sinner's *initia* acceptance by God at conversion is 'not by the works of the law, but by the faith of Jesus Christ' (Gal. 2:16). Justification, that is, free forgiveness for the sake of the saving work of Christ, cannot be earned by human effort. It is accepted in faith. In this sense justification is 'by faith alone'. However, Wesley is careful to emphasize that this by no means excuses the believer from moral obedience, moral discipline, and moral growth. The believer's *final* acceptance to glory at the Judgment is also dependent upon the condition that he or she has been decisively changed for the better in inward character and outward conduct. (Matt. 25:37-40, Rev. 14:13) If these 'good works' are not produced it is a fatal sign that the 'faith' which has been professed is not true, evangelical, saving faith, but a spiritual delusion. Thus *final* justification is not 'by faith alone', but by faith and the good works which faith produces. Likewise, at every stage of the Christian life, from conversion to glory, the human soul cannot turn to God by its own unaided moral effort. Throughout it is entirely dependent upon the enabling grace of God. In this sense salvation is indeed 'by grace alone'. However, Wesley was very careful to avoid the notion, which he regarded as dangerously destructive of moral discipline, that human salvation is solely dependent upon the operation of divine grace, and apart from morally responsible human co-operation. At every stage the soul has freely to accept the calling of grace, so that in the end the decision whether the soul is saved or no depends on human choice, not divine. In this way the formula 'grace alone' is safeguarded against misunderstanding.

The following great hymn, manifestly springing from the first rapture of Charles Wesley's new evangelical experience, is perhaps the best known and best loved of all the Methodist hymns associated with the conversion experience. It contains some very profound theological thought, and some very aspiring spiritual claims, and it is perhaps a pity that through association with a well-loved and enthusiastic tune it is sometimes sung without sufficient reflection.

P.W. i. 105; W.H. 201; M.H.B. 371; M.H. 527; H.P. 216

And can it be, that I should gain
   An interest in the Saviour's blood!   Eph. 1:7, 14
Died he for me? — who caused his pain!   Gal. 2:20
   For me — who him to death pursued.   Acts 9:4–5
Amazing love! how can it be   Isa. 29:14, 1 Jn. 3:1
That thou, my God, shouldst die for me?   Mk. 15:39, Gal. 2:20

'Tis mystery all! the Immortal dies!   1 Cor. 2:7–8, Phil. 2:6–8
  Who can explore his strange design?   Isa. 28:21
In vain the first-born seraph tries   Job. 38:7, Isa. 6:2
  To sound the depths of love divine.   Eph. 3:18–19
'Tis mercy all! Let earth adore;   Hab. 2:20
Let angel minds enquire no more.   1 Pet. 1:12

He left his Father's throne above,   Jn. 6:38, Rev. 22:3
  So free, so infinite his grace!   2 Cor. 8:9
Emptied himself of all but love,   Phil. 2:7 (R.V. marg.)
  And bled for Adam's helpless race: Rom. 5:12, 14, Rev. 5:9
'Tis mercy all, immense and free!   Ps. 145:9, Rom. 11:32
For O my God! it found out me!   Acts 9:15, Gal. 1:15–16

Long my imprisoned spirit lay,   Acts 12:4–6, Jn. 8:34
  Fast bound in sin and nature's night: Rom. 6:17, 1 Cor. 2:14
Thine eye diffused a quickening ray;*   Jn. 1:4
  I woke; the dungeon flamed with light;   Acts 12:7–8
My chains fell off, my heart was free,   Ps. 119:32 (B.C.P), Zech. 9:12
I rose, went forth, and followed thee.   Jn. 8:36, Rom. 6:18

No condemnation now I dread,   Rom. 8:1
  Jesus, and all in him, is mine: Rom. 8:32
Alive in him, my living Head,   1 Cor. 15:22, Col. 1:18
  And clothed in righteousness divine,   Isa. 61:10, Ecclus. 27:8
Bold I approach the eternal throne,   Eph. 3:12, Heb. 10:19–22
And claim the crown, through Christ,   2 Tim. 4:8
  my own.

---

* Cf. Pope, *Eloisa to Abelard*, i. 145: 'Thy eyes diffused a reconciling ray'.

It would appear that on the whole the converts won by the Revival were men and women of a relatively humble station in society, but of a generally 'respectable' manner of life. However, at times a splendid gospel breakthrough was made into the great mass of the down-trodden, the ignorant, and the degraded. A salient example of this was the early preaching to the Kingswood coal-miners, which is commemorated in Charles Wesley's stirring and outspoken 'Hymn for the Kingswood Colliers'. The second verse contains some fine lines which deserve to be remembered.

P.W. i. 287; W.H. 203; M.H.B. 379

Glory to God, whose sovereign grace   Ex. 33:19, Rom. 9:14–15
  Hath animated senseless stones;   Matt. 3:9
Called us to stand before his face,   Deut. 16:16
  And raised us into Abraham's sons!   Matt. 3:9, Gal. 3:7

The people that in darkness lay,   Isa. 60:2
  In sin and error's deadly shade,   Jn. 3:19–20, 1 Jn. 2:11

Have seen a glorious gospel day,   Lk. 1:78, 2 Pet. 1:19
   In Jesu's lovely face displayed.   2 Cor. 4:4, 6

Thou only, Lord, the work hast done,   Ps. 74:13 (B.C.P.), Rom. 9:16
   And bared thine arm in all our sight;   Isa. 52:10
Hast made the reprobates thine own,   Rom. 1:28, 11:32, Tit. 1:16
   And claimed the outcasts as thy right.   Isa. 43:1, Lk. 14:23

Thy single arm, almighty Lord,   Gen. 17:1, Ps. 77:15, 89:13
   To us the great salvation brought,   Isa. 51:9, 52:10, 59:16
Thy Word, thy all-creating Word,   Ps. 33:6, Jn. 1:3
   That spake at first the world from nought.*   Gen. 1:3, Heb. 11:3,
                                              Rev. 4:11

For this the saints lift up their voice,   Isa. 40:9, Acts 4:24
   And ceaseless praise to thee is given;   Ps. 34:1, 71:6, 1 Pet. 4:11
For this the hosts above rejoice,   Rev. 5:9–14, 7:11–12, 15
   We raise the happiness of heaven.   Lk. 15:7, 10

Suffice that for the season past   Heb. 11:25, 1 Pet. 4:3
   Hell's horrid language filled our tongues,   Jas. 3:5–8
We all thy words behind us cast,   Ps. 50:17
   And lewdly sang the drunkard's songs.   Ps. 69:12

But, O the power of grace divine!   Lk. 9:43, 2 Cor. 4:7
   In hymns we now our voices raise,   Eph. 5:19, Col. 3:16
Loudly in strange hosannas join,   Ps. 40:3, Matt. 21:9
   And blasphemies are turned to praise!   1 Tim. 1:13

---

* ' 'Twas great to speak a world from nought'
   (S. Wesley, Jun., 'A Hymn for Sunday' *Poems* (1736) p. 241, line 15.)

42. Communion with Christ

The life of those who have been truly converted is one of communion with Christ. This intense sense of personal fellowship with a personal Saviour is celebrated in beautiful devotional verse. We find that Wesley strongly disowns 'mysticism' as a dangerous error, but it is important to discern what he means by this term. He has in mind such teaching as: (i) 'Quietism', or the notion that the path to interior and spiritual religion is withdrawal from the disciplined means of grace in the Church, into private meditation, (ii) the unevangelical teaching that interior and spiritual religion is to be earned by the discipline of self-denial, (iii) that elite believers can hope to rise above the divine revelation recorded in scripture, and the historic saving work of Jesus Christ, crucified and risen, and so attain to entirely individual and immediate divine illumination. However, the genuine Christian mystic is the one to whom divine grace grants an outstanding and excellent degree of fellowship with God, but securely based on the historic revelation, and saving work in Christ. In this latter sense the Wesley hymns are full of mysticism.

P.W. ix. 362; W.H. 228; M.H.B. 457; H.P. 750

Thou Shepherd of Israel, and mine,	Ps. 23:1, 80:1, Hag. 2:7
The joy and desire of my heart,	Ps. 119:111 (B.C.P.), Eccl. 5:20
For closer communion I pine,	Cant. 5:8
I long to reside where thou art:	Cant. 3:4
The pasture I languish to find,	Ps. 23:2, Cant. 1:7,
	Jn. 10:4
Where all, who their Shepherd obey,	Jn. 10:4, Heb. 5:9
Are fed, on thy bosom reclined,	Isa. 40:11, Jn. 13:23
And screened from the heat of the day.	Isa. 32:2
Ah! show me that happiest place,	Cant. 3:2–3
The place of thy people's abode,	Jn. 14:2, 3
Where saints in an ecstasy gaze,	2 Cor. 12:2
And hang on a crucified God;	Mk. 15:39, Rev. 5:6

131

Thy love for a sinner declare,   Rom. 5:8, 1 Jn. 4:9
   Thy passion and death on the tree;   1 Pet. 2:24, 3:18
My spirit to Calvary bear,   Mk. 8:34, 15:21, Lk. 23:33
   To suffer and triumph with thee.   Rom. 8:17

'Tis there, with the lambs of thy flock,   Isa. 40:11
   There only, I covet to rest,   Matt. 11:28–9
To lie at the foot of the rock,   Isa. 26:4 (R.V. marg.) 32:2
   Or rise to be hid in thy breast;   Cant. 1:13, Jn. 13:23, 25
'Tis there I would always abide,   Jn. 15:4, 1 Jn. 2:17
   And never a moment depart,   Rev. 3:12
Concealed in the cleft of thy side,   Ex. 33:22, Jn. 19:34
   Eternally held in thy heart.   Jer. 31:3, Jn. 15:10

P.W. ii. 263; W.H. 358; M.H.B. 465; H.P. 540

Open, Lord, my inward ear,   Job 33:16
   And bid my heart rejoice;   Ps. 33:21
Bid my quiet spirit hear   1 Pet. 3:4
   Thy comfortable voice;   Isa. 40:2
Never in the whirlwind found,   1 Kgs. 19:11–12
   Or where earthquakes rock the place,
Still and silent is the sound,
   The whisper of thy grace.

From the world of sin, and noise,   Matt. 6:6, Lk. 6:12
   And hurry, I withdraw;   Isa. 52:11, 2 Cor. 6:17
For the small and inward voice   1 Kgs. 19:12, 13
   I wait with humble awe;   Isa. 57:15, 1 Pet. 5:6
Silent am I now and still,   Hab. 2:20
   Dare not in thy presence move;   Ex. 14:13
To my waiting soul reveal   Ps. 130:5
   The secret of thy love.   Eph. 3:19

Thou didst undertake for me,   Isa. 38:14
   For me to death wast sold;   Zech. 11:12, Matt. 27:9
Wisdom in a mystery   1 Cor. 2:7
   Of bleeding love unfold;   Jn. 10:15, 15:13
Teach the lesson of thy cross,   1 Cor. 1:18–20, 23–4
   Let me die with thee to reign;   Jn. 11:16, Rom. 5:17, 6:8,
                                  Phil. 3:10–11

All things let me count but loss,   Phil. 3:7–8
   So I may thee regain.   Jas. 3:19–20

Show me, as my soul can bear,   Ps. 51:5, Jn. 16:12
   The depth of inbred sin!   Jer. 17:9, Rom. 5:12, 14
All the unbelief declare,   Mk. 6:6, Heb. 3:12, 19
   The pride that lurks within;   Ps. 10:4, 1 Jn. 2:16

Take me, whom thyself hast bought,	1 Cor. 6:20
Bring into captivity	2 Cor. 10:5
Every high aspiring thought,	Job 33:17
That would not stoop to thee.	

Lord, my time is in thy hand,	Ps. 31:15
My soul to thee convert;	Ps. 19:7, 51:13, Lk. 22:32
Thou canst make me understand,	Ps. 119:27
Though I am slow of heart;	Lk. 24:25
Thine in whom I live and move,	Acts 17:28
Thine the work, the praise is thine;	Num. 23:23, Ps. 74:13 (B.C.P)
Thou art wisdom, power and love,	1 Cor. 1:24, 1 Jn. 4:9
And all thou art is mine.	Cant. 2:16

In the following most earnest and aspiring prayer for the fulness of divine communion, which is the work of the Spirit in the heart, Charles Wesley is not to be supposed to imply the pantheistic doctrine that human souls are 'drops of divinity', whose destiny is that their separate personal existence will be lost in the impersonal ocean of Deity'. The scriptural Christian doctrine is that the eternal God is a personal Being, and the destiny of human souls in Christ is an eternal life of personal fellowship with that God. Thus, however close be the spiritual communion between the believer and God, the clear distinction of existence between God as the personal Creator, and the personal human soul as created by God, is preserved in heaven.

P.W. i. 164; W.H. 374; M.H.B. 299; H.P. 282

Come, Holy Ghost, all quickening fire,	Matt. 3:11, Jn. 6:63
Come, and in me delight to rest;	1 Pet. 4:14
Drawn by the lure of strong desire,	Ps. 27:4, 38:9, 145:19
O come and consecrate my breast!	Gal. 4:6
The temple of my soul prepare,	1 Cor. 3:16–17
And fix thy sacred presence there.	

If now thy influence I feel,	1 Cor. 12:11
If now in thee begin to live,	Rom. 8:9, Gal. 5:25
Still to my heart thyself reveal,	1 Cor. 2:10, 1 Pet. 4:6
Give me thyself, for ever give:	Jn. 14:16
A point my good, a drop my store,	1 Kgs. 17:12
Eager I ask, I pant for more.	Ps. 42:1

Eager for thee I ask and pant,	Ps. 42:1
So strong the principle divine	
Carries me out with sweet constraint,*	2 Cor. 5:14
Till all my hallowed soul is thine;	Ezek. 18:4
Plunged in the Godhead's deepest sea,	
And lost in thine immensity.	Isa. 40:12, 15

My peace, my life, my comfort thou,   Acts 9:31, Rom. 8:10,
   My treasure, and my all thou art!   Wisd. 7:14, Eph. 4:3
True witness of my sonship, now   Rom. 8:14, 16
   Engraving pardon on my heart,   Jer. 31:33
Seal of my sins in Christ forgiven,   2 Cor. 1:22, Eph. 1:13, 4:30
Earnest of love, and pledge of heaven.   2 Cor. 5:5, Eph. 1:14

Come then, my God, mark out thine heir,   Rom. 8:17, Gal. 3:29, 4:7
   Of heaven a larger earnest give!   Tit. 3:5–7
With clearer light thy witness bear,   Prov. 4:18
   More sensibly within me live;   Rom. 8:11
Let all my powers thine entrance feel,   Eph. 3:16
And deeper stamp thyself the seal.   1 Cor. 15:49, 2 Cor. 3:18,
                                                      Eph. 1:13, 4:30

---

* . . . 'But I love thee
  By love's own sweet constraint, and will for ever
  Do thee all rights of service.'   (Shakespeare, *All's Well that
                                              Ends Well*, ii. 16–19.)

43.   The Life of Trust

f it be once fully realized that in Christ crucified and risen God has provided a convincing pledge that, despite the manifold wrong and tragedy which exist in the world, he is in fact the loving Father, that he has conquered the power of evil, and that he has opened to the believer a sure way in which the sorrows and temptations of life can be not merely endured, but transmuted into the means of spiritual good, a vitally important consequence follows. The believer can look out on life in a difficult world fortified with a courage that nothing can shake. Thus trust in God is the way of life for the converted man or woman. The life of trust is set forth in John Wesley's fine translation, loved by generations of Methodists, of J. A. Rothe's (1688–1758) 'Ich habe nun den Grund gefunden', which had been published by his one-time patron Zinzendorf. See H. B. Bett, *The Hymns of Methodism*, pp. 18–19.

P.W. i. 279; W.H. 189; M.H.B. 375; H.P. 684

Now I have found the ground wherein	Col. 1:23
Sure my soul's anchor may remain,	Heb. 6:19
The wounds of Jesus, for my sin	Isa. 53:5, Zech. 13:6
Before the world's foundation slain;	1 Pet. 3:18, Rev. 13:8
Whose mercy shall unshaken stay,	Ps. 103:17, Heb. 12:27
When heaven and earth are fled away.	Rev. 20:11
Father, thine everlasting grace	Jer. 31:3
Our scanty thought surpasses far,	Isa. 55:8–9, Eph. 3:19
Thy heart still melts with tenderness,	Ps. 103:13, 145:9, Hos. 11:8
Thy arms of love still open are,	Isa. 65:2, Lk. 15:20
Returning sinners to receive,	Isa. 55:7, Mal. 3:7
That mercy they may taste and live.	Ps. 34:8, 1 Pet. 2:3, 25
O Love, thou bottomless abyss,	Rom. 11:33, Eph. 3:18–19
My sins are swallowed up in thee!	Mich. 7:19
Covered is my unrighteousness,	Ps. 32:1, 85:2, Rom. 4:7
Nor spot of guilt remains on me,	1 Tim. 6:14, 2 Pet. 3:14

While Jesu's blood, through earth and skies,	1 Jn. 5:7–8
Mercy, free, boundless mercy, cries.	Ps. 36:5, 57:10, 108:4

With faith I plunge me in this sea,*	Isa. 43:2, Matt. 14:29–30
Here is my hope, my joy, my rest;	Ps. 43:4, Matt. 11:28, Rom. 5
Hither, when hell assails, I flee,	Ps. 55:6, 143:9
I look into my Saviour's breast;	Jn. 13:25, Jude 24
Away, sad doubt, and anxious fear!	Ps. 55:22, Matt. 14:31
Mercy is all that's written there.	Ps. 86:5, 103:8, Dan. 9:18

Though waves and storms go o'er my head,	Isa. 43:2, Jonah 2:3
Though strength, and health, and friends be gone,	Ps. 38:6–11
Though joys be withered all and dead,	Ezek. 24:16, 18, 25
Though every comfort be withdrawn,	2 Cor. 1:8–9
On this my steadfast soul relies,	Ps. 130:5, 6, 141:8, 1 Pet. 5:9
Father, thy mercy never dies.	Ps. 138:8

Fixed on this ground will I remain,	Ps. 57:7, 112:7
Though my heart fail, and flesh decay;	2 Cor. 4:16
This anchor shall my soul sustain,	Heb. 6:19
When earth's foundations melt away;	Ps. 102:25–7, 2 Pet. 3:10
Mercy's full power I then shall prove,	1 Pet. 1:5
Loved with an everlasting love.	Jer. 31:3

---

* Peter indeed plunged, but lacked sufficient faith.

This noble hymn of Christian trust provides an outstanding example of the manner in which Charles Wesley's verses have sometimes been selected and arranged from longer works. The first two verses are from one poem, and are printed in the reversed order from the original, and the second two verses from an entirely separate composition. They were arranged next to one another by Wesley in the 1780 hymnal, and the four verses united, with another in the 1904 book.

P.W. v.17 and iv. 479; W.H. 281, 282; M.H.B. 531; H.P. 681

Light of the world, thy beams I bless,	Jn. 1:9, 8:12, 9:5
On thee, bright Sun of righteousness,	Ps. 112:4, Mal. 4:2
My faith hath fixed its eye;	Ps. 25:15, 141:8, Heb. 12:2
Guided by thee, through all I go,	Ps. 32:8, 78:52, Isa. 30:21
Nor fear the ruin spread below,	Isa. 25:2, 4
For thou art always nigh.	Ps. 145:18

Not all the powers of hell can fright	Ps. 27:3, Isa. 41:13–14
A soul that walks with Christ in light,	1 Jn. 1:7

He walks and cannot fall;	Prov. 3:23, Jer. 31:9
Clearly he sees, and wins his way,	Mk. 8:25, Jn. 14:4
Shining unto the perfect day,	Prov. 4:18
And more than conquers all.	Rom. 8:37
I rest in thine almighty power;	Ps. 37:7, 91:1, Lk. 9:43
The name of Jesus is a tower,	Prov. 18:10
That hides my life above:	Col. 3:3
Thou canst, thou wilt my Keeper be;	Ps. 121:5
My confidence is all in thee,	1 Jn. 5:14
The faithful God of love.	Deut. 7:9, 1 Cor. 10:13, 1 Jn. 4:8
Wherefore, in never-ceasing prayer	1 Thess. 5:17
My soul to thy continual care	1 Pet. 5:7
I faithfully commend;	Ps. 31:6 (B.C.P.)
Assured that thou through life shalt save,	Ps. 23:6
And show thyself beyond the grave	Jn. 14:2–3
My everlasting Friend.	Jer. 31:3

This fine devotional poem is an outstanding example of Charles Wesley's skill in the use of Scripture. It is a paraphrase of Psalm 121, but the language of the paraphrase is itself an assembly of quotations and allusions to many parts of the Bible.

P.W. viii. 235; W.H. 618; M.H.B. 497

To the hills I lift mine eyes,	Ps. 121:1
The everlasting hills;	Deut. 33:15
Streaming thence in fresh supplies	Isa. 30:25, Phil. 1:19
My soul the Spirit feels.	1 Pet. 4:14
Will he not his help afford?	Ps. 121:2
Help while yet I ask, is given:	Ps. 20:2, 121:2, Heb. 4:16
God comes down; the God and Lord	Ex. 3:8, Ps. 72:6, 144:5
That made both earth and heaven.	Ps. 121:2
Faithful soul, pray always; pray,	Lk. 18:1, 1 Thess. 5:17
And still in God confide;	Ps. 57:1, Prov. 3:26
He thy feeble steps shall stay,	Ps. 37:23, 121:3
Nor suffer thee to slide:	Ps. 26:1, 37:31
Lean on thy Redeemer's breast:	Ps. 19:14, Jn. 13:23, 21:20
He thy quiet spirit keeps;	1 Pet. 3:4
Rest in him, securely rest;	Ps. 37:7, Matt. 11:28, 29
Thy watchman never sleeps.	Ps. 121:3, 4
Neither sin, nor earth, nor hell	
Thy Keeper can surprise,	Ps. 121:5

Careless slumbers cannot steal	Ps. 121:3, 4
On his all-seeing eyes;	Gen. 16:13, Job 34:21
He is Israel's sure defence;	Ps. 121:5 (B.C.P.)
Israel all his care shall prove	Deut. 11:12, 1 Pet. 5:7
Kept by watchful providence,	Gen. 22:14, Jer. 31:28, Heb. 11:40
And ever-waking love.	Isa. 50:4
See the Lord, thy Keeper stand	Ps. 121:5, Acts 17:27
Omnipotently near!	Ps. 145:18, Rev. 19:6
Lo! he holds thee by thy hand,	Isa. 42:6
And banishes thy fear;	Isa. 41:10
Shadows with his wings thy head;	Ps. 17:8, 121:5
Guards from all impending harms:	Ps. 121:7
Round thee and beneath are spread	Deut. 33:27
The everlasting arms.	
Christ shall bless thy going out,	Ps. 121:8
Shall bless thy coming in;	
Kindly compass thee about,	Ps. 5:12
Till thou art saved from sin;	Matt. 1:21, Heb. 9:14
Like thy spotless Master, thou,	Lk. 6:40, 1 Pet. 1:19
Filled with wisdom, love, and power,	2 Tim. 1:7
Holy, pure and perfect, now,	Lev. 19:2, Matt. 5:48
Henceforth, and evermore.	Ps. 121:8

44.   Holiness

The new form of life which begins with the New Birth is a progressive growth in grace under the influence of the Spirit, working through the continued discipline of the means of grace, and moral experience. This progression is described as sanctification. It was a salient feature of the teaching of the Wesleys that the proper and expected climax of the life of sanctification is 'entire sanctification'. A number of characteristic terms are used, almost synonymously, to refer to this goal of the Christian life. They are 'scriptural holiness', 'holiness', 'Christian perfection', and 'perfect love'. Of these, 'perfect love' is perhaps the most descriptive of what Wesley had in mind in his teaching. If we may compress the drift of Wesley's teaching into a single formula, 'holiness' or 'Christian perfection' consists in 'entire victory over all *wilful* sin'.

He definitely disowned the notion of 'sinless perfection' as possible in this present life. The believer cannot expect to be lifted by grace clean above every natural human limitation of bodily, nervous, or psychological constitution. One cannot come to a condition where it is impossible to be tempted. However, the 'perfected' believer will immediately recognize the temptation for what it is, and by grace not fall to it. The believer cannot in this life come to such a degree of moral discernment as to be immune to the effect of surprise, inexperience, or human misunderstanding. Nevertheless, the 'perfected' believer, when he discovers that inevitable human limitation has allowed him to slip into error, will not dally with wrong, but will gladly and immediately repent, make restitution, and having learned by experience, will slip that way no more. Thus Christian Perfection is not perfect performance, but perfect love. Therefore the 'perfected' still need to pray for divine forgiveness.

The believer is apt to find within the heart a tension between the new Christian principle of life, and the remains of the old way in obstinate rebellion against it. The gift of 'perfect love' is a divine release from that tension, so that the whole of the powers of the personality flow out in the direction of glad obedience. So the 'perfected' can still grow in grace. The logician may indeed raise the cavil that a 'perfection' which can be improved is not 'perfect'. However, Wesley is not interested in theoretical points of this sort but is a practical moralist. The justification for the doctrine that the only proper goal for Christian growth in grace is 'entire victory over all wilful sin' is that the alternative involves the implication that some degree of knowing compromise with sin is in principle inevitable in the Christian life. This is a denial of God's power 'to save to the uttermost' (Heb. 7:25), and involves a dangerous 'lowering of the sights' of Christian moral discipline.

It is important to remember that Christian Perfection, or Holiness is a divine gift of grace, a work of the Spirit, and not the reward of superior diligence in moral discipline. The 'perfected' are still as completely dependent upon divine grace as other believers. Nevertheless, God will not grant the 'unspeakable gift' (2 Cor. 9:15) unless the believer waits upon him steadfastly, patiently, and wholeheartedly in the devotional and moral discipline of the Christian life. And Wesley also plainly warned that the gift, once granted, can be lost if the believer becomes slack in discipline. There is no room whatever for presumption. Wesley also taught that the gift of Perfect Love is to be expected in a decisive moment of illumination and liberation. Thus some have described the gift of Holiness as 'the second blessing'.

A point of some uncertainty is Wesley's affirmation that all sincere evangelical believers must come in the end to the gift of Perfect Love or Holiness, because it is the divine endowment 'without which no man shall see the Lord' (Heb. 12:14). However, as so many undoubtedly saintly and sincere believers did not appear to attain Perfect Love, Wesley taught that it would be granted at the moment of death, to fit them for heaven. This view must not be confused with the easy-going supposition that the mere death of the body will in some way work advancement in heavenly blessing to those who in this life have been careless in Christian discipleship. Clearly, if a man or woman is alienated from God, that which separates them does not reside in the body of flesh and blood as such, but in the heart, the affections, and the moral will.

Finally, it must be observed that the numerous and searching hymns on the subject of Holiness, which are so characteristic and precious a part of the Wesley heritage, are aspiring prayers for the gift, not claims to have attained. This is a prudent limitation, because modesty about one's own spiritual attainments is surely one of the marks of the true saint.

Wesley records, in his *Plain Account of Christian Perfection* (1767), that he translated the following hymn from the German of Gerhard Tersteegen in Savannah, in 1736 (i.e., well before the evangelical experience at Aldersgate Street). This is cited as part of the evidence that in his early Holy Club period he was consciously living in pursuit of Holiness. Significantly, however, as later published by the more clearly evangelical Wesley, the second half of the fourth verse was changed from the original translation, which read:

> Ah tear it thence, that thou alone
>   May'st reign unrivall'd Monarch there;
> From earthly loves I must be free
> Ere I can find repose in thee.

The purpose of this change is to avoid the implication that Holiness is to be attained by the merit of self-imposed discipline. It is the expected climax of the gracious gift of God.

P.W. i. 71; W.H. 344; M.H.B. 433; H.P. 544

Thou hidden love of God, whose height,	Isa. 45:15, Eph. 3:9, 18
Whose depth unfathomed, no man knows,	
I see from far thy beauteous light,	Heb. 11:13
Inly I sigh for thy repose;	Heb. 4:9, 11
My heart is pained, nor can it be	Ps. 55:4
At rest, till it finds rest in thee.*	
Thy secret voice invites me still	Ps. 25:14, Amos 3:7
The sweetness of thy yoke to prove;	Matt. 11:30
And fain I would; but though my will	Rom. 7:18
Seems fixed, yet wide my passions rove;	Rom. 7:5 (R.V.)
Yet hindrances strew all the way;	1 Thess. 2:18
I aim at thee, yet from thee stray.	Isa. 53:6, 2 Pet. 2:15
'Tis mercy all that thou hast brought	Eph. 2:4
My mind to seek her peace in thee;	Rom. 5:1, Eph. 2:14
Yet while I seek but find thee not,	Job 11:7, 23:3, 8–9
No peace my wandering soul shall see;	Isa. 48:22
O when shall all my wanderings end,	Ps. 119:10
And all my steps to thee-ward tend!	Ps. 37:23
Is there a thing beneath the sun	Eccl. 3:16, 4:7, 5:13, 10:5
That strives with thee my heart to share?	Jer. 3:10
Ah, tear it thence, and reign alone,	Matt. 5:29
The Lord of every motion there!	Jer. 24:7
Then shall my heart from earth be free,	Rom. 6:22
When it hath found repose in thee.	Matt. 11:28–9, Heb. 4:3–5, 9
O hide this self from me, that I	Jas. 5:20
No more, but Christ in me, may live!	Gal. 2:20
My vile affections crucify,	Rom. 1:26, Gal. 5:24
Nor let one darling lust survive!	Rom. 13:14, 1 Pet. 4:2

In all things nothing may I see	1 Cor. 2:2
Nothing desire or seek, but thee!	

Each moment draw from earth away	Jn. 6:44, 12:32
My heart, that lowly waits thy call;	1 Sam. 3:9–10, Isa. 6:8
Speak to my inmost soul, and say,	Matt. 8:8, Mk. 10:49
'I am thy love, thy God, thy all!'	Cant. 2:10, Ps. 50:7, Eph. 4:6
To feel thy power, to hear thy voice,	Heb. 4:7
To taste thy love, be all my choice.	Ps. 34:8, Cant. 2:4,
	Lk. 10:42, 1 Pet. 2:3

---

* S. Augustine, *Confessions*, i.

This Holiness is in essence a very simple thing, yet most profound and searching. It is a heart dominated by the love of God in Christ.

P.W. ii. 77; W.H. 343; M.H.B. 550; M.H. 282; H.P. 536

O for a heart to praise my God,	Ps. 86:12
A heart from sin set free!	Rom. 6:18, 22
A heart that always feels thy blood	1 Jn. 1:7
So freely spilt for me!	Lk. 22:20

A heart resigned, submissive, meek,	1 Pet. 5:5–6
My dear Redeemer's throne,	Isa. 59:20
Where only Christ is heard to speak,	Ps. 95:7, Jn. 5:25, 28
Where Jesus reigns alone.	Rom. 5:21, 1 Cor. 8:6

An humble, lowly, contrite heart,	Ps. 51:10, 17, Isa. 57:15
Believing, true, and clean;	Ezek. 36:25, Jn. 20:27, Heb. 10
Which neither life nor death can part	Rom. 8:38
From him that dwells within.	Jn. 6:56, 14:23, Eph. 3:17

A heart in every thought renewed,	Rom. 12:2
And full of love divine,	Rom. 5:5
Perfect, and right, and pure and good,	Matt. 5:8, Lk. 8:15, 1 Tim. 1:5
A copy, Lord of thine.	Ps. 101:2, Col. 3:10

Thy tender heart is still the same,	Jas. 5:11
And melts at human woe:	Matt. 9:36, Heb. 4:15
Jesu, for thee distressed I am,	Phil. 1:23
I want thy love to know.	Eph. 3:19

My heart, thou know'st, can never rest,*	
Till thou create my peace;	Heb. 2:14
Till, of my Eden re-possessed,	Gen. 3:23–4
From every sin I cease.	1 Pet. 4:1

Fruit of thy gracious lips, on me	Lk. 4:22
Bestow that peace unknown,	Jn. 14:27
The hidden manna, and the tree	Rev. 2:17, 22:2, 14
Of life, and the white stone.	

Thy nature, dearest Lord, impart!	Ps. 45:2, 2 Pet. 1:4
Come quickly from above,	Rev. 3:11, 22:20
Write thy new name upon my heart,	Jer. 31:33, Rev. 3:12
Thy new, best name of love.	1 Jn. 4:8, 16

---

* S. Augustine, *Confessions*, 1.

That the love of God shed abroad in the heart is an all-sufficient solace in the time of tragedy and suffering is the theme of another of John Wesley's translations of the German hymns which he sang with the Moravians in America. The original, Paulus Gerhardt's 'O Jesu Christ, mein schönstes Licht' appeared in Cruger's *Praxis*, 1653. In his *Plain Account of Christian Perfection* he records that the second verse was 'the cry of his heart' as, cruelly disappointed at the failure of his mission, he was in 1738 returning from Savannah.

P.W. i. 138; W.H. 373; M.H.B. 430; M.H. 259; H.P. 696

Jesu, thy boundless love to me	Ps. 100:5, 103:17, 145:8–9
No thought can reach, no tongue declare;*	Isa. 55:8–9, Rom. 11:34,
	Eph. 3:18–19, 2 Cor. 12:4
O knit my thankful heart to thee,	Ps. 86:11 (B.C.P.)
And reign without a rival there!	Rom. 5:21
Thine wholly, thine alone, I am,	Matt. 19:21, 1 Thess. 5:23
Be thou alone my constant flame.	Lev. 6:13
O grant that nothing in my soul	1 Jn. 3:23–4
May dwell, but thy pure love alone;	
O may thy love possess me whole,	1 Pet. 2:9 (R.V.)
My joy, my treasure, and my crown!	Ps. 16:11, Matt. 6:21, Phil. 4:1
Strange fires from my heart remove;	Lev. 10:1
My every act, word, thought, be love.	2 Cor. 10:5
O love, how cheering is thy ray!	
All pain before thy presence flies,	Ps. 73:16–17
Care, anguish, sorrow, melt away,	
Where'er thy healing beams arise;	Mal. 4:2
O Jesu, nothing may I see,	1 Cor. 2:2
Nothing desire, or seek, but thee!	Ps. 38:9
Unwearied may I this pursue,	Isa. 40:30–1
Dauntless to the high prize aspire;	Phil. 3:14
Hourly within my soul renew	Rom. 12:2
This holy flame, this heavenly fire;	Lk. 12:49
And day and night be all my care	Lev. 6:9, 11–12
To guard the sacred treasure there.	Mal. 3:17 (R.V.)
Still let thy love point out my way;	Ps. 32:8, Isa. 30:21
How wondrous things thy love	
hath wrought!	Num. 23:23

Still lead me, lest I go astray;	Ps. 5:8
Direct my word, inspire my thought;	2 Thess. 3:5
And if I fall, soon may I hear	Mich. 7:8
Thy voice, and know that love is near.	Deut. 4:36

In suffering be thy love my peace,	2 Cor. 1:5, 7
In weakness be thy love my power;	2 Cor. 12:9
And when the storms of life shall cease,	Mk. 4:39, Phil. 1:23
Jesus, in that important hour,	Heb. 9:27
In death as life be thou my guide,	Ps. 73:24
And save me, who for me hast died.	2 Cor. 5:14–15

---

* 'If love, alas! be pain; the pain I bear,
  No thought can figure, and no tongue declare.'
  (Prior, *Henry and Emma*, lines 283–4.)

The less thoughtful preachers of Holiness have sometimes represented 'the second blessing' almost as though it were an experience of powerful emotion. Certainly those whose hearts are filled with the love of God enjoy peace with God, and frequently great joy, but the essence of Holiness, according to Wesley, is a moral change. The eminent mark of deep religious experience is not abounding joy, but an upright and reformed character, and a life of strict obedience to the moral law of God. Thus the believer, aspiring after Holiness, is to pray for entire victory over sin, rather than for happiness.

P.W. ii. 130–2; W.H. 375; M.H.B. 558; H.P. 747

Saviour from sin, I wait to prove	Matt. 1:21
That Jesus is thy healing name,	Acts 4:10
To lose, when perfected in love,	1 Jn. 2:5, 4:12
Whate'er I have, or can, or am:	Phil. 3:7–8
I stay me on thy faithful word,	Tit. 3:8
The servant shall be as his Lord.	Matt. 10:25

My heart, which now to God aspires,	Ps. 84:2
The following moment cleaves to dust;	Ps. 22:15
My firm resolves, my good desires,	
My holy frames — no more I trust,	1 Cor. 4:4, 2 Cor. 11:17
Poor, feeble, broken reeds, to you;	Isa. 36:6
My goodness melts as morning dew.	Hos. 6:4, 13:3

I feel that thou wouldst have me live,	Ezek. 18:32, 33:11
And waitest now thy grace to show:	Isa. 30:18, Jn. 5:6
When I am willing to receive	Jas. 4:6
The grace, I all thy life shall know;	Acts 2:28, 1 Jn. 1:2
And thou art striving now with me,	Gen. 32:24
To get thyself the victory.	Ps. 98:1

| Answer that gracious end in me | Rom. 14:9 |

For which thy precious life was given,	Mk. 10:45, 1 Pet. 1:19
Redeem from all iniquity,	Hos. 14:2
Restore, and make me meet for heaven;	Col. 1:12
Unless thou purge my every stain,	Ps. 51:7, Heb. 9:14
Thy suffering and my faith are vain.	1 Cor. 15:2, Gal. 2:21

'Tis not a bare release from sin,	
Its guilt and pain, my soul requires;	Rom. 6:1–2, 15
I want a Spirit of power within;	Acts 1:8, 2 Tim. 1:7
Thee, Jesus, thee my heart desires,	Ps. 37:4, 38:9
And pants, and breaks to be renewed,	Ps. 42:1, Ps. 51:10
And washed in thine all-cleansing blood.	Rev. 1:5

I ask not sensible delight,	Job. 13:15, 2 Cor. 4:8–9
The joy and comfort of thy grace;	2 Cor. 1:4, 8–9
Still let me want thy blissful sight,	Ex. 33:22–3, Job 23:3, 8–9
Let me go mourning all my days;	Ps. 38:6, 42:9, 43:2
With trembling awe thy ways adore;	Deut. 28:65, Ps. 2:11
But save me, that I sin no more.	1 Jn. 3:9

———————

P.W. i. 328; W.H. 361; M.H.B. 387; H.P. 740

My God! I know, I feel thee mine,	Cant. 2:16, 6:3
And will not quit my claim,	Cant. 3:4
Till all I have is lost in thine,	Phil. 3:7–8
And all renewed I am.	Eph. 4:23, Col. 3:10

I hold thee with a trembling hand,	Phil. 2:12
But will not let thee go,	Gen. 32:26
Till steadfastly by faith I stand,	Acts 2:42, 1 Cor. 16:13
And all thy goodness know.	Rom. 2:4

When shall I see the welcome hour,	Heb. 3:13
That plants my God in me!	Col. 2:7, Jas. 1:21
Spirit of health, and life, and power,	2 Tim. 1:7
And perfect liberty!	2 Cor. 3:17

Jesus, thine all-victorious love	Rom. 8:37
Shed in my heart abroad;	Rom. 5:5
Then shall my feet no longer rove,	Heb. 12:13
Rooted and fixed in God.	Col. 2:7, Jas. 1:21

Love can bow down the stubborn neck,	Deut. 10:16
The stone to flesh convert,	Ezek. 11:19, 36:26
Soften, and melt, and pierce, and break	Joel 2:12–13
An adamantine heart.	Zech. 7:12

O that in me the sacred fire	Lev. 1:7, Isa. 6:6–7,
Might now begin to glow,	Matt. 3:11, Lk. 12:49

Burn up the dross of base desire,	Isa. 1:25, Mal. 3:2–3
And make the mountains flow!	Isa. 64:1–3
O that it now from heaven might fall,	Gen. 19:24, Lk. 17:29
And all my sins consume!	Lk. 3:17
Come, Holy Ghost, for thee I call,	Matt. 3:11, Lk. 3:16
Spirit of burning, come!	Isa. 4:4
Refining fire, go through my heart,	Mal. 3:2–3
Illuminate my soul;	Heb. 10:32
Scatter thy life through every part,	2 Cor. 9:9
And sanctify the whole.	1 Thess. 5:23
My steadfast soul, from falling free,	1 Cor. 15:58, Jude 24
Shall then no longer move;	Col. 1:23
But Christ be all the world to me,	Gal. 6:14
And all my heart be love.	Rom. 5:5

P.W. ii. 319; W.H. 391, 393; M.H.B. 562, 570; M.H. 281; H.P. 726

God of all power, and truth, and grace,	Ps. 31:5, 1 Pet. 5:10
Which shall from age to age endure,	Ps. 102:12, 26–7
Whose word, when heaven and earth	
shall pass,	Mk. 13:31
Remains and stands for ever sure.	Isa. 40:8
That I thy mercy may proclaim,	Exod. 34:6
That all mankind thy truth may see,	1 Tim. 2:4
Hallow thy great and glorious name,	Ezek. 36:22–3
And perfect holiness in me.	2 Cor. 7:1
Thy sanctifying Spirit pour,	Joel 2:28–9, Rom. 15:16
To quench my thirst, and make me clean;	Jn. 4:14, 7:37, 39
Now Father, let the gracious shower,	Ezek. 34:26, 36:25, 27
Descend, and make me pure from sin.	Jn. 16:8, 1 Tim. 5:22
Purge me from every sinful blot,	Ps. 51:7, Ezek. 36:25
My idols all be cast aside;	Isa. 2:20, 31:7
Cleanse me from every evil thought,	Matt. 15:19
From all the filth of self and pride.	Ezek. 22:15, 36:25
Give me a new, a perfect heart,	Ps. 101:2, Ezek. 36:26
From doubt, and fear, and sorrow free;	Matt. 21:21, 1 Jn. 4:18
The mind which was in Christ impart,	1 Cor. 2:16, Phil. 2:5
And let my spirit cleave to thee.	Acts 11:23
Open my faith's interior eye,	Eph. 1:18, Heb. 11:1, 27
Display thy glory from above;	Ps. 148:13
And all I am shall sink and die,	1 Cor. 15:31
Lost in astonishment and love.	Isa. 52:14, Matt. 7:28

Now let me gain perfection's height,	Matt. 5:48, Eph. 4:13
Now let me into nothing fall;	2 Cor. 12:11, 1 Jn. 4:17
Be less than nothing in thy sight,	Isa. 40:17
And feel that Christ is all in all!	Col. 3:11
O that I now, from sin released,	Rom. 6:6–7
Thy word might to the utmost prove,	Heb. 7:25
Enter into the promised rest,	Heb. 4:1
The Canaan of thy perfect love!	Gen. 17:8, Deut. 12:10–11, 1 Jn. 4:12, 17

45.   The Means of Grace

The whole process of salvation, from the first stirrings of penitence to the climax of holiness, is a work of divine grace. At every stage we are dependent upon the initiative of God's love, God's action, God's power. In the last resort the would-be believer, and the believer, has to wait upon God for him to do his work. Our part is to respond. However, this certainly does not mean that Christian discipleship is passive. God has provided a spiritual 'trysting-place' where those who would receive his grace must wait. Attached to this divinely-appointed place of waiting there is a promise, that those who in obedience and fidelity wait there will assuredly receive God's grace. This place of waiting is provided by 'the means of grace', that is to say, worship and spiritual fellowship, prayer, private and public, the reading and study of the Bible, the preaching of the word, and the climax of all in the sacraments.

Thus within the Church there is a path of spiritual discipline actively to be followed by all who would receive the grace of God. Those who are careless of this discipline may sometimes be surprisingly visited by the grace of God, for the sovereign God is not limited in his action to the means of grace which he, for our own good, has instituted. Nevertheless, the discipline of the means of grace is an essential part of the Christian life, and only those who in an obedient, faithful, and expectant spirit use the means can enjoy the security of the divine promise. The true and health-giving spiritual balance in this matter is that the Christian is to use the means of grace, but not to trust diligence in the use of them to accomplish salvation by the merit of self-discipline. We are to trust only the saving work of God in Jesus Christ, and in the operation of the Holy Spirit through the means.

The following verses quote 'Be still, and know that I am God' (Ps. 46:10) because this was the favourite proof-text of Wesley's 'quietist' opponents. These were wrong-headed would-be evangelicals whose error consisted in the notion that the way to wait upon God was to avoid the use of the disciplined means of grace, and to remain in isolated inactivity until God should move, because one could not use the means of grace without trusting in them. Wesley naturally abhorred this error of 'stillness' because it involved the overthrow of the discipline of regular Church-going, reception of Holy Communion, diligent private devotions, and membership of the Society. See also the note on page 153.

P.W. i. 233; W.H. 91, 92

Long have I seemed to serve thee, Lord,	Dan. 10:1
With unavailing pain;	Gal. 5:6, 6:15
Fasted, and prayed, and read thy word,	Mk. 9:29, Acts 17:11
And heard it preached in vain.	Heb. 4:2
Oft did I with the assembly join,	Heb. 10:25
And near thine altar drew;	Ps. 26:6 (B.C.P.), Heb. 13:10
A form of godliness was mine,	2 Tim. 3:5
The power I never knew.	
Where am I now, and what my hope?	Job 17:15
What can my weakness do?	2 Cor. 12:9
Jesus, to thee my soul looks up,	Isa. 17:7, 45:22, Mk. 8:25
'Tis thou must make it new.	2 Cor. 5:17
I see the perfect law requires	Jas. 1:25
Truth in the inward parts,	Ps. 51:6
Our full consent, our whole desires,	Ps. 38:9, Rom. 7:16
Our undivided hearts.	Ps. 119:10, Hos. 10:2,
	Matt. 22:37
Still for thy loving-kindness, Lord,	Ps. 48:8 (B.C.P.)
I in thy temple wait;	
I look to find thee in thy word,	Lk. 24:2, Jn. 5:39, Acts 8:35
Or at thy table meet.	Lk. 24:35, 1 Cor. 10:16
Here, in thine own appointed ways,	Ps. 37:34, Isa. 64:5
I wait to learn thy will;	Ps. 119:33
Silent I stand before thy face,	Ps. 37:7 (R.V. marg.), Hab. 2:20
And hear thee say, 'Be still!'	Ps. 46:10
'Be still! and know that I am God!'—	Ex. 14:13, Ps. 46:10
'Tis all I live to know;	Phil. 3:10
To feel the virtue of thy blood,	Heb. 10:22, 12:24, 1 Pet. 1:2
And spread its praise below.	Ps. 9:14, Mk. 5:20
I wait my vigour to renew,	Isa. 40:31
Thine image to retrieve,	2 Cor. 3:18
The veil of outward things pass through,	Heb. 10:20
And gasp in thee to live.	Ps. 42:1

Fruitless, till thou thyself impart,   1 Cor. 3:6–7, Phil. 2:16
  Must all my efforts prove;
They cannot change a sinful heart;   Jer. 13:23, Rom. 7:23–4
  They cannot purchase love.   Ps. 49:7–8, Rom. 6:23

I do the thing thy laws enjoin,   Acts 10:4
  And then the strife give o'er;   Heb. 4:10
To thee I then the whole resign,   Phil. 3:4–7
  I trust in means no more.   Rom. 11:6, Gal. 2:16

46. Prayer

Prayer as a means of grace is not to be thought of as a means whereby I hope to harness God's power to my human scheme. That implies the denial of the initiative of grace. Prayer is the means whereby I trust to be taken up into God's plan, and used and empowered by his grace for the accomplishment of his good purposes. It is for this reason that authentic Christian prayer always implies the perhaps unspoken clause, 'If it be Thy will'. In this we follow our Lord himself, whose prayer in Gethsemane voices that sacrifice of divine obedience which was accomplished in the Cross (Lk. 22:42).

On the one hand, it is the command of our Lord, and the general witness of Scripture, and of Christian experience, that we are to pray in expression of all various human needs, and to pray believingly and persistently. At the same time, our knowledge of what is God's good will for the world, the Church, our loved ones, and ourselves, is limited, so that we have to face the possibility that even believing and earnest prayer may not apparently be answered, at least in the way we would wish (2 Cor. 12:8–9). Thus we are certainly to pray for the sick, and Christian experience witnesses to many wonders of healing by divine power. Yet that prayer is bound to be denied in the end, for it is part of God's good plan that we should all die, and leave for the unseen world. But more particularly are we to pray for the gift of penitence and faith, and for growth in grace, both for the Church, and individuals, and ourselves.

But how, it may be asked, is the troubled but earnest enquirer after religious experience to pray for the divine gift of faith, if he or she is aware chiefly of doubt? The answer lies in the initiative of divine grace. God's prevenient grace (i.e., the grace that *goes before* the conscious religious experience), offers to all that small initial 'faith as a grain of mustard seed' which enables the sincere searcher to pray: 'Lord, I believe: help thou mine unbelief'. And God can answer this prayer with the gift of stronger faith, which in turn enables more adequate prayer in those who respond. If God's people are praying it

151

may well open the way for his grace to accomplish many blessings which it is not his will to grant if they are not praying.

The following stirring verses remind us that the Christian's warfare is a spiritual, not a merely social or political conflict. Christian action can only accomplish spiritual good if God is guiding it, and his power flowing through it. In fact, it must be the action of spiritually sensitive, that is, of praying men and women.

P.W. v. 40; W.H. 266, 267, 268; M.H.B. 484, 541; M.H. 250; H.P. 719

Soldiers of Christ, arise,	2 Tim. 2:3
And put your armour on,	Eph. 6:11
Strong in the strength which God supplies	Isa. 26:4, 40:29, Phil. 4:19
Through his eternal Son;	2 Tim. 2:1, Heb. 1:8
Strong in the Lord of hosts,	Isa. 47:4, Eph. 6:10
And in his mighty power,	Lk. 9:43, Eph. 1:19
Who in the strength of Jesus trusts	Ps. 40:31, Eph. 1:12
Is more than conqueror.	Rom. 8:37
Stand then in his great might,	Jer. 10:6, Eph. 6:10, 14
With all his strength endued;	Lk. 24:49
But take, to arm you for the fight,	1 Tim. 6:12, 1 Pet. 4:1
The panoply of God;	Eph. 6:13
That, having all things done,	Eph. 6:13, Phil. 4:13
And all your conflicts passed,	Ps. 34:19, Phil. 1:30
Ye may o'ercome through Christ alone,	1 Jn. 5:4, 5, Rev. 2:7, 21:7
And stand entire at last.	Jas. 1:4
But, above all, lay hold	Eph. 6:16
On faith's victorious shield;	
Armed with that adamant and gold, *	
Be sure to win the field:	1 Cor. 15:57
If faith surround your heart,	1 Cor. 7:37
Satan shall be subdued,	Rom. 16:20
Repelled his every fiery dart,	Eph. 6:16
And quenched with Jesu's blood.	1 Jn. 1:7
In fellowship, alone,	Ps. 111:1 (B.C.P.), Matt. 6:6
To God with faith draw near,	Heb. 4:16, 10:22
Approach his courts, besiege his throne,	Ps. 100:4, Isa. 62:7, Lk. 18:7
With all the powers of prayer:	Jas. 5:16–18
Go to his temple, go,	Ps. 48:9, Acts 2:46
Nor from his altar move;	Ps. 26:6, 43:4
Let every house his worship know,	Acts 2:46
And every heart his love.	Acts 4:32
Pour out your souls to God,	Ps. 42:4, Lam. 2:19, 3:20
And bow them with your knees,	Ps. 95:6, Eph. 3:14
And spread your hearts and hands abroad,	Ex. 9:29, 33
And pray for Zion's peace;	Ps. 122:6

Your guides and brethren bear	1 Thess. 5:25, Heb. 13:7
For ever on your mind;	Phil. 2:2
Extend the arms of mighty prayer,	1 Kgs. 8:22, 1 Tim. 2:8
Ingrasping all mankind.	Mal. 1:11, 1 Tim. 2:1
From strength to strength go on,	Ps. 84:7
Wrestle and fight and pray,	1 Cor. 9:26, Eph. 6:12
Tread all the powers of darkness down,	Mal. 4:3, Lk. 22:53, Col. 1:13
And win the well-fought day;	1 Tim. 6:12, 2 Tim. 4:7
Still let the Spirit cry,	Rev. 22:17
In all his soldiers, 'Come',	
Till Christ the Lord descend from high,	1 Thess. 4:16
And take the conquerors home.	Rom. 8:37, 1 Thess. 4:17

---

* 'Satan, with vast and haughty strides advanced,   (Milton, *Paradise Lost*,
  Came towering, armed in adamant and gold'.   vi. 109–110.)

We notice how daringly Wesley turns Satan's equipment against him!

The following verses reflect the dispute which unfortunately arose between the Wesleys and the Moravians, whose fellowship had done so much to bring them to the evangelical experience, and whose hymns, as translated by John Wesley, constitute a characteristic and valuable element in the Methodist heritage of devotion and hymnody. It would be most unfair to charge the Moravians as such with carelessless of discipline in the use of the means of grace, and in morality. However, every movement of fervent religion is liable to be defaced by the proverbial 'lunatic fringe' of extremists, and some who called themselves Moravians had fallen into the error of 'stillness', and even of antinomianism, and greatly troubled the early Methodist Societies. It was this which caused the breach between the original Fetter Lane Society, and Wesley's United Society, and the separation of the Methodists from the Moravians, see Wesley's *Journal*, 1739, Nov. 1–9, Dec. 13–31, 1740, Jan. 1, April 19–30, June 19–28, July 18–20. This illustrates how Wesley was carrying on 'a war on two fronts', against unevangelical formalism and legality on the one hand, and on the other, against the relaxation of discipline, devotional, moral and churchly, in the supposed interest of 'spiritual' religion. This is of salient importance for understanding his preaching.

P.W. iv. 325; W.H. 118

Author of faith, to thee I cry,	Heb. 12:2
To thee, who wouldst not have me die,	Ezek. 18:31–2, 33:11
But know the truth, and live;	Ps. 119:144
Open mine eyes to see thy face,	Ex. 33:11
Work in my heart the saving grace,	Eph. 2:8, 3:20
The life eternal give.	Rom. 6:23
Shut up in unbelief I groan,	Rom. 11:32 (R.V.)
And blindly serve a god unknown,	Acts 17:23
Till thou the veil remove;	2 Cor. 3:14
The gift unspeakable impart,	2 Cor. 9:15
And write thy name upon my heart,	Jer. 31:33, Rev. 3:12
And manifest thy love.	1 Jn. 4:9
I know the work is only thine,	Ps. 74:13 (B.C.P.)
The gift of faith is all divine;	Eph. 2:8
But if on thee we call,	Rom. 10:12–13
Thou wilt the benefit bestow,	Ps. 116:12
And give us hearts to feel and know	Jer. 24:7
That thou hast died for all.	2 Cor. 5:15
Thou bidd'st us knock and enter in,	Matt. 7:7, 13, 11:28
Come unto thee, and rest from sin,	Heb. 4:10, 1 Pet. 4:1
The blessing seek and find;	Joel 2:12–14, Matt. 7:7
Thou bidd'st us ask thy grace, and have;	Ps. 27:8, Heb. 4:16
Thou canst, thou would'st, this moment save	1 Tim. 2:4, 2 Pet. 3:9
Both me and all mankind.	Jn. 3:16
Be it according to thy word!	Ps. 119:41
Now let me find my pardoning Lord,	Mic. 7:18
Let what I ask be given;	Lk. 11:9
The bar of unbelief remove,	Heb. 3:19
Open the door of faith and love,	Acts 14:27
And take me into heaven.	Rev. 4:1

47. The Preaching of the Gospel

A genuine Christian sermon, such as is a fitting part of Christian worship, is much more than a lecture upon the meaning of the Bible, or on Christian doctrine or morals. Certainly the sermon is not to be thought of as the occasion for the preacher to air his or her personal opinions, or display his or her personality and powers of persuasion. Ideally the sermon should take up some part of God's redeeming message, witnessed to in the Bible, and apply it devotionally and personally, and in a challenging manner, to the condition of the hearers in such a way that the Holy Spirit may use the medium of the speaker to convey the gift of penitence and faith to the worshippers. Christian preaching has come to its proper fulfilment when the hearer forgets to say: 'The preacher gave us a good sermon this morning', and comes away with an awareness: 'Christ spoke to me this morning'.

It is for this reason that, on the one hand, although different preachers of various experience and cast of mind may on different occasions declare various portions of God's truth, yet the preacher is under an obligation to declare nothing other than the scriptural faith of the Church. Similarly, the congregation is not normally invited to have a 'question hour', in which they can in turn air their views, because the business of the sermon is devotional rather than instructional, though of course there is an important place in the activity of the Church for instruction and discussion.

We have to admit that preaching does not always rise to the level of a means of grace. This is because the power to bring the hearers to the gift of faith, and build them up in grace, does not arise from human talent. In the last resort it is the mysterious work of the Spirit through the preacher. Thus sometimes a preacher of apparently limited gifts and unimpressive personality may be surprisingly used by God for the advance of the gospel. By contrast, a large congregation may sometimes be gathered by the effective use of Church organization and propaganda, and by the ministry of a personally attractive preacher. Yet sadly it does not always follow from this that the Church is being built up spiritually, and sinners converted to God. So we say that, in the manner of true evangelical power, God *'gives* the Word'. He gives it in his own way, and he gives it in response to the believing prayers of the Church. So times of spiritual revival cannot be 'professionally organized'. They have to be prayed for. Preaching as a means of grace grows out of prayer as a means of grace.

Charles Wesley's fine treatment of the parable of the Great Feast declares the mission and office of the gospel preacher under the title 'Exhorting sinners to return to God'.

P.W. iv. 274; W.H. 2; M.H.B. 323; M.H. 102; H.P. 460

Come, sinners, to the gospel feast,	Isa. 25:6, Lk. 14:16
Let every soul be Jesu's guest;	Rev. 3:20
Ye need not one be left behind,	Matt. 18:12, 13
For God hath bidden all mankind.	Acts 17:30
Sent by my Lord, on you I call,	Lk. 10:1, 14:17
The invitation is to all:	1 Tim. 2:4, 2 Pet. 3:9
Come, all the world; come, sinner, thou!	Jn. 3:16–17, Rom. 11:15
All things in Christ are ready now.	Lk. 14:17
Do not begin to make excuse,	Lk. 14:18
Ah! do not you his grace refuse;	Heb. 10:29
Your worldly care and pleasures leave,	Lk. 8:14
And take what Jesus hath to give.	Jn. 4:10
Your grounds* forsake, your oxen quit,	Lk. 14:18–20
Your every earthly thought forget,	Col. 3:2
Seek not the comforts of this life,	Heb. 11:25
Nor sell your Saviour for a wife.	Deut. 13:6, 8, Lk. 14:20, 26
'Have me excused', why will ye say?	Lk. 14:18
Why will ye for damnation pray?	Jas. 3:5, 8
Have you excused—from joy and peace?	Gal. 5:22
Have you excused—from happiness?	Ps. 144:15
Excused, alas! why should you be	Lk. 14:18
From health, and life, and liberty,	Lk. 4:18
From entering into glorious rest,	Heb. 4:1
From leaning on your Saviour's breast?	Jn. 13:25, 21:20
Yet must I, Lord, to thee complain,	Lk. 14:21
The world hath made thy offers vain;	Mal. 3:14
Too busy, or too happy they,	Matt. 13:22, Lk. 14:18–20
They will not, Lord, thy call obey.	Tit. 1:16
Go then, my angry Master said,	Lk. 14:21
Since these on all my mercies tread,	Heb. 10:29
Invite the rich and great no more,	Lk. 14:12

But preach my gospel to the poor.	Matt. 11:5, Lk. 4:18, 14:21
Come then, ye souls by sin oppressed,	Matt. 11:28–9, Rom. 6:20–1
Ye restless wanderers after rest,	Ps. 55:6, 116:7
Ye poor, and maimed, and halt, and blind,	Lk. 14:21
In Christ a hearty welcome find.	Lk. 15:22–4
Come, and partake the gospel feast;	Isa. 25:6, Matt. 26:29
Be saved from sin; in Jesus rest;	Matt. 11:28–9, 2 Thess. 1:7
O taste the goodness of your God,	Ps. 34:8, 1 Pet. 2:3
And eat his flesh, and drink his blood!	Jn. 6:53–6
Ye vagrant souls, on you I call;	Lk. 14:21, 23
O that my voice could reach you all!	Isa. 40:9, Rom. 10:14–15, 18
Ye all are freely justified,	Acts 13:39
Ye all may live, for God hath died.	Ezek. 33:11, Jn. 10:10, 1 Thess. 5:10
My message as from God receive,	Ps. 68:11, 2 Cor. 5:20
Ye all may come to Christ, and live;	1 Tim. 2:4, 2 Pet. 3:9
O let his love your hearts constrain,	2 Cor. 5:14
Nor suffer him to die in vain!	Gal. 2:21
His love is mighty to compel;	Lk. 14:23, Eph. 1:19, 2:4
His conquering love consent to feel,	Cant. 8:6–7
Yield to his love's resistless power,**	Lk. 14:23, Rom. 9:19
And fight against your God no more.	2 Chron. 13:12, Acts 5:39
See him set forth before your eyes,	Gal. 3:1
Behold the bleeding Sacrifice!	Heb. 9:14, 26, Rev. 5:6
His offered benefits embrace,	Ps. 68:19, Rom. 6:23
And freely now be saved by grace.	Eph. 2:8
This is the time; no more delay!	Lk. 14:17
This is the acceptable day,	Isa. 61:2, Lk. 4:19
Come in, this moment, at his call,	Lk. 14:17
And live for him who died for all.	2 Cor. 5:14, 15

---

* i.e. fields
** 'Masters' demands come with a power resistless'.

(Milton, *Samson Agonistes*, line 1404.)

The compelling sanction behind the evangelist's witness to the atoning work of Christ is the personal testimony that he himself has been wonderfully converted.

P.W. v. 115, iii. 6; W.H. 40, 5; M.H.B. 329, 311

Ye neighbours, and friends of Jesus, draw near!	Lk. 15:6, Jn. 15:14, 15
His love condescends by titles so dear	2 Cor. 5:20
To call, and invite you his triumph to prove,	2 Cor. 2:14
And freely delight you in Jesus's love.	Cant. 2:3–4

Thy faithfulness, Lord, each moment we find,	Isa. 11:5, Lam. 3:23
So true to thy word, so loving and kind;	Jer. 31:3, Rev. 21:5
Thy mercy so tender to all the lost race,	Ps. 145:9
The foulest offender may turn and find grace.	Isa. 1:18, 55:7, Zech. 13:1

The mercy I feel to others I show,	Ps. 40:9–10
I set to my seal that Jesus is true!	Jn. 3:33
Ye all may find favour who come at his call:	Jn. 6:37
O come to my Saviour, his grace is for all.	Rom. 11:32, 1 Tim. 2:4, 2 Pet. 3:9

O let me commend my Saviour to you!	Lk. 22:32
The publicans' Friend, and Advocate too;	Matt. 11:19, 1 Jn. 2:1
For you he is pleading his merits and death,	Rom. 3:25, 1 Jn. 2:2, 4:10
With God interceding for sinners beneath.	Heb. 7:25, 9:11–14

To us, and to them, is published the word;	Acts 10:37, 13:49
Then let us proclaim our life-giving Lord,	Isa. 61:1, Jn. 6:33
Who now is reviving his work in our days,	Hab. 3:2, Acts 17:30
And mightily striving to save us by grace.	2 Cor. 13:3, Gal. 2:8, Eph. 1:19

O Jesus, ride on till all are subdued,	Ps. 45:4, Heb. 2:8, Rev. 19:11
Thy mercy make known, and sprinkle thy blood,	Isa. 52:15, Hab. 3:2, Heb. 12:24, 1 Pet. 1:2
Display thy salvation, and teach the new song,	Ps. 40:3, Lk. 2:30, Rev. 5:9, 14:3
To every nation, and people, and tongue.	Isa. 66:18, Mic. 4:2

The spiritual equipment of the Christian minister, which enables him or her to exercise an effective ministry, is the gift of God, who commissions the minister.

P.W. ii. 343; W.H. 744; M.H.B. 791; H.P. 772

Jesus, thy wandering sheep behold!	Ezek. 34:6
See, Lord, with yearning pity see	Matt. 9:36
Lost sheep that cannot find the fold,	Jn. 10:16
Till sought and gathered in by thee.	Ezek. 11:17, Lk. 15:5, 1 Pet. 2:25

Lost are they now, and scattered wide,	Ezek. 34:5, 6, Jn. 10:12
In pain, and weariness, and want;	Ezek. 34:21
With no kind shepherd near to guide	Num. 27:17, Matt. 15:24
The sick, and spiritless, and faint.	Ezek. 21:7, Matt. 9:36

Thou, only thou, the kind and good,	Ps. 23:1, 80:1, Jn. 10:11
And sheep-redeeming Shepherd art:	Ezek. 34:23, 37:24
Collect thy flock, and give them food,	Ezek. 28:25, 39:28, Jn. 10:9
And pastors after thine own heart.	Jer. 3:15

Give the pure word of general grace,	Ps. 68:11, 1 Tim. 2:4
And great shall be the preachers' crowd;	Acts 5:14, 14:1
Preachers, who all the sinful race	Isa. 1:4, 18, Acts 17:30
Point to the all-atoning blood.	Rom. 3:23–25, 5:11,
	Heb. 9:13–14
Open their mouth, and utterance give;	Ezek. 3:27, Acts 2:4, Eph. 6:19
Give them a trumpet-voice, to call	Isa. 58:1, Jn. 3:16
A world, who all may turn and live	Rom. 10:18, 2 Pet. 3:9
Through faith in him who died for all.	Rom. 3:25, 2 Cor. 5:14
Thy only glory let them seek;	Jn. 7:18
O let their hearts with love o'erflow!	Deut. 6:5, Matt. 22:37
Let them believe, and therefore speak,	Ps. 116:10, 2 Cor. 4:13
And spread thy mercy's praise below.	Matt. 9:31
Mercy for all be all their song,	Ps. 59:16, 101:1
Mercy which every soul may claim,	Ex. 34:6–7, 2 Pet. 3:9
Mercy which doth to all belong,	Rom. 11:32
Mercy for all in Jesus' name.	1 Pet. 1:3

P.W. xii. 260; W.H. 734; M.H.B. 792; H.P. 771

Lord, if at thy command	Matt. 10:7, Mk. 3:14, 4:14
The word of life we sow,	Eccles. 11:6, Phil. 2:16
Watered by thy almighty hand,	Jer. 31:12, Acts 11:21
The seed shall surely grow:	Mk. 4:27
The virtue of thy grace	2 Cor. 9:10
A large increase shall give,	Mk. 4:20, 1 Cor. 3:6, 7
And multiply the faithful race	Isa. 9:3, Acts 6:1
Who to thy glory live.	1 Cor. 10:31, 1 Pet. 2:9
Now then the ceaseless shower	1 Kgs. 18:1, 41, Ps. 65:10
Of gospel-blessings send,	Deut. 32:2, Ezek. 34:26
And let the soul-converting power	Ps. 19:7
Thy ministers attend.	Mk. 16:15, 17
On multitudes confer	Acts 5:14
The heart-renewing love,	Acts 4:32, Rom. 12:2
And by the joy of grace prepare	Tit. 3:7
For fuller joys above.	

In one of his 'Hymns for a Preacher of the Gospel' Wesley fittingly reminds us that those who in a moment of vision and zeal have embarked upon the gospel ministry need to be spiritually vigilant to 'stir up the gift of God which is in them'. It is sadly easy to grow stale in the work, with passage of time. Here is a challenging prayer of consecration.

P.W. v. 105; W.H. 433; M.H.B. 390; H.P. 767

O that I was as heretofore — Rev. 2:5
When first sent forth in Jesu's name — Lk. 10:1, Rom. 10:15
I rushed through every open door, — 1 Cor. 16:9, 2 Cor. 2:12
And cried to all, 'Behold the Lamb!' — Jn. 1:29, 36
Seized the poor trembling slaves of sin, — Deut. 28:65, Rom. 6:20
And forced the outcasts to come in. — Ps. 147:2, Isa. 11:12, 56:8, Lk. 14:23

The God who kills, and makes alive, — Rom. 7:9–13, 1 Cor. 15:22
To me the quickening power impart, — Rom. 4:17, Eph. 2:1
Thy grace restore, thy work revive, — Ps. 23:3, 51:12, Hab. 3:2
Retouch my lips, renew my heart, — Isa. 6:7, 2 Cor. 4:16
Forth with a fresh commission send, — Jonah 3:1, Jn. 21:15–17
And all thy servant's steps attend. — Ps. 37:23

Give me the faith which can remove, — Matt. 17:20, 21:21
And sink the mountain to a plain, — Zech. 4:7
Give me the child-like praying love, — Ps. 26:8
That longs to build thine house again; — Neh. 1:4, 2:4–5
The love which once my heart o'erpowered, — 2 Cor. 5:14
And all my simple soul devoured. — Ps. 69:9

I want an even strong desire, — Rom. 10:1
I want a calmly-fervent zeal, — Rom. 12:11
To save poor souls out of the fire, — Amos. 4:11, Jude 23
And snatch them from the verge of hell, — Isa. 5:14
And turn them to the pardoning God, — Ex. 34:6–7, Mich. 7:18
And quench the brands in Jesu's blood.* — Zech. 3:2, Eph. 1:7, 1 Jn. 1:7, Rev. 1:5

I would the precious time redeem, — Eph. 5:16, Col. 4:5
And longer live for this alone — 1 Pet. 4:2
To spend, and to be spent for them — 2 Cor. 12:15
Who have not yet my Saviour known, — Jn. 1:26
Fully on these my mission prove, — Rom. 15:19, 2 Tim. 4:17
And only breathe, to breathe thy love. — Rom. 14:8

My talents, gifts, and graces, Lord, — Matt. 25:15, Rom. 12:6
Into thy blessed hands receive, — Ps. 31:5
And let me live to preach thy word, — Acts 20:24
And let me to thy glory live, — Ps. 115:1, Eph. 1:12, 14
My every sacred moment spend — Ps. 31:15, 2 Cor. 12:15
In publishing the sinner's friend. — Mk. 1:45, 5:20, Lk. 7:34, Jn. 15:14, 15

Enlarge, inflame, and fill my heart — 2 Cor. 6:11
With boundless charity divine, — 1 Cor. 13:7–8, 13, Eph. 3:19
So shall I all my strength exert, — Eccl. 9:10
And love them with a zeal like thine, — Jn. 2:17, 1 Jn. 4:11
And lead them to thine open side, — Jn. 19:34–5

The sheep for whom their Shepherd died.   Jn. 10:11, 15, Heb. 13:20,
                                                           1 Pet. 5:2

---

* 'Thou who didst save him, snatch the smoking brand
  From out the flames, and quench it in thy blood'.

                                        (Young, *Night Thoughts*, iv. 605–6.)

48. Baptism

The Wesleys carried out their mission in a country where practically everyone, even the ungodly, had been baptized as an infant, apart from the small minority who had been brought up in denominations which do not baptize infants. Therefore the chief Methodist interest in this matter was the practical one, strongly to affirm that those who possessed formal membership of the Church needed to come by a conversion experience to a deeply-committed personal religion. Nevertheless, they also continued plainly to affirm that Baptism is the divinely-appointed rite of incorporation into the Church, and is the occasion of a work of grace in the heart of the one baptized. That is to say, Baptism is in the proper sense of the word a means of grace. Furthermore, the children of the Christian community are to be baptized, upon a promise of Christian nurture. John Wesley affirmed and defended the baptismal doctrine of the Book of Common Prayer, but would not allow the notion of Baptismal Regeneration to be used as a cave of refuge in which the formal Churchman sought to evade the challenge of the evangelist for conversion (*Sermon:* XIV. l, iv. 2, 3, XXXIX iv. 4).

His doctrine may indeed lack logical clarity, but is adapted to the practical good of the situation.

P.W. x. 322; W.H. 893

Jesus, in earth and heaven the same,	Matt. 28:18
Accept a parent's vow,	1 Sam. 1:11, Prov. 31:2
To thee, baptized into thy name,	Matt. 28:19, Acts 8:16
I bring my children now;	1 Cor. 7:14, 2 Tim. 1:5
Thy love permits, invites, commands,	Matt. 19:14, 28:19
My offspring to be blessed;	Mk. 10:16
Lay on them, Lord, thy gracious hands,	Matt. 19:15, 1 Pet. 2:3
And hide them in thy breast.	Isa. 40:11
To each the hallowing Spirit give	Acts 2:38, 8:17, Rom. 1:4
Even from their infancy;	Acts 16:33, 2 Tim. 1:5

Into thy holy church receive	Matt. 28:19, Acts 2:41f.
Whom I devote to thee;	Matt. 18:5
Committed to thy faithful care,	2 Tim. 1:12
Protected by thy blood,	Acts 20:28, 1 Pet. 1:19
Preserve by thine unceasing prayer,	Heb. 7:25
And bring them all to God.	1 Pet. 3:18

49.   The Lord's Supper

The interests of evangelistic preaching and of sacramental worship have often sadly parted company one with another, in a manner quite unfaithful to the witness of the New Testament. This was decidedly not the case with Methodism in its first and most creative days, whatever may have happened in some Methodist circles later. The background of the preaching of the Wesleys was an England in which sacramental devotion was frequently at a low ebb. Except in certain strictly traditionalist circles the sacrament was usually administered at Christmas, Easter, and Pentecost only, being the three days laid down in the Prayer-Book as the minimum. Deeply engrained in the general mind of the laity was the feeling that to go to communion was the business only of the few and pious in the congregation. Furthermore, civil office was in general open only to members of the Church of England, with the consequence that a certificate that one had received the Holy Communion according to the rites of the Established Church was a common qualification for a government post. This unspiritual abuse helped to cast an air of formality upon the Lord's Supper. It was in these somewhat unpropitious circumstances that the Methodist preaching was accompanied by a remarkable wave of sacramental fervour.

The Methodist Society not being a separate Church, it was one of the Rules that the Methodist was to be regular in attendance at Sunday worship in the Parish Church. Wesley made great efforts to maintain this discipline, and was in his Journal constantly able to observe with satisfaction that when he took his people to the Church there were more communicants than there had been for years.* When in London he obtained a building in which he could conduct public worship there were amazing scenes of sacramental devotion (Journal, May 29–June 5, 1743).

There is a sad irony in the circumstance that Wesley's attempted loyalty to the Church of England in fact undermined early Methodist sacramentalism. He would not allow his normally unordained

164

preachers to administer the sacraments in the Methodist Society. Therefore the spiritual affections and loyalties of Methodists came to centre increasingly around their own distinctive acts of worship and fellowship, which were non-sacramental. When Wesley's firm hand of leadership was removed antipathy between Methodists, and Anglican parish clergy whom fervent Methodists considered to be lacking in spiritual understanding and zeal, caused the rank and file of Methodists more and more to absent themselves from the Parish Church. Hence the separated Methodist Church was left as a body where the generally accepted mark of full membership was membership of the Class-meeting, rather than the status of communicant.

We find, then, that eucharistic hymns are strongly represented among the writings of the Wesleys. Dr. Daniel Brevint, a divine of the old seventeenth-century High Church school, while in exile during the rule of Cromwell, had written a devotional manual, 'The Christian Sacrament and Sacrifice'. This much appealed to John Wesley, who characteristically abbreviated it. His brother Charles, equally characteristically, proceeded to versify this matter into 166 'Hymns for the Lord's Supper'. A number of thes are among the finest, and most theologically interesting, of the Wesley hymnody. Wesley published the extract from Brevint, together with the hymns, in a small volume which had wide circulation in early Methodism. This work is generally regarded as definitive for the sacramental teaching of the Wesleys.

Brevint's first heading to be considered is 'Concerning the Sacrament, as it is a Memorial of the Sufferings and Death of Christ'. The word 'memorial' or 'remembrance' has often been misunderstood, and taken in a much reduced sense. The scriptural term 'memorial' has a much richer meaning than that of a memento of the past. It stands for the means by which the effect of God's historic redeeming act in the past is kept alive in present experience. Thus in the Old Testament the Passover meal was first eaten by the Israelites, family by family, on the night in which they were delivered by God out of Egyptian slavery into renewed nationhood. And to eat the Passover from year to year was a declaration that the Israelites of succeeding generations were part of the People of God, sharing still in the historic deliverance. Thus it was the 'memorial'. So in the New Testament our Lord's redeeming sacrifice of victorious moral obedience came to its climax at the time of the Passover, 'in the night in which he was betrayed', at the Last Supper, and in Gethsemane. Christ marked this time of redemption by instituting the renewed Christian Passover, the Sacrament of the Lord's Supper, in the company of his Church, which is the new and true Israel. So the Lord's Supper is likewise a 'memorial', and to partake of it is a declaration that the

Church of succeeding centuries is one body with that original Church which witnessed God's redeeming action in Christ crucified and risen, and that it shares that redemption.

---

* See J. E. Rattenbury, 'The Eucharistic Hymns of J. and C. Wesley', p. 5.

P.W. iii. 228; W.H. 900; H.L.S. 20; M.H.B. 181; H.P. 550

Lamb of God, whose bleeding love	Lk. 22:44, Jn. 19:34, Gal. 2:20
We thus recall to mind,	Lk. 22:19, 1 Cor. 11:24
Send the answer from above,	Heb. 7:25–6, 9:14, 26
And let us mercy find;	2 Tim. 1:18, Heb. 4:16
Think on us, who think on thee,	Mk. 14:72, 16:7, Heb. 4:15
And every struggling soul release:	2 Cor. 4:8–10, 12:7–9
O remember Calvary,	Lk. 23:33
And bid us go in peace.	Lk. 7:50, 8:48
By thine agonizing pain	Heb. 5:7
And sweat of blood we pray,	Lk. 22:44
By thy dying love to man,	Lk. 23:34, Jn. 19:26f. Gal. 2:2
Take all our sins away;	Jn. 1:29, 1 Jn. 3:5
Burst our bonds, and set us free,	Nah. 1:13, Jn. 8:36, Gal. 5:1
From all iniquity release:	Ps. 85:2, Mic. 7:18
O remember Calvary,	Lk. 23:33
And bid us go in peace.	Lk. 7:50, 8:48
Let thy blood, by faith applied,	Rom. 3:25, 1 Pet. 1:2
The sinner's pardon seal,	Acts 5:30.f, Eph. 1:7, 2 Tim. 2
Speak us freely justified,	Rom. 3:24, 4:5
And all our sickness heal:	Matt. 8:16–17, Mk. 2:10–11
By thy passion on the tree	Acts 5:30, 10:39, Gal. 3:13
Let all our griefs and troubles cease;	Isa. 53:4, 2 Thess. 1:7
O remember Calvary,	Lk. 23:33, 1 Pet. 3:18
And bid us go in peace.	Lk. 7:50, 8:48
Never will we hence depart,	Jn. 6:68
Till thou our wants relieve,	Ps. 23:1
Write forgiveness on our heart,	Jer. 31:33f., Heb. 8:10, 12
And all thine image give:	Rom. 8:29, Col. 3:10
Still our souls shall cry to thee,	Lk. 18:7
Till perfected in holiness:	2 Cor. 7:1
O remember Calvary,	Lk. 23:36
And bid us go in peace.	Lk. 7:50, 8:48

'The believer, being prostrate at the Lord's Table, as at the very foot of his cross, should with earnest sorrow confess and lament all his sins, which were the nails and spears that pierced his Saviour. . . . Let us fall amazed at that stroke of divine justice, that could not be satisfied but by the death of God! . . . How deep and holy is this mystery!' (Brevint, ii.8).

P.W. iii. 229; H.L.S. 21; W.H. 701; M.H.B. 191; H.P. 166

God of unexampled grace,	Rom. 5:20, Eph. 2:7, 1 Pet. 5:10
Redeemer of mankind,	Jn. 3:16f., Acts 13:47, Gal. 3:13
Matter of eternal praise	1 Tim. 1:17, Rev. 5:9, 13
We in thy passion find:	Acts 1:3
Still our choicest strains we bring,	Ps. 108:1 (B.C.P.)
Still the joyful theme pursue,	Ps. 95:1
Thee the Friend of sinners sing,	Matt. 11:19, Lk. 7:34
Whose love is ever new.	Jer. 31:3, Lam. 3:22f.
Endless scenes of wonder rise	Isa. 29:14, 1 Cor. 2:7–8
With that mysterious tree,	Acts 10:39, 1 Pet. 1:11–12, 2:24
Crucified before our eyes	Gal. 3:1
Where we our Maker see:	Jn. 1:3
Jesus, Lord, what hast thou done?	Isa. 25:1, 52:14–15, 53:1
Publish we the death divine,	Mk. 15:39, Phil. 2:6, 8
Stop, and gaze, and fall, and own	Jn. 19:25
Was never love like thine!	Jn. 10:11, 15:13,
	Rom. 5:8, 10, Eph. 2:4
Never love nor sorrow was	Lam. 1:12
Like that my Saviour showed;	Isa. 63:9
See him stretched on yonder cross,	Isa. 65:2, Rom. 10:21
And crushed beneath our load!	Isa. 53:4, 6, 2 Cor. 5:21
Now discern the Deity,	Rom. 1:4, 1 Cor. 2:14, 1 Jn. 4:2
Now his heavenly birth declare;	Isa. 53:8, Acts 8:33
Faith cries out, 'Tis he, 'tis he,	1 Cor. 12:3
My God, that suffers there!	Mk. 15:39

'The main intention of Christ herein was . . . to invite us to his sacrifice, not as done and gone many years since, but as to grace and mercy, still lasting, still new, still the same as when it was first offered for us.' (Brevint ii. 7).

P.W. iii. 219; H.L.S. 5; W.H. 708

O thou eternal Victim, slain	Rev. 13:8
A sacrifice for guilty man,	Heb. 9:26, 1 Jn. 2:2, 4:10
By the eternal Spirit made	Heb. 9:14, 9:28
An offering in the sinner's stead,	Isa. 53:6, 1 Pet. 2:24, 3:18
Our everlasting Priest art thou,	Heb. 7:3, 10:12
And plead'st thy death for sinners now.	1 Cor. 15:3, Heb. 7:25
Thy offering still continues new,	Ex. 29:42, Heb. 10:12, 14
Thy vesture keeps its bloody hue,	Isa. 63:1–3, Rev. 19:13
Thou stand'st the ever-slaughtered Lamb,	Rev. 5:6, 13:8
Thy priesthood still remains the same,	Ex. 40:15, Heb. 7:24
Thy years, O God, can never fail,	Ps. 102:27, Heb. 1:12
Thy goodness is unchangeable.	Ps. 52:1

O that our faith may never move,	1 Cor. 15:58, 1 Pet. 5:9
But stand unshaken as thy love!	Jer. 31:3, Heb. 12:27
Sure evidence of things unseen,	Heb. 11:1
Now let it pass the years between,	Ps. 77:10–11
And view thee bleeding on the tree,	Gal. 3:1, 13
My God, who dies for me, for me!	Mk. 15:39, Gal. 2:20

The Holy Spirit represents the principle of present, continuing, personal religious experience. It is his operation which secures that the sacrament is an effective memorial, and means of grace. 'Any other sacrifice by time may lose its strength: but Thou, O eternal Victim, offered up to God through the Eternal Spirit, remainest always the same.' (Brevint ii. 9).

P.W. iii. 226, H.L.S. 16, W.H. 899, M.H.B. 765, H.P. 298

Come, thou everlasting Spirit,	Jn. 14:16, Heb. 9:14
Bring to every thankful mind*	Jn. 14:26, 1 Cor. 14:16, 17
All the Saviour's dying merit,	Rom. 3:25, 1 Jn. 2:2
All his sufferings for mankind!	2 Cor. 5:15
True Recorder of his passion.	1 Pet. 1:11
Now the living faith impart;	1 Cor. 12:3, 9
Now reveal his great salvation;	Isa. 56:1, Rom. 1:17
Preach his gospel to our heart.	Rom 10:9–10
Come, thou Witness of his dying;	Heb. 10:15
Come, Remembrancer divine!	Jn. 14:26
Let us feel thy power, applying	Rom. 8:16, 1 Cor. 12:3
Christ to every soul, — and mine!	Ps. 71:23, 66:16, Ezek. 18:4

It is a pity that national feeling perhaps prevents the wider use of these verses, which so admirably express the idea that for a community of Christians to celebrate the memorial of redemption by our Lord's death represents their claim to be an authentic part of the one original Church, the new and true Israel of God.

---

* Drink this is remembrance that Christ's blood was shed for thee, and be thankful.
                                                  (Communion Service, B.C.P.)

P.W. iii. 224; H.L.S. 13; W.H. 897

Come, all who truly bear	Acts 9:15, 1 Pet. 4:16
The name of Christ your Lord,	Acts 11:26, 2 Tim. 2:19
His last mysterious supper share,	Mk. 14:17–25
And keep his kindest word.	1 Cor. 11:24f.
Hereby your faith approve	Rom. 14:18
In Jesus crucified:	1 Cor. 2:2
'In memory of my dying love,	1 Cor. 11:24
Do this', he said, — and died.	1 Cor. 11:23

The badge and token this,	Eph. 1:13–14
The sure confirming seal,	
That he is ours, and we are his,	Cant. 2:16, 2 Tim. 2:19
The servants of his will;	Eph. 6:6, Rev. 7:3
His dear peculiar ones,	Ps. 135:4, 1 Pet. 2:9
The purchase of his blood,	Acts 20:28
His blood which once for all atones,	Rom. 5:11, Heb. 7:27, 9:28
And brings us now to God.	1 Pet. 3:18
Then let us still profess	1 Tim. 6:12, Heb. 4:14, 10:23
Our Master's honoured name;	Jn. 5:23, Phil. 2:9, Jas. 2:7
Stand forth his faithful witnesses,	Acts 1:8, 2:32, 5:32
True followers of the Lamb,	Jn. 1:36f., Rev. 14:4
In proof that such we are,	2 Cor. 8:24
His saying we receive,	Jn. 3:33
And thus to all mankind declare	Matt. 28:19, Acts 1:8
We do in Christ believe.	Ps. 6:16
Part of his church below,	Phil. 3:20 (R.V.)
We thus our right maintain:	Eph. 2:19–20
Our living membership we show,	Jn. 15:5, 1 Jn. 5:12
And in the fold remain;	Jn. 10:16, 1 Cor. 12:27
The sheep of Israel's fold,	Matt. 19:28, Gal. 6:16
In England's pastures fed;	Ps. 23:2, Jn. 10:9
And fellowship with all we hold,	Acts 2:42, 1 Jn. 1:7
Who hold it with our Head.	Col. 2:19

Brevint's next two sections are united by Wesley under the title: 'As it is a Sign and a Means of Grace'. The general principle of the means of grace is that God has appointed certain acts of devotion and worship as the place where men and women are to wait upon him, if they desire him to come and visit them with his grace. This principle comes to its climax in the sacraments, which are to an eminent degree the means of grace. It is not to be supposed that 'sacramental grace' is a different quality of grace, more saving in its effect than the grace declared in the preaching of the Word, and prayer. The grace of God is the unmerited love of God, and the effectual power of God, and God is always the same, through whatever means he chooses to operate. The special place of the sacraments ordained by our Lord is that there is a special divine promise attached to them.

God has pledged himself to give his grace through these particular means to all who will faithfully use them. When the Church comes together with the intention of doing what Christ commanded should be done, and takes the bread and wine as he ordained, and says over them his solemn words, and then in faith partakes of the same, God's people may be assured of an effectual manifestation of the Lord's presence, and of his saving power.

Thus the sacraments as means of grace answer to the principle of a secure standing before God as covenanted members of the Church. It does not follow from this that those who do not receive the sacraments are spiritually lost, for the sovereign God is not tied to the means of grace which he has ordained. God in his infinite mercy can save all those he sees fit to save, whether or no they have obeyed his ordinance. Nevertheless, those who do not use the sacraments have cut themselves off from the secure divine promise. This is an example of the general principle that it is the business of the Christian preacher to declare the terms of salvation, but not to venture upon any judgment as to whether particular individuals are 'saved' or no. Thus to be a communicant is the generally accepted mark of full committed Church membership.

We totally disown the unenlightened opinion that to go to communion is a mark that one thinks oneself to have attained a creditable standard of Christian discipleship. Even the most devout person has no merit to plead in the presence of the holy God, for all are dependent on grace. Nevertheless, although an enquiring person can with a good conscience attend Christian worship, prayer, and fellowship, and listen to Christian preaching, without the implication that he or she is a committed Christian, to come to the Lord's Table without a sincere commitment of Christian discipleship is a spiritually false and harmful step. Evangelistic preaching as a means of grace is the Church reaching out to those who are perhaps not yet full believers. The Lord's Supper as a means of grace is the covenanted Church of believers meeting together, seeking to grow in grace.

However, we know that there are in the fellowship of the Church disciples of very varying degree of spiritual growth. There are many in the Church who have a sincere desire to follow Christ as their Lord and Saviour, and who in this sense are Church members 'in good standing', who yet have not come to the gift of evangelical saving faith, or to a conscious personal experience of Christ. They are in fact incompletely 'converted'. Folk in this condition can rightly be communicants, and at the Lord's Table may come to a full personal experience of Christ. In this sense Wesley can describe the Lord's Supper as a 'converting ordinance'. *Journal:* June 27–8, 1740.

The Lord's Supper is a 'sign' and also a 'means'. In fact, the sacrament is what is called an 'operative symbol'. It is a symbol which focuses and portrays certain truths, and also performs spiritual saving acts which correspond to those truths. Though Protestants do not usually call marriage a sacrament the idea of an 'operative symbol' may be illustrated from a marriage. The ceremony consists of a number of symbolic actions which give outward expression to ideas of love, trust, and consent, such as reciting the vows, the giving and receiving of the ring, and signing the register. Yet these actions do not only express ideas. Taken together they actually marry the couple. Thus the marriage is both a 'sign' and a 'means'. The Lord's Supper is to the Christian the supreme example of this principle. It is a 'sign' which in hallowed symbolism focuses to the mind the ideas of Christ's sacrificial obedience unto death, and his resurrection and living presence. And it is also a 'means' by which the Church of today, and individual believers, receive a share of the effect of Christ's atoning sacrifice, and the experience of his victorious and life-giving presence. This fact of 'taking a share' in Christ's death and resurrection is expressed in the symbolism of 'eating his body' and 'drinking his blood'.

P.W. iii. 266; H.L.S. 71

Draw near, ye blood-besprinkled race,	Ex. 24:8, 1 Pet. 1:2
And take what God vouchsafes to give;	Isa. 55:1–3, Rom. 6:23
The outward sign of inward grace,*	
Ordained by Christ himself, receive:	1 Cor. 11:23f.
The sign transmits the signified,	Jn. 6:54–57
The grace is by the means applied.	Heb. 13:9–10

---

* 'An outward and visible sign of an inward and spiritual grace given unto us, ordained by Christ himself, as a means whereby we receive the same.'
                    (Catechism, B.C.P., Sec. answer on the Sacraments.)

P.W. iii. 266, 263; H.L.S. 72, 65; M.H.B. 767; H.P. 602

Come, Holy Ghost, thine influence shed,	Rom. 5:5
And realize the sign;	Lk. 24:30f., 35
Thy life infuse into the bread,	Jn. 6:35, 51, 58, Rom. 8:10
Thy power into the wine.	1 Cor. 10:16
Effectual let the tokens prove,	Eph. 3:7
And made, by heavenly art,	1 Cor. 12:6
Fit channels to convey thy love	Rom. 5:5
To every faithful heart.	Acts 2:41–2
Now, on the sacred table laid,	1 Cor. 10:21
Christ's flesh becomes our food,	Jn. 6:55
His life is to our souls conveyed	Jn. 6:57
In sacramental blood.	Mk. 14:24
Blest be the Lord, for ever blest,	Ps. 34:1, Rom. 9:5
Who bought us with a price,	1 Cor. 6:20, 7:23
And bids his ransomed servants feast	Isa. 25:6, 55:1f., Mk. 10:45
On his great sacrifice.	Heb. 10:10, 12

It is spiritually unprofitable to dispute as to the precise manner in which partaking of the consecrated elements conveys grace to the believer. It is sufficient that God has promised so to do, and that we may find his promise verified in our experience. Thus we may confidently rejoice in the sacramental gift of Christ's body and blood, yet without affirming the scholastic theory of transubstantiation advanced to explain the manner of the gift. 'Indeed, in what manner this is done, I know not; it is enough for me to admire. . . . I know that this bread hath nothing in itself, which can impart grace, holiness, and salvation. But I know also, that it is the ordinary way of God to produce his greatest works at the presence, though not by the power, of the most useless instruments.' (Brevint iv. 3)

P.W. iii. 255; H.L.S. 57; M.H. 332

O the depth of love divine,	Eph. 3:18–19
Th' unfathomable grace!	Rom. 11:33f.
Who shall say how bread and wine	Jn. 6:52
God into man conveys!	
How the bread his flesh imparts,	Jn. 6:51
How the wine transmits his blood,	1 Cor. 10:16
Fills his faithful people's hearts	Eph. 1:1
With all the life of God!	Eph. 3:19
Let the wisest mortal show	Isa. 55:8–9, 1 Cor. 1:19–21
How we the grace receive,	1 Cor. 10:17
Feeble elements bestow	1 Cor. 10:16
A power not theirs to give.	Zech. 4:6, 10
Who explains the wondrous way,	Jn. 6:52, 60
How through these the virtue came?	
These the virtue did convey,	Jn. 6:58
Yet still remain the same.	
How can heavenly spirits rise,	Heb. 12:23
By earthly matter fed,	Ps. 78:25
Drink herewith divine supplies,	Phil. 1:19
And eat immortal bread?	Jn. 6:48–50
Ask the Father's wisdom how;	Prov. 8:1, 22, Wisd. 7:22
He that did the means ordain!	1 Cor. 1:30, 11:23–5
Angels round our altars bow	Heb. 12:22, 13:10
To search it out in vain.	1 Pet. 1:12
Sure and real is the grace,	2 Tim. 2:19
The manner be unknown;	1 Cor. 2:7
Only meet us in thy ways,	Ex. 25:22, 30:6, Ps. 25:4–5
And perfect us in one.	Heb. 10:14
Let us taste the heavenly powers;	Heb. 6:5
Lord, we ask for nothing more:	1 Tim. 6:6
Thine to bless, 'tis only ours	1 Chron. 17:27
To wonder and adore.	Rom. 11:33f.

Thus the sacrament is a heavenly meal which conveys to us all that Christ accomplished for our salvation, and which sustains our spiritual life. 'And as bread and wine keep up our natural life, so doth our Lord Jesus, by a continual supply of strength and grace, represented by bread and wine, sustain that spiritual life which he hath procured by his cross.' (Brevint iii. 3)

P.W. iii. 244; H.L.S. 40; M.H.B. 764; M.H. 315; H.P. 596

Author of life divine,	Acts 3:15 (R.V. marg.)
Who hast a table spread,	Ps. 23:5, 1 Cor. 10:21
Furnished with mystic wine	Jn. 2:10, 1 Cor. 10:16, 11:25f.
And everlasting bread,	Jn. 6:35, 51, 1 Cor. 11:23f.
Preserve the life thyself hast given,	Ps. 64:1, Jn. 6:33, 57
And feed and train us up for heaven.	Jn. 6:47–50, 54, 58,
	Heb. 12:9–10
Our needy souls sustain	Ps. 72:13
With fresh supplies of love,	Phil. 4:19
Till all thy life we gain,	Jn. 6:33
And all thy fulness prove,	Eph. 3:19
And strengthened by thy perfect grace,	1 Pet. 5:10
Behold without a veil thy face.	2 Cor. 3:16,18, 4:6

'Now it is Christ himself, with his body and blood, once offered to God upon the cross, and ever since standing before him as slain, who fills the Church with the perfumes of his sacrifice, whence faithful communicants return home with the first-fruits of salvation. . . . Since it pleaseth Christ to work thereby, O my God, whensoever thou shalt bid me go and wash in Jordan, I will go; and will no more doubt of being made clean from my sins. . . . And when Thou sayest, Go, take and eat this bread which I have blessed, I will doubt no more of being fed with the bread of life.' (Brevint iv. 4)

P.W. iii. 273; M.H.B. 761; H.L.S. 81; H.P. 614

Jesu, we thus obey	1 Cor. 11:23–4
Thy last and kindest word,	
Here in thine own appointed way	Isa. 55:6
We come to meet our Lord:	Matt. 28:9
The way thou hast enjoined,	Heb. 9:20
Thou wilt therein appear;	Lk. 24:34, 35
We come with confidence to find	Eph. 3:12
Thy special presence here.	Gen. 28:16–17
Our hearts we open wide,	Cant. 5:2, Rev. 3:20
To make the Saviour room;	Lk. 2:7
And lo! the Lamb, the Crucified,	Jn. 1:29, 36, Rev. 5:6
The sinner's Friend, is come!	Matt. 11:19

His presence makes the feast;	Lk. 24:30–1, 41–3, Rev. 3:20
And now our bosoms feel	Lk. 24:32
The glory not to be expressed,	1 Pet. 1:8
The joy unspeakable.	
With pure celestial bliss	Jn. 16:22
He doth our spirits cheer,	
His house of banqueting is this,	Cant. 2:4
And he hath brought us here:	
He doth his servants feed	Lk. 12:37, Jn. 6:27, 51
With manna from above,	Ex. 16:15, Jn. 6:31ff.
His banner over us is spread,	Cant. 2:4
His everlasting love.	Jer. 31:3
He bids us drink and eat	Jn. 6:50f.
Imperishable food,	
He gives his flesh to be our meat,	Jn. 6:53
And bids us drink his blood:	
Whate'er the Almighty can	Gen. 17:1, Rev. 19:6
To pardoned sinners give,	Isa. 55:1, 7
The fulness of our God made man	Col. 2:9
We here with Christ receive.	

'This great and holy mystery communicates to us the death of our blessed Lord, both as offering himself to God, and as giving himself to man. . . . The holy sacrament is, after the sacrifice for sin, the true sacrifice of peace-offerings, and the table purposely set to receive those mercies that are sent down from his altar.' (Brevint iv. 7)

P.W. iii. 323, 282; H.L.S. 142, 92

Come we that record	Jn. 19:35
The death of our Lord,	
The death let us bear,	Heb. 13:12–13
By faithful remembrance his sacrifice share.	1 Cor. 11:24, 25,
	Heb. 10:12, 14, 13:15
In rapturous bliss	1 Cor. 14:15–16
He bids us do this,	1 Cor. 11:24, 25
The joy it imparts	1 Pet. 1:8
Hath witnessed his gracious design in	
our hearts.	Col. 3:16
Receiving the bread,	Jn. 6:48, 56
On Jesus we feed:	
It doth not appear,	
His manner of working; but Jesus is here!	Matt. 18:20, 28:20,
	Lk. 24:35
O that all men would haste	Isa. 25:6, Lk. 14:17
To the spiritual feast,	Jude 12 (R.V.)

At Jesus's word
Do this, and be fed with the love of our Lord!   Cant. 2:3, 4, 1 Cor. 11:23, 24

    Bring near the glad day   Heb. 10:25
    When all shall obey   2 Cor. 10:5
    Thy dying request,   1 Cor. 11:24f.
And eat of thy supper, and lean on thy breast.   Jn. 13:23

    To all men impart
    One way and one heart,   Jer. 32:39
    Thy people be shown   2 Cor. 6:16, 1 Pet. 2:9–10
All righteous and spotless and perfect in one.   1 Cor. 11:33–34, Heb. 10:14,
                                                     1 Jn. 4:12

Thus, as the Wesleys are careful to point out, the Lord's Supper is the Church's commemorative sacrifice. To say this is not in the slightest degree to take away from the unique historic position and spiritual value of the sacrifice of the Cross. By the true spiritual sacrifice of a life of sinless obedience to the Father, coming to its climax in a death of divine obedience, performed by God the Son as man, and on behalf of all mankind, God has done everything which needs to be done to release from the guilt and conquer the power of sin. Nothing needs to be added, or can be added, to this one redeeming act. As the Book of Common Prayer well states the evangelical position: Christ 'made there, by his one oblation of himself once offered, a full, perfect, and sufficient sacrifice, oblation, and satisfaction for the sins of the whole world'.

Thus the sacrament is in no sense a 'repetition' of Calvary. Yet it is a commemoration. It is the appointed means whereby the body of worshipping believers make themselves one with Christ as he offers his sacrifice, so that the Church of today, in every place, may share in the redeeming effect of that which God performed once and for all in the death and resurrection of Christ. The relation between the sacrifice of the Cross and the Church's continuing commemorative sacrifice may perhaps be illustrated in this way. The action of a great musician in the composition of some outstanding work is a unique historic act of creative genius. By the nature of things it can never be repeated. Yet the composer has left behind a musical score, which musicians of a later time can rehearse for a new performance. This performance is another creative act, derived from the first, by which the effect of the first is mediated to the hearers. It is in fact a 'commemoration'. So the celebration of the sacrament is 'a rehearsal of the score' of the sacrifice of the Cross. It is a commemorative sacrifice.

'This Victim having been offered up in the fulness of times, and in the midst of the world, which is Christ's great temple, and having been thence carried up to heaven, which is his sanctuary; from thence spreads salvation all around, as the burnt-offering did its smoke. And thus his Body and Blood have everywhere, but especially at this Sacrament, a true and real Presence. When he offered himself upon earth, the vapour of his atonement went up and darkened the very sun; and, by rending the great veil, it clearly showed he had made a way into heaven.' (Brevint, iv. 5)

It is to be observed that, following the Wesleys, the sacramental Real Presence of Christ is not to be thought of as an invisible essence or quantity inhering in the consecrated bread and wine as such. The Presence is in the whole sacramental action, and in the hearts of the worshippers. It is the profound experience of the worshipping Church that to join in the sacramental celebration, and actually to receive the consecrated elements, is an action which carries with it an especial divine guarantee that the universal presence of Christ will be made known with saving effect.

P.W. iii. 301; W.H. 902; H.L.S. 116; M.H.B. 771; H.P. 629

Victim divine, thy grace we claim	Mk. 15::39, Heb. 9:14–15
While thus thy precious death we show;	1 Cor. 11:26, 1 Pet. 1:19
Once offered up, a spotless Lamb,	Ex. 12:5, Heb. 9:12, 1 Pet. 1:1
In thy great temple here below,	Heb. 2:14, 17
Thou didst for all mankind atone,	Lev. 16:16, Jn. 1:29, Rom. 5:1
And standest now before the throne.	Acts 7:56, Heb. 8:1, Rev. 5:6
Thou standest in the holiest place,	Heb. 9:12, 24, Rev. 5:6
As now for guilty sinners slain;	Isa. 53:5–6, 1 Pet. 3:18
The blood of sprinkling speaks, and prays,	Ex. 24:8, Heb. 12:24
All-prevalent for helpless man;	1 Pet. 1:2, Rev. 5:5
Thy blood is still our ransom found,	Matt. 20:28, 1 Tim. 2:6
And spreads salvation all around.	Ps. 98:3, 1 Pet. 1:18–19
The smoke of thy atonement here	Gen. 8:20–21, Eph. 5:2
Darkened the sun and rent the veil,	Matt. 27:51, Lk. 23:44f.
Made the new way to heaven appear,	Heb. 9:8, 10:20
And showed the great Invisible;	Jn. 1:18, Heb. 11:27
Well pleased in thee our God looked down,	Ps. 102:19, Isa. 42:1, 21
And called his rebels to a crown.	Ezek. 2:3, Dan. 9:9,
	2 Cor. 5:20, 2 Tim. 4:8,
	Jas. 1:12, 1 Pet. 5:4
We need not now go up to heaven,	Deut. 30:11–12, Rom. 10:6
To bring the long-sought Saviour down;	Matt. 13:17, 1 Pet. 1:10–11
Thou art to all already given,	Jn. 3:16
Thou dost even now thy banquet crown:	Cant. 2:4
To every faithful soul appear,	Jn. 20:27, 2 Tim. 4:8
And show thy Real Presence here!	Matt. 18:20, 28:20

And setting forth the derived and commemorative sacrifice of the Lord's Supper we have verses based on Brevint, *Extract*, vi. 2. 'All comes to this, (1) That the sacrifice (upon the cross) in itself can never be repeated; (2) That nevertheless, this sacrament, by our remembrance, becomes a kind of sacrifice, whereby we present before God the Father that precious oblation of his Son once offered. And thus we do every day offer unto God the meritorious sufferings of our Lord, as the only sure ground whereon God may give, and we obtain, the blessing we pray for.'

P.W. iii. 309; H.L.S. 125; W.H. 394; M.H.B. 723; H.P. 554

O God of our forefathers, hear,	Ex. 3:6, 2 Tim. 1:3
And make thy faithful mercies known;	Ps. 89:1, 24
To thee through Jesus we draw near,	Heb. 10:22
Thy suffering, well-beloved Son,	Mk. 1:11, 12:6, Heb. 5:8
In whom thy smiling face we see,	Num. 6:26, 2 Cor. 4:6
In whom thou art well pleased with me.	Eph. 1:6
With solemn faith we offer up,	Ps. 116:17, 1 Pet. 2:5
And spread before thy glorious eyes,	1 Kgs. 8:54, 1 Tim. 2:8
That only ground of all our hope,	Heb. 11:1
That precious bleeding sacrifice,	1 Pet. 1:19
Which brings thy grace on sinners down,	Heb. 4:16
And perfects all our souls in one.	Jn. 17:23
Acceptance through his only name,	Acts 4:12, Eph. 1:6
Forgiveness in his blood we have;	Eph. 1:7, Col. 1:14
But more abundant life we claim	Jn. 10:10
Through him who died our souls to save,	1 Pet. 1:9, 2:24f.
To sanctify us by his blood,	Heb. 13:12
And fill with all the life of God.	Jn. 6:51, Eph. 3:19
Father, behold thy dying Son,	1 Jn. 2:1–2
And hear his blood that speaks above;	Heb. 12:24
On us let all thy grace be shown,	Eph. 2:7
Peace, righteousness, and joy, and love;	Rom. 14:17, Gal. 5:22
Thy kingdom come to every heart,	Matt. 6:10
And all thou hast, and all thou art.	Lk. 15:31, Rev. 11:17, 16:5

Finally, if in the sacrament we make ourselves one with Christ our Head as he offers his sacrifice of obedience, it follows that by his grace we must make our own sacrifice of moral and spiritual obedience to God, if our identification with Christ is to be done in deed and in truth. The response to the gift of the sacrament is therefore practical Christian consecration, in inward character and outward conduct.

'On the one side, neither our persons nor works can be presented to God, otherwise than as these additional offerings, which of

themselves fall to the ground, unless the great Sacrifice sustains
them. And on the other hand, this great Sacrifice sustains and
sanctifies only those things that are . . . hallowed upon his altar, and
together with him consecrated to God.' (Brevint vii. 9)

P.W. iii. 321; W.H. 427; H.L.S. 139; M.H.B. 566; H.P. 727

God of all-redeeming grace,	Tit. 2:13–14
By thy pardoning love compelled,	2 Cor. 5:14
Up to thee our souls we raise,	Ps. 25:1, 86:4, 143:8
Up to thee our bodies yield.	Rom. 6:13, 12:1
Thou our sacrifice receive,	Isa. 56:7
Acceptable through thy Son,	Phil. 4:18, 1 Pet. 2:5
While to thee alone we live,	Rom. 14:8
While we die to thee alone.	
Just it is, and good, and right*	
That we should be wholly thine,	Deut. 1:36
In thy only will delight,	Ps. 40:8
In thy blessed service join.	Rom. 12:1
O that every thought and word	
Might proclaim how good thou art,	Ps. 34:8, Isa. 12:4
Holiness unto the Lord	Ex. 28:36, Zech. 14:20
Still be written on our heart.	Jer. 31:33

---

* The 1780 hymn-book reads the more familiar 'Meet it is, and just and right', which
appears to echo the B.C.P. Communion Service.

'Let us take care to attend on this sacrifice in such a manner (1) as
may become faithful disciples, who are resolved to die for and with
their Master; (2) as true members that cannot outlive their Head.'
(Brevint vii. 10)

P.W. iii. 335; H.L.S. 157; W.H. 428; M.H.B. 382; H.P. 698

Let him to whom we now belong	Deut. 14:2, 1 Pet. 2:9 (R.V.)
His sovereign right assert,	Ex. 33:19
And take up every thankful song,	Eph. 5:19–20
And every loving heart.	1 Jn. 4:19
He justly claims us for his own	1 Cor. 6:20, 7:23
Who bought us with a price:	Acts 20:28, 2 Pet. 2:1
The Christian lives to Christ alone,	Phil. 1:21
To Christ alone he dies.	Rom. 14:8
Jesu, thine own at last receive;	Rom. 15:7
Fulfil our heart's desire,	Ps. 37:4, Rom. 10:1
And let us to thy glory live,	1 Cor. 10:31, 2 Thess. 2:14
And in thy cause expire.	Phil. 2:17, 2 Tim. 4:6–7

Our souls and bodies we resign,	Rom. 12:1
With joy we render thee	Ps. 27:6, 116:12, Matt. 22:21
Our all, no longer ours, but thine	Rom. 14:4
Through all eternity!	2 Tim. 1:12

'To this effect, the faithful worshipper, presenting that soul and body, which God hath given him, at the altar, may say: "Lo, I come!" if this soul and body may be useful to anything, "to do Thy will", O God. And if it please Thee to use that power that Thou hast over dust and ashes, over weak flesh and blood . . . lo, here they are, to suffer also Thy good pleasure. . . . Hereafter no man can take away anything from me, no life, no honour, no estate: since I am ready to lay them down, as soon as I perceive Thou requirest them at my hands. . . . And if Thou be pleased, either that I live yet a while, or not, . . . I will give up all Thou art pleased to ask, until at last I "give up the ghost".' (Brevint vii. 11)

P.W. iii. 333; H.L.S. 155; W.H. 430; M.H.B. 574; H.P. 791

Father, Son, and Holy Ghost,	Matt. 28:19
One in Three, and Three in One,	1 Jn. 5:7*
As by the celestial host	Rev. 4:8
Let thy will on earth be done;	Matt. 6:10
Praise by all to thee be given,	Ps. 67:35
Glorious Lord of earth and heaven!	Ps. 145:11–12, Isa. 24:23, 33:21
Vilest of the fallen race,	Lam. 1:11, 1 Tim. 1:15
Lo, I answer to thy call;	1 Sam. 3:10, Isa. 6:8
Meanest vessel of thy grace,	2 Cor. 4:7, Eph. 2:8
Grace divinely free for all,	Rom. 6:23, 1 Tim. 2:4
Lo, I come to do thy will,	Ps. 40:8, Heb. 10:7, 9
All thy counsel to fulfil.	Ps. 20:4,** 2 Thess. 1:11
Take my soul and body's powers,	Rom. 12:1
Take my memory, mind, and will,	Rom. 12:2–3
All my goods, and all my hours,	Deut. 8:18
All I know, and all I feel,	Eccles. 2:26
All I think, and speak, and do;	
Take my heart—but make it new.	Ezek. 36:26
Now, O God, thine own I am,	Ps. 119:94, 1 Cor. 6:9
Now I give thee back thine own,	1 Chron. 29:14
Freedom, friends, and health, and fame,	
Consecrate to thee alone;	2 Chron. 29:31, 31:6
Thine I live, thrice happy I,	Ps. 144:15, 146:5
Happier still, for thine I die.	Rom. 14:8, Phil. 1:23
Father, Son, and Holy Ghost,	Matt. 28:19
One in Three, and Three in One,	1 Jn. 5:7

As by the celestial host	Rev. 4:8
Let thy will on earth be done;	Matt. 6:10
Praise by all to thee be given,	Ps. 67:3, 5
Glorious Lord of earth and heaven.	Ps. 145:11–12, Isa. 24:23, 33:21

---

* We observe that this text, which comes from late copies of the Vulgate, is omitted in modern versions of the Bible. For the purposes of this study, however, it is surely legitimate to trace references to the text as Wesley read it. John Wesley certainly knew the text had been controverted, and following the learned critic Bengel had accepted it (*Notes on the New Testament*).

** It would appear that this phrase is derived from this text, though the sense is changed.

50. The Church

The Church is the corporate and disciplined society of all those who are joined to Christ. The purpose and mission of the Church is to praise God, and to witness to all mankind regarding the truth of the gospel by the ministry of Word and Sacraments, and by the manner of her life. The Church is the new and true Israel, the People of God, and the inheritor of God's promises to old Israel. The roots of the Church are found in that nucleus of faithful Israelites who were able by faith to accept Jesus as the long-promised Messiah. Thus the old and new Israel are continuous, though the Christian faith is not just a revised edition of the old Jewish religion of the Law. The preparation of the moral Law leads up to the gospel of divine redemption in Christ crucified and risen. The Wesley hymnody rejoices in a strong sense of continuity with the original and normative New Testament Church.

P.W. v. 479–81; W.H. 16

Happy the souls that first believed,	Prov. 16:20
To Jesus and each other cleaved;	Acts 11:23
Joined by the unction from above,	1 Jn. 2:20
In mystic fellowship of love.	Acts 2:42
Meek, simple followers of the Lamb,	Rev. 14:4
They lived, and spake, and thought the same;	1 Cor. 1:10, Phil. 2:2
They joyfully conspired to raise	
Their ceaseless sacrifice of praise.*	Heb. 13:15
To Jesus they performed their vows,	Ps. 61:8
A little church in every house;	Acts 2:46, Philem. 2
Brake the commemorative bread,	1 Cor. 11:24
And drank the Spirit of their Head.	1 Cor. 10:4, Col. 1:18
With grace abundantly endued,	Tit. 3:6
A pure, believing multitude,	Acts 4:32
They all were of one heart and soul,	Jer. 32:39
And only love inspired the whole.	Phil. 2:2, Col. 2:2

O what an age of golden days!**
O what a choice, peculiar race!   Ex. 19:5, 1 Pet. 2:9
Washed in the Lamb's all-cleansing blood,   Rev. 1:5
Anointed kings and priests to God!   Rev. 1:6

Ye different sects, who all declare,   1 Cor. 1:10, 13
'Lo, here is Christ!' or, 'Christ is there!'   Matt. 24:23
Your stronger proofs divinely give,   1 Jn. 2:5, 3:14
And show me where the Christians live.***

---

* 'this our sacrifice of praise and thanksgiving'. (Communion Service, B.C.P.)
** For the classical myth of the Golden Age: Virgil, *Eclogues*, iv. 7–10, etc.
*** Antoinette Bourignon, a Quietist who died in 1680, asks in the Introduction to her *Light of the World:* 'Where are the Christians? Let us go to the country where the Christians live'. See also, Wesley, *Notes on the New Testament*, on Acts 2:42.

The glorious divine promise that, despite the opposition of the powers of evil, the Church will not fail in her mission, is confidently celebrated in a paraphrase of Psalm 48.

P.W. viii. 111–14; W.H. 572; M.H.B. 699; H.P. 438

Great is our redeeming Lord   Ps. 34:22, 48:1, 96:4, 145:3
  In power, and truth, and grace;   Ps. 106:8, Acts 4:33
Him by highest heaven adored,   Heb. 12:22–3, Rev. 4:8–11
  His church on earth should praise: Ps. 48:1
In the city of our God,   Ps. 46:4, 87:1, 3
  In his holy mount below,   Ps. 48:2, Isa. 2:2, Zech. 8:3
Publish, spread his praise abroad,   Deut. 32:3, Ps. 48:10
  And all his greatness show.   1 Chron. 29:11, Ps. 150:2

Monarchs with their armies met,   2 Kgs. 18:13, 35, Ps. 48:4
  Jerusalem to assail;   Isa. 10:10–11, 36:18–20
Sworn to o'erthrow the sacred seat   Deut. 12:5, 14, 1 Kgs. 6:13
  Where God vouchsafes to dwell: Ps. 68:16, 18
Lo! their boast is turned to shame!   2 Kgs. 19:32–7, Ps. 48:5–6
  Struck with sore amaze and dread,   Ex. 15:15–16, Mal. 1:14
Marching towards her wall they came,   Ps. 48, 4
  They came, they saw, they fled!*

For thy lovingkindness, Lord,   Ps. 36:10, 48:9
  We in thy temple stay;   Lk. 24:53, Acts 2:46
Here thy faithful love record,   Ps. 40:10, Isa. 63:7
  Thy saving power display: Rom. 1:16
With thy name thy praise is known;   Ps. 48:10
  Glorious thy perfections shine,   Ps. 50:2
Earth's remotest bounds shall own   Isa. 42:10, 49:6, Acts 1:8
  Thy works are all divine.   Ps. 145:17

Sons of God, triumphant rise,   Ps. 48:11
  The city's walls surround!   2 Kgs. 6:17, Ps. 48:12

Lo! her bulwarks touch the skies,	Ps. 48:13, Gal. 4:26
How high, yet how profound!	
Tell the number of her towers,	Ps. 48:12
All her palaces declare,	Ps. 48:13, 122:7
Guarded by angelic powers,	Rev. 21:12
And God in person there!	Mal. 3:1, Rev. 21:22
See the gospel-church secure,	Eph. 2:20, 1 Pet. 2:6
And founded on a Rock!	Deut. 32:4, Isa. 32:2
All her promises are sure;	Matt. 16:18, 28:20
Her bulwarks who can shock?	Isa. 26:1, Heb. 8:6
Count her every precious shrine;	Ps. 48:12–13
Tell, to after-ages tell,	Ps. 44:1, 48:13
Fortified by power divine,	Matt. 28:18, Lk. 24:49
The church can never fail.	Matt. 16:18
Zion's God is all our own,	Ps. 48:14
Who on his love rely;	2 Chron. 16:8
We his pardoning love have known,	Neh. 9:17, Mic. 7:18
And live to Christ, and die:	Rom. 14:8
To the new Jerusalem	Heb. 12:22, Rev. 3:12, 21:2
He our faithful guide shall be:	Ps. 48:14
Him we claim, and rest in him,	Heb. 4:9–11
Through all eternity.	Ps. 48:14, Rev. 14:13

---

cf. Julius Caesar's boast: veni, vidi, vici (I came, I saw, I conquered), (Suetonius, *Divus Julius*, 37:2.)

God will work through the Church an age-long redeeming purpose, destined to unify all mankind to his glory. This is worked out in a paraphrase of Isaiah 66:10–23.

P.W. ix. 466–71; W.H. 460

All ye that Sion love	Ps. 26:8, Isa. 66:10
Rejoice in her increase,	Isa. 29:19
Yourself begotten from above	Jn. 3:7 (R.V. marg.)
To taste her happiness;	Isa. 66:11, Heb. 6:5
Who wept her state decayed,	Neh. 2:3
Let every mournful soul	Isa. 66:10
In her prosperity be glad	Zech. 1:17
With joy for ever full.	Isa. 66:12, 1 Jn. 1:4
Father of boundless grace,	Ps. 145:9, Jn. 3:16
Thou hast in part fulfilled	1 Tim. 2:4, Heb. 2:8
Thy promise made to Adam's race,	Gen. 3:15
In God incarnate sealed:	Jn. 1:14, 6:27
A few from every land	Isa. 66:18, Acts 2:5
At first to Salem came,	
And saw the wonders of thy hand,	Deut. 7:19
And saw the tongues of flame!	Isa. 66:15, Acts 2:3

Yet still we wait the end, — 1 Cor. 1:7, 1 Thess. 1:10
The coming of our Lord, — Acts 1:11, Rev. 3:11, 22:7, 12
The full accomplishment attend — Rev. 17:17
Of thy prophetic word: — Mk. 13:26
Thy promise deeper lies — Acts 13:32f., 2 Pet. 3:9
In unexhausted grace, — Jer. 31:3, Jas. 4:6
And new-discovered worlds arise — Isa. 66:19, 2 Pet. 3:13
To sing their Saviour's praise. — Rev. 15:3

Beloved for Jesu's sake, — Rom. 11:28, Eph. 1:6
By him redeemed of old, — Ps. 74:12
All nations must come in, and make — Isa. 66:20
One undivided fold; — Jn. 10:16
While gathered in by thee, — Jn. 11:52, Eph. 1:10
And perfected in one, — Jn. 17:23
They all at once thy glory see — 2 Cor. 4:6
In thine eternal Son. — Heb. 1:8

Jesus, we wait to see — Rom. 8:19
That spotless church of thine, — Cant. 4:7, Eph. 5:27
The heaven-appointed ministry, — Isa. 66:21, 2 Pet. 3:14
The hierarchy divine:
Command her now to rise — Amos 9:11
With perfect beauty pure, — Ps. 50:2, Rev. 21:2, 27
Long as the new-made earth and skies — Isa. 66:22
To flourish and endure.

The Church is the Body of Christ, the outward life and activity of which expresses to the world the inward loving life of the Spirit of Christ.

P.W. i, 356, 361–2; W.H. 515–18; M.H.B. 720; M.H. 530; H.P. 764

Christ from whom all blessings flow, — Eph. 1:3
Perfecting the saints below, — Eph. 4:12, Heb. 10:14
Hear us, who thy nature share, — 2 Pet. 1:4
Who thy mystic body are. — 1 Cor. 12:27, Eph. 2:16, 4:4

Join us, in one spirit join, — 1 Cor. 6:17, Eph. 2:18, 4:4
Let us still receive of thine; — Jn. 16:14
Still for more on thee we call, — Ps. 86:5
Thou, who fillest all in all. — Eph. 1:23

Build us in one body up, — Eph. 2:22, 1 Pet. 2:5
Called in one high calling's hope; — Eph. 1:18, 4:4, Phil. 3:14
One the Spirit whom we claim; — Eph. 4:4
One the pure baptismal flame. — Lk. 3:16, Acts 2:3

One the faith, and common Lord, — Eph. 4:5
One the Father lives, adored, — Eph. 4:6
Over, through, and in us all, — Rom. 9:5, 11:36, Col. 3:11
God incomprehensible.* — Job. 11:7, Isa. 55:8–9

Husband of thy church below,	Jer. 31:32, Eph. 5:23
Christ, if thee our Lord we know,	1 Cor. 12:3, Phil. 2:11
Unto thee, betrothed in love,	Hos. 2:19, 20
Always faithful let us prove.	1 Cor. 4:2, Rev. 2:10
Steadfast let us cleave to thee;	Acts 11:23, Heb. 3:14, 6:19
Love the mystic union be;	Phil. 2:2
Union to the world unknown!	1 Jn. 3:1
Joined to God, in spirit one.	1 Cor. 6:17
Move, and actuate, and guide:	1 Cor. 12:11
Divers gifts to each divide;	1 Cor. 12:4
Placed according to thy will,	Rom. 12:6, Eph. 1:5
Let us all our work fulfil.	Acts 14:26
Many are we now and one,	Rom. 12:5
We who Jesus have put on;	Rom. 13:14, Gal. 3:27
There is neither bond nor free,	Gal. 3:28
Male nor female, Lord, in thee!	
Love, like death, hath all destroyed,	Cant. 8:6
Rendered all distinctions void;	Rom. 10:12**
Names, and sects, and parties fall:	1 Cor. 1:12–13
Thou, O Christ, art all in all!	Col. 3:11

---

* Athanasian Creed, 9, 12.
** Prior, *Solomon, the Vanity of Knowledge,* ii. 241–2:
    Or grant, thy passion has these names destroyed,
    That love, like death, makes all distinctions void.

Methodism started not as a Church, holding public worship, but as a chain of fellowships, organized in circuits. It is natural, therefore, to find that the Wesley hymnody expresses a deep sense of fellowship. It is to be noted that by 'fellowship' is meant something much more profound than the spirit of personal human friendship existing within the Society, valuable though that is. In its proper sense fellowship indicates the discipline of close pastoral oversight, exercised by the members one upon another.

P.W. v. 467; W.H. 485; M.H.B. 718; M.H. 310; H.P. 760

Jesu, we look to thee,	Heb. 12:2
Thy promised presence claim!	Matt. 28:20
Thou in the midst of us shalt be,	Matt. 18:20, Lk. 24:36
Assembled in thy name.	Jn. 20:19, Acts 4:31, 11:26, Heb. 10:25
Thy name salvation is,	Matt. 1:21, Acts 4:10, 12
Which here we come to prove;	Rom. 12:2, Heb. 3:9
Thy name is life, and health, and peace,	Ps. 67:2, Eph. 2:14
And everlasting love.	Jer. 31:3, 1 Jn. 5:12

We meet, the grace to take   Eph. 2:8, Phil. 1:7
Which thou hast freely given;   Rom. 3:24, 12:6, Jas. 4:6
We meet on earth for thy dear sake,   Matt. 18:19, 1 Jn. 1:7
That we may meet in heaven.   Mk. 10:29–30, Heb. 12:22–4

Present we know thou art,   Matt. 18:20, 28:20
But O thyself reveal!   Jn. 20:19, 26, Gal. 1:16
Now, Lord, let every bounding heart   Ps. 28:8 (B.C.P.)
The mighty comfort feel.   Isa. 40:1–2, Jn. 14:18

O may thy quickening voice   Ps. 119:50, Rom. 4:17
The death of sin remove;   Jn. 5:25, Rom. 6:23, Eph. 5:14
And bid our inmost souls rejoice   Jn. 16:22, 1 Pet. 1:6, 8
In hope of perfect love!   1 Jn. 4:17, 18, Col. 1:28,
                                               1 Pet. 5:10

P.W. iv. 252; W.H. 500; M.H.B. 745; M.H. 301; H.P. 753

All praise to our redeeming Lord,   1 Cor. 1:30, Gal. 3:13
  Who joins us by his grace,   1 Cor. 1:10, Eph. 2:5–6, 4:6
And bids us, each to each restored,   Eph. 2:15
  Together seek his face.   Ps. 27:8

He bids us build each other up;   Eph. 4:12
  And, gathered into one,   Jn. 11:52, Eph. 1:10
To our high calling's glorious hope   Eph. 1:18
  We hand in hand go on.   2 Kgs. 10:15, Gal. 2:9

The gift which he on one bestows,   1 Cor. 12:4, 11
  We all delight to prove;   Isa. 58:14, Rom. 12:2
The grace through every vessel flows,   Acts 9:15, 2 Tim. 2:21
  In purest streams of love.   2 Cor. 6:6, 1 Tim. 1:5

Even now we think and speak the same,   Rom. 12:16, 1 Cor. 1:10
  And cordially agree;   2 Kgs. 10:15, Jer. 32:39
Concentred all, through Jesu's name,   1 Cor. 1:10, 5:4
  In perfect harmony.   Ps. 133:1, Eph. 2:13–15

We all partake the joy of one,   1 Cor. 12:26
  The common peace we feel,   Eph. 2:17, 1 Pet. 5:14
A peace to sensual minds unknown,   1 Cor. 2:14
  A joy unspeakable.   1 Pet. 1:8

And if our fellowship below   1 Jn. 1:3
  In Jesus be so sweet,   Cant. 5:13
What heights of rapture shall we know,   2 Cor. 12:4
  When round his throne we meet!   Rev. 14:3

P.W. ii. 138; W.H. 504; M.H.B. 721; M.H. 193; H.P. 773

Jesus, united by thy grace,	Eph. 4:7, 13
And each to each endeared,	Eph. 5:1–2, 1 Thess. 2:8
With confidence we seek thy face,	Ps. 27:8, Heb. 4:16
And know our prayer is heard.	Matt. 18:19, 1 Jn. 5:14–15
Still let us own our common Lord,	Rom. 10:12
And bear thine easy yoke,	Matt. 11:30
A band of love, a threefold cord,	Eccl. 4:12, Hos. 11:4
Which never can be broke.	Col. 2:19, 3:14
Make us into one spirit drink;	1 Cor. 12:13
Baptize into thy name;	Matt. 28:19, Acts 2:38, 8:16
And let us always kindly think,	Phil. 2:2, 3:16
And sweetly speak the same.	1 Cor. 1:10
Touched by the lodestone of thy love,	Phil. 2:1–2, 1 Jn. 4:7, 19
Let all our hearts agree,	Jer. 32:39, Ezek. 11:19
And ever towards each other move,	Gal. 5:13, 1 Pet. 3:8
And ever move towards thee.	Jn. 15:9, 10
To thee, inseparably joined,	Jn. 15:4–9, 1 Cor. 6:17
Let all our spirits cleave;	2 Kgs. 18:6, Acts 11:23
O may we all the loving mind	1 Cor. 2:16, Phil. 2:5
That was in thee receive!	
This is the bond of perfectness,	Col. 3:14
Thy spotless charity;	Heb. 9:14
O let us, still we pray, possess	.
The mind that was in thee!	1 Cor. 2:16, Phil. 2:5

A characteristic fellowship-meeting of early and traditional Methodism was the Love-feast. This was a gathering opened with praise and prayer, leading up to a simple ceremonial token meal of bread or special cake, and of water drunk from a loving-cup, followed by an extended opportunity for giving Christian testimony. This form of fellowship was taken over from the Moravians, who had developed Love-feasts with a view to reviving what they took to be the customs of the ancient Church. Charles Welsey wrote a long hymn for the Love-feast, divided into sections, to be sung at intervals during the proceedings. It breathes a particularly strong sense of fellowship within the ancient Church.

P.W. i. 350–2; W.H. 519–522; M.H.B. 713, 748; H.P. 756

Come, and let us sweetly join	Ps. 95:1
Christ to praise in hymns divine!	Eph. 5:19
Give we all with one accord,	Acts 4:24
Glory to our common Lord;	Acts 10:36
Hands and hearts and voices raise;	Lam. 3:41

Sing as in the ancient days;   2 Sam. 23:1, Jas. 5:13
Antedate the joys above,*   Mk. 14:25f.
Celebrate the feast of love.   Jude 12

Strive we, in affection strive;   Lk. 13:24, Col. 4:12 (R.V.)
Let the purer flame revive,   Hab. 3:2, Lk. 12:49
Such as in the martyrs glowed,   Acts 7:55, Rev. 2:13, 17:6
Dying champions for their God: Acts 7:59, Heb. 11:4, 35–8
We like them may live and love;   2 Cor. 6:9, Heb. 12:1–2
Called we are their joys to prove,   Heb. 12:22ff., Jas. 1:2, 1 Pet.
Saved with them from future wrath,   1 Thess. 1:10
Partners of like precious faith.   2 Pet. 1:1

Sing we then in Jesu's name,   Eph. 5:19
Now as yesterday the same;   Heb. 13:8
One in every time and place,   Matt. 28:19–20
Full for all of truth and grace: Jn. 1:14
We for Christ, our Master, stand,   Matt. 23:8, 10, Phil. 4:1
Lights in a benighted land: Matt. 5:14–16, Phil. 2:15
We our dying Lord confess;   Mk. 15:39, Lk. 23:40–43
We are Jesu's witnesses.   Acts 1:8, 22, 22:15

Witnesses that Christ hath died,   1 Cor. 1:23f., 1 Pet. 5:1
We with him are crucified;   Gal. 2:20
Christ hath burst the bands of death,   Acts 2:24
We his quickening Spirit breathe;   Rom. 8:11, 1 Cor. 15:45
Christ is now gone up on high,   Acts 1:9, Eph. 4:8
Thither all our wishes fly;   Col. 3:1–2
Sits at God's right hand above;   Mk. 16:19
There with him we reign in love!   Rom. 5:17, 2 Tim. 2:12,
                                            Rev. 20:4

Come, thou high and lofty Lord!   Isa. 57:15
Lowly, meek, incarnate Word!   Matt. 11:29, Jn. 1:14
Humbly stoop to earth again,   Phil. 2:8
Come and visit abject men!   Ps. 113:6, Matt. 8:8, Lk. 7:6
Jesus, dear expected guest,   Jn. 2:2, Lk. 10:38
Thou art bidden to the feast,
For thyself our hearts prepare,   Ps. 10:17, 23:5
Come, and sit, and banquet there!   Cant. 2:4, Isa. 25:6, Rev. 3:2(

Let us join, 'tis God commands,   Jn. 13:34
Let us join our hearts and hands;   Jer. 50:5
Help to gain our calling's hope,   Eph. 4:4
Build we each the other up: 1 Thess. 5:11
God his blessings shall dispense,   Eph. 1:3
God shall crown his ordinance;   Mal. 3:7
Meet in his appointed ways;   Isa. 64:5
Nourish us with social grace.   Eph. 5:29–30

Plead we thus for faith alone,   Lk. 17:5, Rom. 3:28, Gal. 2:1(
Faith which by our works is shown: Jas. 2:18, 22, 26

God it is who justifies;	Rom. 8:33
Only faith the grace applies;	Eph. 2:8
Active faith that lives within,	Eph. 3:17
Conquers earth, and hell, and sin,	Heb. 11:33
Sanctifies, and makes us whole,	Mk. 5:34, Jn. 17:17
Forms the Saviour in the soul.	Gal. 4:19, Heb. 10:14
Let us for this faith contend,	Jude 3
Sure salvation is its end:	1 Pet. 1:9
Heaven already is begun,	Mk. 1:15, Heb. 6:5
Everlasting life is won.	Lk. 18:30
Only let us persevere,	Eph. 6:18
Till we see our Lord appear,	2 Tim. 4:8, Tit. 2:13
Never from the rock remove,	Deut. 32:15, 18, 1 Cor. 10:4
Saved by faith, which works by love.	Gal. 5:6
Hence may all our actions flow,	1 Cor. 13:7–8
Love the proof that Christ we know;	1 Jn. 5:2
Mutual love the token be,	
Lord, that we belong to thee:	Jn. 13:35, 1 Jn. 3:14, 4:7
Love, thine image, love impart!	Rom. 8:29, 1 Cor. 15:49
Stamp it on our face and heart!	
Only love to us be given!	1 Cor. 12:31, 13:13
Lord, we ask no other heaven.	Ps. 73:25

---

* Our joys below it can improve,
  And antedate the bliss above.

(Pope, *Ode on St. Cecilia's Day*, VII:122–3)

51. Eternal Life

The saving work of God in the divine Son made man represents the invasion of this world by the divine, the timeless, the universal. In the same way, the union with God in Christ by 'the faith that works by love' possesses the quality of the universal, the timeless. Started in this life, it cannot be broken off by the death of the body. Thus the gift of God is eternal life. Eternal life is much more than infinite duration. It is a quality of life, life with God. Yet by virtue of that quality it looks beyond the grave to an everlasting life of blessed fellowship with God, and with all his redeemed.

P.W. ii. 242; W.H. 384; M.H.B. 565; H.P. 731

I know that my Redeemer lives,	Job 19:25
And ever prays for me;	Heb. 7:25
A token of his love he gives,	2 Cor. 1:22, 5:5
A pledge of liberty.	Lev. 25:10, 2 Cor. 3:17
I find him lifting up my head,	Ps. 3:3
He brings salvation near,	Isa. 56:1, Rom. 13:11
His presence makes me free indeed,	Jn. 8:36
And he shall soon appear.	Heb. 9:28, 1 Pet. 5:4, Rev. 3:11, 22:7, 12
He wills that I should holy be,	Lev. 19:2, 1 Thess. 4:3
What can withstand his will?	Acts 11:17, Rom. 9:19
The counsel of his grace in me	Eph. 1:11
He surely will fulfil.	
Jesus, I hang upon thy word:	Lk. 19:48 (R.V.)
I steadfastly believe	Acts 2:42, 1 Pet. 5:9
Thou wilt return and claim me, Lord,	Jn. 14:3
And to thyself receive.	
Thy love I soon expect to find,	Ps. 62:5
In all its depth and height;	Eph. 3:18–19
To comprehend the Eternal Mind,	Isa. 55:8–9, Eph. 3:19
And grasp the infinite.	Eccles. 3:11 (R.V. marg.)
When God is mine, and I am his,	Cant. 6:3
Of paradise possessed,	2 Cor. 12:4

| I taste unutterable bliss, | 1 Pet. 1:8 |
| And everlasting rest. | 2 Thess. 2:16, Heb. 4:9–11 |

The bliss of those that fully dwell,	Jn. 15:4, 10
Fully in thee believe,	1 Pet. 1:8
'Tis more than angel-tongues can tell,	1 Cor. 13:1
Or angel-minds conceive.	1 Pet. 1:12

Thou only know'st, who did'st obtain,	Matt. 11:27, Lk. 10:22
And die to make it known;	Rom. 5:8
The great salvation now explain,	Heb. 2:3
And perfect us in one!	Jn. 17:23

P.W. i. 370; W.H. 403; M.H.B. 563; H.P. 736

Lord, I believe a rest remains	Heb. 4:9
To all thy people known,	Jer. 31:34
A rest where pure enjoyment reigns,	1 Pet. 1:8, Jude 24
And thou art loved alone.	Ps. 73:25

A rest where all our soul's desire	Ps. 73:25
Is fixed on things above;	Col. 3:1
Where fear, and sin, and grief expire,	
Cast out by perfect love.	1 Jn. 4:18

O that I now the rest might know,	Heb. 4:10–11
Believe and enter in!	Heb. 4:3
Now, Saviour, now the power bestow,	Lk. 24:49, Acts 1:8
And let me cease from sin.	1 Pet. 4:1

Remove this hardness from my heart,	Ezek. 36:26
This unbelief remove:	Mk. 9:24
To me the rest of faith impart,	Heb. 4:3, 10
The sabbath of thy love.	Gen. 2:2

I would be thine, thou knowest I would,	Jn. 21:15–17
And have thee all my own;	Hos. 2:23
Thee, O my all-sufficient good!	2 Cor. 3:5
I want, and thee alone.	Ps. 73:25

Thy name to me, thy nature grant!	Gen. 32:29, Ex. 3:13
This, only this be given:	
Nothing beside my God I want,	Ps. 73:25
Nothing in earth or heaven.	

Come, Father, Son, and Holy Ghost,	Matt. 28:19, 2 Cor. 13:14
And seal me thine abode!	Cant. 8:6, Jn. 14:23
Let all I am in thee be lost,	Phil. 1:21
Let all be lost in God.	

P.W. v. 134; W.H. 440; M.H.B. 584

Thou, Jesu, thou my breast inspire,	Job 32:8
And touch my lips with hallowed fire,*	Isa. 6:7
And loose a stammering infant's tongue;	Isa. 32:4
Prepare the vessel of thy grace,	2 Tim. 2:21
Adorn me with the robes of praise,	Isa. 61:3
And mercy shall be all my song;	Ps. 89:1
Mercy for all who know not God,	Rom. 11:32, 1 Tim. 1:13
Mercy for all in Jesu's blood,	Rev. 5:9
Mercy, that earth and heaven transcends;	Ps. 148:13, Jer. 31:37
Love that o'erwhelms the saints in light,	Col. 1:12
The length, and breadth, and depth,	
and height	Eph. 3:18
Of love divine, which never ends!	Jer. 31:3
A faithful witness of thy grace,	Lk. 12:42, Acts 1:8, Col. 1:7
Well may I fill the allotted space,	Acts 26:16
And answer all thy great design;	1 Tim. 2:7
Walk in the works by thee prepared;**	Eph. 2:10 (R.V.)
And find annexed the vast reward,	Rev. 14:13
The crown of righteousness divine.	2 Tim. 4:8
When I have lived to thee alone,	Rom. 14:8
Pronounce the welcome word, 'Well done!'	Matt. 25:21
And let me take my place above;	Jn. 14:2, 3
Enter into my Master's joy,	Matt. 25:21
And all eternity employ	Rev. 7:15
In praise, and ecstasy, and love.	

---

*   O thou my voice inspire
Who touched Isaiah's hallowed lips with fire!   (Pope: *Messiah*, ll. 5–6)
** B.C.P. Second Thanksgiving after Communion.

P.W. iv. 262; W.H. 71; M.H.B. 610; H.P. 819

Leader of faithful souls, and guide,	Isa. 55:4
Of all that travel to the sky,	Ps. 73:24, Heb. 11:16
Come and with us, even us, abide,	Lk. 24:29
Who would on thee alone rely,	2 Chron. 16:8
On thee alone our spirits stay,	Isa. 50:10
While held in life's uneven way.	Matt. 7:13–14
We have no abiding city here,	Heb. 13:14
But seek a city out of sight;	Heb. 11:10, 16
Thither our steady course we steer,	Heb. 12:1–2
Aspiring to the plains of light,	
Jerusalem, the saints' abode,	Heb. 12:22f.
Whose founder is the living God.	Heb. 11:10

Patient the appointed race to run,	Heb. 12:1
This weary world we cast behind;	Ps. 63:1 (R.V.), 1 Jn. 2:15
From strength to strength we travel on,	Ps. 84:7
The new Jerusalem to find;	Rev. 21:2
Our labour this, our only aim,	Phil. 3:13
To find the new Jerusalem.	
Through thee, who all our sins hast borne,	Isa. 53:6, Heb. 9:28, 1 Pet. 2:24
Freely and graciously forgiven,	Lk. 7:42, Rom. 3:24
With songs to Zion we return,	Isa. 35:10
Contending for our native heaven;	Phil. 3:20 (R.V.), Heb. 12:22
That palace of our glorious King,	Matt. 5:35
We find it nearer while we sing.	Ps. 40:2–3, Acts 16:25
Raised by the breath of love divine,	Acts 17:25
We urge our way with strength renewed;	Isa. 40:31
The church of the first-born to join,	Heb. 12:23
We travel to the mount of God,	Ex. 18:5, Heb. 12:22
With joy upon our heads arise	Isa. 35:10, 51:11
And meet our Captain in the skies.	1 Thess. 4:17, Heb. 2:10

On account of the theological interest of the fifth line of the second verse, we venture to print as Charles Wesley originally wrote it what is perhaps the best-loved hymn on the present theme, and his most emphatic statement on the divine gift of holiness. It is this line which caused John Wesley to omit this verse when he included the hymn in the 1780 hymnal, and the editors of American hymnals to modify the line. The very bold petition 'Take away our power of sinning' is a reference to a famous passage in St. Augustine (*De civitate Dei* xxii, 30) in which he is discussing the spiritual condition of unfallen Adam, as compared with the better condition of the redeemed. 'The first immortality, which Adam lost by sinning, was the ability not to die (*posse non mori*), the new immortality will be the inability to die (*non posse mori*). In the same way, the first freedom of choice conveyed the ability not to sin (*posse non peccare*); the new freedom will confer the inability to sin (*non posse peccare*) . . . It surely cannot be said that God himself has not freedom of choice, because he is unable to sin?' Thus unfallen Adam was morally free in the sense that he was not fated to sin. The perfected in Christ will be morally free in a higher and fuller sense. They will share in the moral freedom of God who, being entirely good, cannot sin.

The underlying issue is what is meant by 'freedom'. In ordinary parlance freedom is assumed to be liberty of choice between different courses. However, the Christian freedom which is offered in the Gospel is much more than this. There is within the heart a frustrating inward tension which secures that whereas part of the personality sincerely desires to serve Christ, another part is kicking against that obedience. Christian freedom is a work of grace which will release the believer from that frustration. The divine gift of holiness, or perfect love, is that of a personality in which all the powers flow out in glad and whole-hearted obedience. This more exalted Christian liberty is not a bare freedom of choice, but freedom of unimpeded action. Clearly, the climax of this holiness would be a character entirely confirmed in good, and in this sense incapable of sinning.

The difficulty which has troubled some is that whereas St. Augustine is talking about the condition of the perfected saints in glory, of which this is doubtless true, Charles Wesley is praying that it may happen on earth! Is it indeed possible for the believer to speak as though the love and joy of heaven had actually come down to earth? We observe, firstly, that Wesley's line is an aspiring prayer that this degree of holiness may be granted, not a presumptuous claim that he had attained. And secondly, a raptured poet must not be expected always to express himself in the language of common sense, such as may be taken literally. Even hymn writers must be allowed on occasion some degree of enthusiastic poetic licence! Nevertheless, the phrase is perhaps over-bold.

P.W. iv. 219; W.H. 385; M.H.B. 431; M.H. 283; H.P. 267

Love divine, all loves excelling,*	Ps. 36:7, Jn. 15:13
Joy of heaven to earth come down,	1 Kgs. 6:13, Job 38:7
Fix in us thy humble dwelling,	Isa. 57:15, Mal. 3:1
All thy faithful mercies crown;	Ps. 103:4
Jesu, thou art all compassion,	Matt. 9:36
Pure unbounded love thou art,	1 Jn. 4:8, 16
Visit us with thy salvation,	Lk. 1:68
Enter every trembling heart.	Deut. 28:65
Breathe, O breathe thy loving Spirit	Jn. 20:22, 2 Tim. 1:7
Into every troubled breast,	Lk. 24:38
Let us all in thee inherit,	Rom. 8:17
Let us find that second rest:	Heb. 4:8–9
Take away our power of sinning,**	1 Jn. 3:9
Alpha and Omega be,	Rev. 1:8
End of faith as its beginning,	Heb. 12:2
Set our hearts at liberty.	Ps. 119:32 (B.C.P.)
Come, almighty to deliver,	Isa. 63:1
Let us all thy life receive,	Jn. 6:33, 10:10
Suddenly return, and never,	Mal. 3:1
Never more thy temples leave.	Ps. 68:16, Ezek. 10:18
Thee we would be always blessing,	Ps. 34:1, Lk. 24:53
Serve thee as thy hosts above,	Rev. 22:3
Pray, and praise thee without ceasing,	1 Thess. 5:16–17
Glory in thy perfect love.	1 Jn. 2:5, 4:12

Finish then thy new creation,	2 Cor. 5:17
Pure and sinless let us be,***	Cant. 4:7, Eph. 5:27
Let us see thy great salvation,	Heb. 2:3, 2 Pet. 3:14
Perfectly restored in thee;	Ps. 51:12, Isa. 49:6, 58:12
Changed from glory into glory,	2 Cor. 3:18
Till in heaven we take our place,	Jn. 14:2–3
Till we cast our crowns before thee,	Rev. 4:10
Lost in wonder, love, and praise.	Rev. 8:1

---

* It is usually considered that the opening lines of this hymn are reminiscent of Dryden's 'Song of Venus' in *King Arthur*, Act II. Sc. v. ll. 1–4:

      Fairest Isle, all isles excelling,
        Seat of pleasures and of loves;
      Venus here will choose her dwelling,
        And forsake her Cyprian groves.

** S. Augustine, *De Civitate Dei*, xxii: 30.

*** We observe that this line is changed to the more familiar 'Pure and spotless let us be' in John Wesley's 1780 hymnal, and succeeding hymnals. This reading accords more closely with the Scripture references given, and is perhaps also reminiscent of a famous quotation on the unity of the Church in St. Cyprian: 'To this one Church the Holy Spirit points in the Song of Songs, in the person of our Lord, saying, "My dove, my spotless one, is but one; she is the only one of her mother, elect of her that bare her" (Cant. 6:9)' *De catholicae ecclesiae unitate*, 4.

52. The Communion of Saints

All those who are joined to God in Christ are joined to one another. This has the splendid consequence that the whole world Church is only a small part of the universal fellowship of all believers, for most of the Christians who have ever lived are in heaven. The departed, who await the final mysterious glory of the general resurrection, are certainly not in a state of suspended animation. They praise and serve God in glory, and look with interest and blessing upon the struggling Church in this world. Thus the Church Triumphant in heaven is one body with the Church Militant on earth. Spiritually vital Christianity has always possessed a clear doctrine of this, the Communion of Saints. The only certain thing about human life is death, and any form of Christian teaching which does not hold a strong and intelligible message of hope and comfort at the grave-side is bankrupt.

'In the purpose of God, his Church and heaven go both together, that being the way that leads to this, as the holy place to the holiest, both of which are implied in what Christ calls the kingdom of God.' (Brevint v. 2)

P.W. iii. 286; H.L.S. 96; W.H. 15; M.H.B. 818; M.H. 535; H.P. 816

Happy the souls to Jesus joined,	1 Cor. 6:17
And saved by grace alone;	Eph. 2:8
Walking in all thy ways we find	Deut. 8:6, Ps. 128:1
Our heaven on earth begun.	Heb. 6:5
The church triumphant in thy love,	2 Cor. 2:14
Their mighty joys we know;	Heb. 12:22f.
They sing the Lamb in hymns above,	Rev. 7:9–10
And we in hymns below.	Eph. 5:19
Thee in thy glorious realm they praise,	Rev. 5:13, 15:3–4
And bow before thy throne;	Rev. 14:3
We in the kingdom of thy grace,	Eph. 3:14–15, Col. 1:13
The kingdoms are but one.	Rev. 11:15

The holy to the holiest leads,	Ex. 26:33, Heb. 9:3, 24
From hence our spirits rise,	Col. 3:2
And he that in thy statutes treads	Ezek. 11:20, 33:15, 36:27
Shall meet thee in the skies.	Gen. 5:24, 1 Thess. 4:17

The magnificent traditional Methodist funeral hymn has perhaps suffered a little because it is too robust and unsentimental for the taste of some, and has unfortunately circulated in some hymnals in an emasculated form.

P.W. vi. 215; W.H. 949; M.H.B. 824; M.H. 302; H.P. 812

Come, let us join our friends above	Heb. 12:23
That have obtained the prize,	Phil. 3:14
And on the eagle-wings of love	Ex. 19:4
To joys celestial rise;	Matt. 25:21
Let all the saints terrestrial sing	Ps. 66:1, 4
With those to glory gone,	Ps. 73:24
For all the servants of our King	Heb. 12:22f.
In earth and heaven are one.	Rev. 19:5, 22:3
One family we dwell in him,	Jer. 31:1
One church above, beneath,	Eph. 3:15
Though now divided by the stream,	Isa. 43:2
The narrow stream of death:	
One army of the living God,	1 Sam. 17:26
To his command we bow:	Ps. 33:9
Part of his host hath crossed the flood,	Josh. 3:14–17
And part is crossing now.	2 Tim. 4:6
Ten thousand to their endless home	Rev. 5:11
This solemn moment fly;	Eccl. 12:5
And we are to the margin come,	Josh. 3:8
And we expect to die:	2 Tim. 4:6, Heb. 9:27
His militant, embodied host	1 Cor. 12:27, Eph. 6:11–12
With wishful looks we stand,	Deut. 34:1–4
And long to see that happy coast,	
And reach that heavenly land.	Heb. 11:16
Our old companions in distress	1 Cor. 7:26, 2 Cor. 4:8–10
We haste again to see,	Heb. 10:32ff.
And eager long for our release,	Phil. 1:23
And full felicity:	Rev. 7:16–17
Even now by faith we join our hands	Heb. 11:1, 2, 12:1, 2
With those that went before;	
And greet the blood-besprinkled bands	Heb. 12:24, 1 Pet. 1:2
On the eternal shore.	2 Cor. 5:1, Rev. 5:9
Our spirits too shall quickly join,	1 Cor. 6:17
Like theirs, with glory crowned,	Heb. 12:23, 1 Pet. 5:4

And shout to see our Captain's sign,   Isa. 18:3, Matt. 24:30
    To hear his trumpet sound: 1 Cor. 15:52, 1 Thess. 4:16
O that we now might grasp our guide,   Ps. 48:14
    O that the word were given!   Ps. 68:11
Come Lord of hosts the waves divide,   Ex. 14:16, 21–2
    And land us all in heaven!   Jn. 14:2, 3, Heb. 12:22f.,
                                                1 Pet. 1:4

53.   The Second Advent

The climax of the Christian history of this world is the Second Advent of our Lord in glory, bringing the Last Judgment. Clearly, this awesome and mysterious event is outside our present factual experience. The End is what happens when the train of events which we have come to regard as accustomed and natural is broken off, and the human race is faced with spiritual experiences which we cannot measure by comparison with the present. Therefore the theology of The End has to be set forth in symbolical language, in the language of imaginative poetry rather than of matter-of-fact description. In consequence, those parts of the Bible in which God has revealed to faith this part of his truth are framed in vivid imagery.

In approaching this part of Scripture the wise and reverent expositor will, we believe, seek to avoid two opposite extremes. The one is to interpret this imagery with excessive literalism, through the feeling that this is the only way in which it can be taken seriously as a divine revelation. We need to remember that the Hebrew mind, which framed these Scriptures, was lacking in visual imagination. Indeed, the Hebrews had a religion which forbade the portrayal of 'images'. Thus it would never have occurred to the author of the Revelation to try to draw a picture of the Four Horsemen of the Apocalypse, after the manner of Dürer. What we have in the strange visions of the Revelation are symbols of ideas, framed in words. We are not to suppose that the visions of heavenly conflict in the Revelation must necessarily disclose events which are to take place visibly. The opposite error is to dismiss these parts of the Bible as concerned with matters of vague and unimportant, or even of repulsive, speculation. The Christian expectation that at the end of the ages Christ will be revealed as the manifest Master of the whole human situation, so that history will end in a manner worthy of God, is an essential part of the Christian faith. To minimize this expectation in Christian teaching is to emasculate the Gospel, and rob it of its power to breathe courage into the hearts of believers, as they face the black prospects of a sinful world which manifestly can only be rescued from catastrophe by the mysterious intervention of divine redeeming power.

The New Testament word *parousia* which is in some places translated 'Advent', in some places 'Coming', and in some 'Presence' is a vivid symbol drawn from the historic idea of kingship. The sovereignty of the monarch extends in principle to every part of his dominions, and at all times, but when on a royal progress he appears before the citizens to administer justice the sovereignty is impressively demonstrated at a certain place by a personal appearance. This personal appearance is the 'Royal Presence', the 'Advent'. So Christ is a spiritual Being, not confined to time or place. When he manifests that presence in an impressive personal experience we speak of it as his 'Coming', his 'Advent'. To say that Christ 'comes' does not involve the idea that he moves from another place, for he is universally present. It means that men and women become impressively aware of his universal presence.

Our Lord is in fact present with us now, but sincere believers will be the first to admit that our awareness of this splendid fact is often dim and variable. The unbelieving world in effect ignores his presence and rule, either with easy-going apathy, or disdain, or hostility. The Christian hope of Christ's Second Advent in glory reflects God's promise that the climax of Christian history will consist in the manifestation of this frequently obscure Christ to every human soul in sovereign majesty. Thus God will show himself to be God.

Our Lord clearly advised his disciples that it is spiritually unprofitable to seek to forecast the time of this awesome event (Mark 13:32–37; Luke 17:20–21; Acts 1:6–7). Rather must they live spiritually alert, in a state of constant and disciplined expectation. And it would appear that the event, when it occurs, will not be confined to some particular place, but will be world-wide (Matthew 24:26–7; Luke 17:23–4). Therefore one would suggest, without being dogmatic in denial, that it is perhaps an excess of literalism to insist that the fulfilment of the promise of Acts 1:11 must necessarily be, as it were, the Ascension in reverse, with an 'eastern-style' Figure descending upon the Mount of Olives. We may say that Christ's Second Advent in glory will be a manifestation of his living presence and majesty at least as impressive as his resurrection-appearances in glory, but confronting the whole human race, and for eternity.

It is clear that if the human race is now being judged according as each soul accepts or rejects Christ, this judgment which is at present provisional, and frequently hidden from our knowledge, will at the Royal Presence of Christ in glory issue in a judgment which is open and final. In that clear light evil will fully be shown up to be evil.

Those who have hardened themselves in the pursuit of evil, and perhaps prospered in this life, will be shown up to be what they truly are. On the other hand, those who have loved Christ, served and suffered with him, and hoped in his cause in the day of adversity, will see the desire of their hearts come true.

In this connection, as we turn to the final selection of hymns, we observe that though Wesley believed in hell he was not a 'hell-fire preacher'. The famous 1780 hymnal sets out his programme of evangelical experience and evangelistic preaching. The note of warning of dreadful final punishment for the obstinately disobedient is certainly there, but fear of divine punishment is not advanced as the cardinal reason for repentance, and for seeking forgiveness in Christ. The leading reasons for 'Exhorting Sinners to return to God' are 'The Pleasantness of Religion' and 'The Goodness of God'. The same may be said of our Lord. There is in the background of his teaching that awful foreboding of the unspeakably dreadful fate which the finally impenitent will bring upon themselves. Yet he was not a second John the Baptist, an austere preacher of fiery judgment. He was an humane and approachable figure, so that the implacable enemy of sin could earn the title of 'the friend of publicans and sinners'.

P.W. vi. 141; W.H. 56

He comes! he comes! the Judge severe,*	Matt. 25:31f., 2 Cor. 5:10
The seventh trumpet speaks him near;	Rev. 11:15
His lightnings flash, his thunders roll,	Matt. 24:27, Rev. 8:5, 11:19
How welcome to the faithful soul!	2 Tim. 4:8, Rev. 6:10
Shout, all the people of the sky,	1 Thess. 4:16
And all the saints of the Most High!	Dan. 7:18
Our Lord, who now his right obtains,	Rev. 11:15
For ever and for ever reigns.	

---

* 'He comes, he comes, the hero comes,
    Sound your trumpets, beat your drums'
The patriotic song by Henry Cary, on the occasion of 'The War of Jenkins' Ear' (1739) which opened with these words, provided the model for this hymn which was sung to the popular tune.

P.W. v. 284; W.H. 65

Ye virgin souls arise,	Matt. 25:1, 7, Rev. 14:4
With all the dead awake!	Dan. 12:2, 1 Cor. 15:52
Unto salvation wise,	Eph. 5:14, 2 Tim. 3:15

Oil in your vessels take,	Matt. 25:4
Upstarting at the midnight cry,	Matt. 25:6
'Behold the heavenly Bridegroom nigh!'	

He comes, he comes to call	Matt. 25:32, Rev. 1:7
The nations to his bar,	Rom. 14:10, 2 Cor. 5:10
And raise to glory all	1 Cor. 15:43
Who fit for glory are;	Col. 1:12
Make ready for your full reward,	Matt. 25:40, Rev. 22:12
Go forth with joy to meet your Lord.	Matt. 25:6, 21, 23

Ye that have here received	
The unction from above,	1 Jn. 2:20
And in his Spirit lived,	Gal. 5:25
Obedient to his love,	Matt. 22:37
Jesus shall claim you for his bride:	Eph. 5:23, Rev. 21:2, 9
Rejoice with all the sanctified.	Acts 20:32, 26:18

Rejoice in glorious hope	Rom. 5:2
Of that great day unknown,	Matt. 24:36, Acts 1:7
When all shall be caught up	1 Thess. 4:17
And stand before his throne:	Rev. 7:9
Ye pure in heart, obtain the grace	Matt. 5:8
To see without a veil his face!	1 Cor. 13:12, 2 Cor. 3:16, 18, 1 Jn. 3:2

P.W. vi. 143; W.H. 66; M.H.B. 264; M.H. 364; H.P. 241

Lo! He comes with clouds descending,	Dan. 7:13, Mk. 14:62, Rev. 1:7
Once for favoured sinners slain!	Rom. 5:8, Heb. 9:28
Thousand thousand saints attending,	Deut. 33:2, Dan. 7:10
Swell the triumph of his train:	Ps. 47:1, Jude 14
Hallelujah!	Rev. 19:6
God appears, on earth to reign!	Rev. 20:6

Every eye shall now behold him	Rev. 1:7
Robed in dreadful majesty;	Matt. 19:28, 25:31
Those who set at nought and sold him,	Matt. 26:15, Mk. 9:12
Pierced, and nailed him to the tree,	Zech. 12:10, Ps. 22:16
Deeply wailing	Matt. 13:42, Rev. 1:7
Shall the true Messiah see.	Matt. 24:4–7, 24, 27

The dear tokens of his passion	Lk. 24:40, Jn. 20:27
Still his dazzling body bears;	Rev. 5:6
Cause of endless exultation	Rev. 5:11–14, 7:15
To his ransomed worshippers;	Mk. 10:45, Rev. 5:9
With what rapture	2 Thess. 1:10
Gaze we on those glorious scars!	Isa. 63:1, 3

Yea, amen! let all adore thee,	Rev. 1:7, 11:15, 22:3
High on thine eternal throne	Matt. 19:28, 25:31
Saviour, take the power and glory,	Rev. 11:17
Claim the kingdom for thine own:	Lk. 22:30, Rev. 11:15
Jah, Jehovah,	Ex. 3:14, 6:3, Ps. 68:4
Everlasting God, come down!	Ex. 3:8, Ps. 144:5, Isa. 9:6, Jer. 10:10, Rom. 16:26

Index of first lines of hymns

Brackets indicate that the first line as generally known is not the same as in this book.

Index of passages
of Scripture paraphrased